SAP® F

Financial Accounting

SAP® FI

Financial Accounting

By

V. Narayanan

Reprinted 2015

FIRST EDITION 2010 Reprinted 2013

ISBN : 978-81-8333-323-8

LIMITS OF LIABILITY AND DISCLAIMER OF WARRANTY

The information contained in this book is to the best of the author's knowledge true and correct. The author has made every effort to ensure accuracy of this publications, but cannot be held responsible for any loss or damage arising from any information in this book.

All trademarks referred to in the book are acknowledged as properties of their respective owners.

Distributors:

COMPUTER BOOK CENTRE
12, Shrungar Shopping Centre, M.G. Road,
BANGALORE-560001 Ph: 25587923, 25584641

MICRO BOOKS
Shanti Niketan Building, 8, Camac Street
KOLKATTA-700017 Ph: 22826518/9

BUSINESS PROMOTION BUREAU
8/1, Ritchie Street, Mount Road,
CHENNAI-600002 Ph: 28410796, 28550491

BPB PUBLICATIONS
B-14, Connaught Place, NEW DELHI-110001
Ph : 23325760, 23723393, 23737742

BPB BOOK CENTRE
376, Old Lajpat Rai Market, DELHI-110006
Ph: 23861747

MICRO MEDIA
Shop No.5, Mahendra Chambers, 150 D.N. Rd,
Next to Capital Cinema V.T. (C.S.T.) Station,
MUMBAI-400001 Ph: 22078296, 22078297

DECCAN AGENCIES
4-3-329, Bank Street,
HYDERABAD-500195 Ph: 24756400, 24756967

INFO TECH
G-2, Sidhartha Building , 96, Nehru Place,
NEW DELHI-110019
Ph: 26438245, 26415092, 26234208

INFO TECH
Shop No. 2, F-38, South Extention Part-I
NEW DELHI-110049
Ph: 24691288

Published by **Manish Jain** for BPB Publications, B-14, Connaught Place, New Delhi-110001 and Printed by him at Akash Press, New Delhi.

Trademark Acknowledgement

Disclaimer

The contents of this book are the views of the author, together with inputs from his friends' experiences in consulting in SAP. The views expressed in this book should not be construed as that SAP. Omissions and factual inaccuracies, if any, to correctly depict SAP in the book, are purely incidental and not intentional.

Dedication

To my dear wife: Meena

About the Author

A Post Graduate in Sciences, a Chartered Financial Analyst (CFA) and a Project Management Professional (PMP), V. Narayanan has more than 25 years of work experience in accounting, banking, finance and Information Technology. Trained in SAP FICO, he is a practicing SAP FI/CO Consultant-cum-Project Manager. He has been instrumental in managing SAP implementations (new, roll-outs, upgrades etc) for a number of international clients. Experienced in various versions of R/3 as well as mySAP ERP (SAP ERP, now) and new dimension products of SAP, he currently works in 'SAP Consulting', in one of the multinational IT consulting companies in India. Trained by Thames Valley University of UK, he is also a professional trainer and a visiting faculty in the areas of ERP, SAP, banking etc.

Armed with an excellent understanding of SAP Financial Accounting and Controlling, and with good cross-module expertise, he has authored a number of best-selling books on SAP Financial Accounting & Controlling.

Acknowledgment

A book like this requires a lot of inputs from experts so that the end-product is authentic. I have been fortunate enough to have a number of SAP experts - cutting across various application areas - as my friends and well wishers who were more than willing to provide me with helpful tips, clarifications and reviews in shaping up the several questions presented in this book. I consciously avoided listing them here for the simple reason that it may be possible that inadvertently I leave one or more names, and that may look inappropriate in spite them helping me. Instead, I extend a loud 'thanks' to all of them.

As you will see inside the book, very uncommon to a book like this, I have peppered the entire volume with a large number of screen-shots taken from SAP application for easy understanding. Thanks to Mr. Hariharan of Maagnus Infotech, Chennai, India, for allowing me to make use of their SAP system for generating these screen-shots.

I certainly need to thank Mr. Manish Jain of BPB Publishers for suggesting to bring out a book like this, which I was not even contemplating earlier.

Preface

As with my first book 'SAP FI: Transactions Made EASY' ('SAP R/3 FI Transactions' in the international market), this book is also different from the rest of the lot in the market: aiming at providing an enrichment of knowledge in SAP Financial Accounting, in an easy and simple way.

This is an enlarged and revised edition of my earlier book 'SAP FI/CO Demystified' ('SAP FI/CO Questions & Answers' in the international market), though this volume concentrates only on SAP FI (Financial Accounting). Whatever way you look at this, either as the second edition of the earlier book or as the new one, this book brings you a lot more information on SAP FI than the previous one.

The book unravels the complexity of SAP FI application and its component modules, through numerous 'Questions & Answers' (440 to be exact!). The questions are collected, grouped and explained in a logical way so that you progress seamlessly from the basic to the advanced topics. To visualize what is dealt in a particular question, there is help by way of numerous illustrations in the form of screen-shots, diagrams, and examples throughout the book. The screen-shots (from SAP ERP ECC6), in particular, will help you to comprehend as if you are in-front of a computer running SAP FI application!

The contents of the book are arranged in nine chapters:

- Organizational Units & Basic Settings
- General Ledger Accounting (FI-G/L) including new G/L
- Accounts Payable (FI-A/P) & Accounts Receivable (FI-A/R)
- Bank Accounting (FI-BL)
- Asset Accounting (FI-AA)
- Lease Accounting (FI-LA)
- Travel Management (FI-TV)
- SAP FI Tables
- SAP FI Transaction Codes

The chapter 'Organizational Units & Basic Settings' has 121 questions covering the basics in Financial Accounting. To help understanding how you need to set up the several organizational elements within FI, and their assignment, an organizational map is provided before we even start the questions. Besides the organizational structure, the chapter also discusses most of the basic settings like fiscal year, posting periods, currencies, document types, document number ranges, taxes, and even the Schedule Manager.

The 'General Ledger Accounting' chapter brings out the important aspects of both 'classical

G/L' and 'new G/L'. With 69 questions, this chapter takes you from chart of accounts, to G/L accounts, to the latest in G/L accounting including document splitting, segment accounting, parallel valuation, closing cockpit etc.

The customer /vendor masters, purchase cycle, terms of payment, payment program, tolerances, sales cycle, credit management, dunning etc are covered in the chapter 'Accounts Payable & Accounts Receivable' in 88 questions.

There are 34 questions in 'Bank Accounting' covering bank directory, house banks, bank chain, lockbox processing, bank statements (electronic & manual), checks etc.

The chapter on 'Asset Accounting' consists of 88 questions covering types of assets including assets under construction and low value assets, asset numbering, asset class, asset masters, acquisition, transfers, retirements, scrapping, depreciation, asset history sheet, asset explorer etc.

The 'Lease Accounting' discusses the leasing types, classifications, value IDs, lease accounting engine etc in 10 questions.

The 'Travel Management' chapter discusses travel requests, travel planning, travel expenses, the entire process flow in travel management, trips, planning manager, travel manager, technical options of setting up various components of travel management etc. There are 30 questions in this chapter.

Besides the questions, you will also see two chapters dedicated for 'SAP FI Tables' and 'SAP FI Transaction Codes' which will act as your one-stop reference.

- The 'SAP FI Tables' chapter lists 95 of the most important tables in SAP FI.
- A total of 430+ Transaction Codes are listed in two sections (configuration and others) in the chapter 'SAP FI Transaction Codes'.

Unlike an alphabetical listing of Transaction Codes / Tables which is the convention, this book attempts something functional and useful: these information are arranged the way you need, as most of the time you may not know the Transaction Code or Table to look at, but you know the functionality or task for which you are trying to find out the information.

So, how to use this book?

The answer is simple.

Read in any way you want. Pick-up a chapter and read all the questions or simply pick-up a question, go to the relevant page and see the answer. Use the book as a reference or a study-guide or a just a reading material, but make sure you understand a particular question or concept before moving on to the next.

All the 440 questions listed in this book, will certainly improve your understanding of the subject, whether it is for job interviews in SAP, especially in Financial Accounting, or just to use the application in a better manner in your current job.

Contents

Organizational Units & Basic Settings

General Ledger (FI-GL)

General Ledger Accounting (New)

Accounts Payable (FI-A/P) & Accounts Receivable (FI-A/R)

Bank Accounting (FI-BL)

Asset Accounting (FI-AA)

Lease Accounting (FI-LA)

Travel Management (FI-TV)

SAP® FI Financial Accounting

Before getting into the questions, please look at the FI organizational structure depicted below and understand how it is structured. When moving through the questions, at any point of time, if you have a clarification on the arrangement of the various organizational elements, do visit this page again. To be successful as a FI or CO consultant you need to have a thorough grasp on this basic fundamental block in SAP FI / CO.

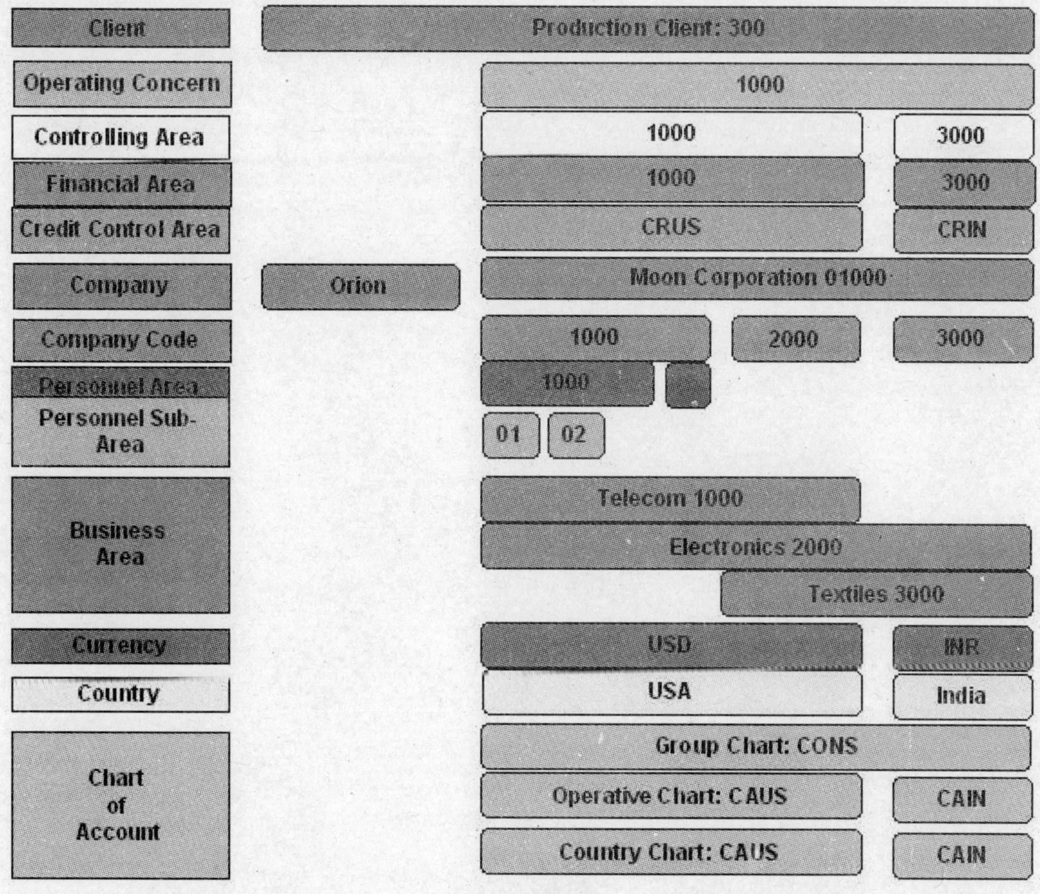

Figure 0.1: FI Organizational Structure

The questions are arranged into several areas within FI, including:

- Organizational Units & Basic Settings
- General Ledger Accounting (FI-G/L)
- General Ledger Accounting (New)
- Accounts Payable (FI-A/P) & Accounts Receivable (FI-A/R)
- Bank Accounting (FI-BL)
- Asset Accounting (FI-AA)
- Lease Accounting (FI-LA)
- Travel Management (FI-TV)

1

Organizational Units & Basic Settings

The questions in this section relate to the basics in SAP Financial Accounting and will help you to understand how to design / define the organizational units, the relationships, assignments and the interdependencies among them, the various configuration units/settings like fiscal year, posting period, chart of accounts etc as detailed below:

- Company
- Company codes
- Fiscal year
- Posting period
- Currency
- Exchange rate
- Tax

1. What is an 'Enterprise Structure' in SAP?

The '**Enterprise Structure**', helps you to portray the specific organizational structure of your business in the SAP System. SAP, in its standard version, comes delivered with sample organizational units (for accounting, logistics, human resources etc): do not expect SAP to 'provide' all that would be required for your business requirement, but it is a good practice to try to match the structure provided by SAP with that of your specific requirement, and extend the SAP structures wherever you need more or different units. It is very critical that you define the structure correctly as you will not be able to change these after the business 'go-live'. It is also necessary that you restrict the access to these structures through appropriate 'authorization profiles'. Remember to define only the required structure. Nothing more, nothing less!

2. What do you mean by 'Organizational Units' in SAP?

The '**Organizational Units**' in SAP, are the elements or structures representing the business functions, and are used in reporting. For example, Client (across the various modules), Company Code (FI), Controlling Area (CO), Plant (Logistics), Sales Organization (SD), Purchasing Organization (MM), Employee Group (HR) etc.

3. What are all 'Organizational Units' to be defined in SAP FI?

The various '**Organizational Units**' in SAP FI (Version: SAP ERP/ECC6) are:

- Company (Non-required)
- Company Code (Mandatory)
- Business Area (Mandatory)
- Consolidation Business Area (Mandatory)
- Functional Area (Mandatory)
- Credit Control Area (Mandatory)
- Functional Management (FM) Area (Mandatory)
- Profit Centre (Mandatory)
- Segment (Optional)

You will be defining these units under '*SAP Customizing Implementation Guide>Enterprise Structure>Definition>Financial Accounting*' (Version: SAP ERP ECC6):

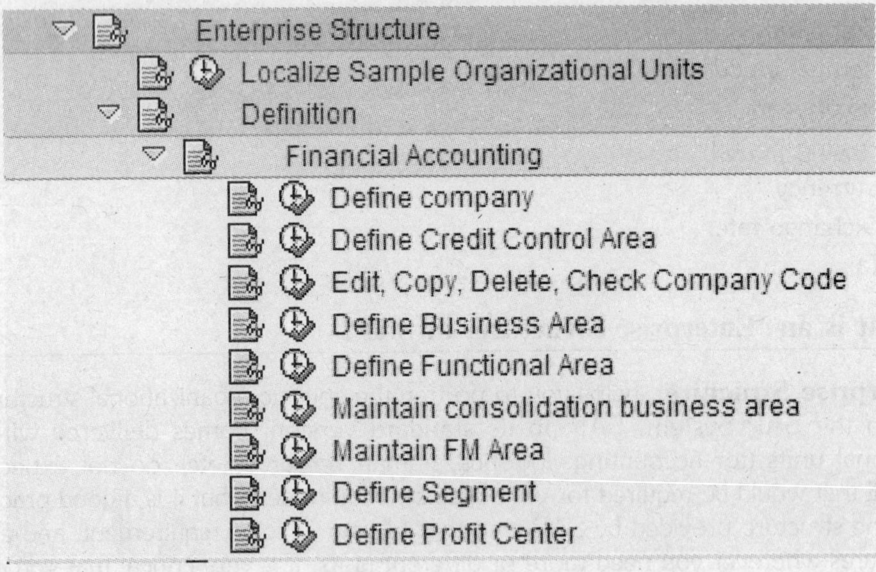

Figure 1.1: FI Organizational Units

Transaction Code
SPRO

4. What is a 'Company'?

A **Company** in SAP is represented by a 6-character alphanumeric code and usually represents the organizational unit in accounting depicting the business enterprise as per the particular country's commercial law requirements. A Company can include one or more Company Codes. The creation/definition of a Company, in SAP, is optional, but the consolidation functions in SAP are based on the Company. SAP provides you with the sample Company 'G00000' with all the foreign key relationships. It is recommended that you keep the pre-set company ID G00000 if you only require one company: by this you can reduce the number of tables which you need to adjust.

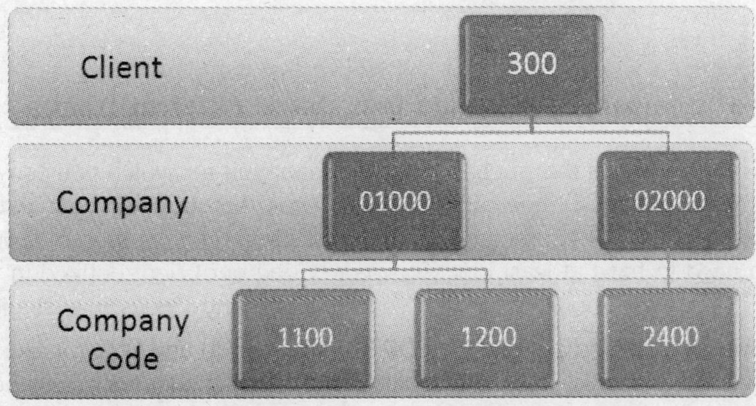

Figure 1.2: Company & Company Code

Company	01000
Company name	Moon Corporation
Name of company 2	

Detailed information	
Street	West Pomenade
PO Box	
Postal code	60000
City	Frankfurt
Country	DE
Language Key	DE
Currency	EUR

Figure 1.3: Define a Company

Note that all the Company Codes for a Company must work with the same operational chart of accounts and fiscal year, though the currencies used in each of the Company Codes can be different.

(When you enter the Transaction, do not be confused when the screen shows 'Change View "Internal Trading Partners": Overview'. This is where you define the Company).

Transaction Code
OX15

5. What is a 'Company Code', and how this is different from a 'Company'?

A **Company Code** in SAP is the smallest organizational unit for which you can draw individual Financial Statements (Balance Sheet and Profit & Loss Account) for your external statutory reporting. It is denoted by a 4-character alphanumeric code. The creation of Company Code is mandatory: you need to have at least one Company Code per Client defined in the system, for implementing FI. You may, however, define several Company Codes in a single Client.

SAP comes delivered with Company Code 0001 in clients 000 and 001 for Germany (Country Code: DE). All country-specific parameters (like payment methods, tax calculation procedures, chart of accounts etc) are preset in this company code for this country. In case, you want to create a Company Code for the USA and its legal requirements, note to run the *country installation program*, first, in client 001: the country of Company Code 0001 is then set to "US" (from "DE") and all country-specific parameters related to it are set to USA.

You may define a Company Code by copying from an existing one (*Copy, Delete, Check Company Code Option*). In fact SAP recommends this approach (less time consuming than creating new), as this has the advantage that you also copy the existing company code-specific parameters: you may then change certain data in the relevant application.

You may also define the Company Code anew (the second option in the following figure), from scratch.

Activities

Perf...	Name of Activity
	Copy, delete, check company code
	Edit Company Code Data

Figure 1.4: Options to define a Company Code

6. What needs to be done if you define a Company Code by 'Copy' function?

When you copy an existing Company Code, all the Company Code-specific specifications of the 'source' ('From Company Code') are copied to your new company code 'target' ('To Company Code').

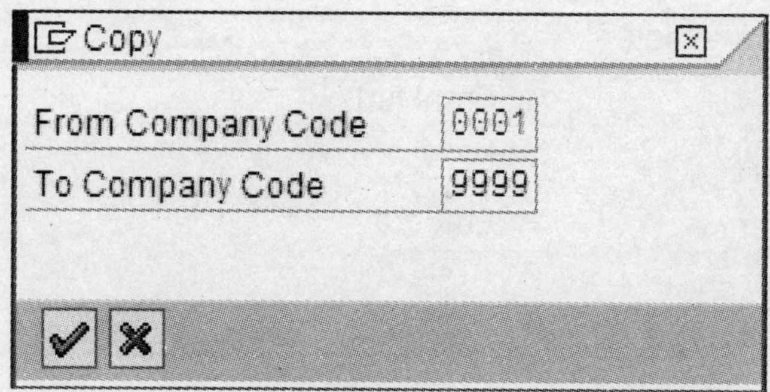

Figure 1.5: Define a Company Code (by 'Copy' function)

Note that the target Company Code should not have been defined earlier, as the same will be defined automatically during the copying procedure.

So, how to do this?

- Create the company code using the function "Copy Company Code".
- Enter / modify Company Code data (name, description, address, and currency) with the function "Edit Company Code Data"
- Use the **Transaction Code OBY6** to modify any other 'Global Parameters' which need to be different from that of the 'source' Company Code.

Transaction Code
EC01

7. How to create a new Company Code from scratch?

You can use the function "Edit Company Code Data" to create a Company Code, from scratch. In this case, the Company Code "global data" is not copied.

Once you create the new Company Code using this option, then you need to maintain the Global Parameters using the **Transaction Code OBY6**.

Company Code	9999
Company Name	Model Company

Additional data	
City	Frankfurt
Country	DE
Currency	EUR
Language	

Figure 1.6: Define a Company Code (by 'Edit Company Code Data' function)

8. How to change the Company Code key?

Use the "Replace" function in the **Transaction Code EC01**, to change the Company Code key. But, this is only possible if no postings have been made in the Company Code that is to be replaced with the new Company Code key.

9. What are all the important 'Global Parameters' for a Company Code?

The 'Global Parameters' for a Company Code are segregated into to two sections:

- **Accounting Organization**

  The parameters under this section include the chart of accounts, Credit Control Area, FM area, company, fiscal year variant etc. This is also the area wherein you will normally set the Company Code as 'productive' before 'going-live'.

Accounting organization			
Chart of Accts	INT	Country Chart/Accts	
Company		FM Area	
Credit Control Area	EURO	Fiscal Year Variant	K4
Ext. co. code	☐	Global CoCde	
Company code is productive	☐	VAT Registration No.	

Figure 1.7: 'Accounting Organization' parameters under 'Global Parameters'

- **Processing Parameters**

  The Processing Parameters include settings like field status variant, fiscal year variant, whether you want the system to propose fiscal year during document entry, Company Code-Controlling Area assignment, what would be the calculation base for discount/ tax etc, whether you will need financial statements per business area, maximum exchange rate deviation allowed etc.

Processing parameters

Document entry screen variant		☐ Business area fin. statements
Field status variant	0001	☑ Propose fiscal year
Pstng period variant	0001	☐ Define default value date
Max. exchange rate deviation	10 %	☐ No forex rate diff. when clearing in LC
Sample acct rules var.		☐ Tax base is net value
Workflow variant	0001	☐ Discount base is net value
Inflation Method		☑ Financial Assets Mgmt active
Crcy transl. for tax		☐ Purchase account processing
CoCd->CO Area	2	☐ JV Accounting Active
Cost of sales accounting actv.		☐ Hedge request active
☐ Negative Postings Permitted		☐ Enable amount split
☐ Cash Management activated		☐ Tax Rep. Date Active

Figure 1.8: 'Processing Parameters' under 'Global Parameters'

Transaction Code
OBY6

10. Can you assign more than one 'Company Code' to a 'Company'?

Yes, you can assign more than one Company Code to a Company. But, all such Company Codes should use the same operating *Chart of Accounts* and same *FiscalYear*, even though they all can have different *Local Currencies*.

11. What is a 'Business Area'?

Business Areas correspond to specific business segments of a company, and may cut across different Company Codes (for example product lines). They can also represent different responsibility areas (for example, branch units). You can create financial statements for business areas, which can be used for various internal reporting purposes.

Business Area	Description
2000	Plant engineering & constructi
3000	Automotive
3400	Metal, wood & paper
3500	Aerospace
4000	Chemicals
5000	Consumer products: non-food

Figure 1.9: Business Area

Transaction Code
OX03

12. How to enable Business Area Financial Statements (FS)?

There are two ways in which you can enable the financial statements for the business areas:

- Enabling the business area financial statements in the Global Parameters of Company Codes (one by one for each of the Company Codes)

Processing parameters	
Document entry screen variant [ ]	[ ] Business area fin. statements

Figure 1.10: Enable Business Area Financial Statements (OBY6)

Transaction Code
OBY6

- Enabling the business area financial statements for more than one Company Code, at the same time.

Co	Company Name	City	Business area FS
0001	P A.G.	Walldorf	☐

Figure 1.11: Enable Business Area Financial Statements (OB65)

Transaction Code
OB65

When you set this indicator, the Business area field is always ready for input (when documents are posted), independent of the field control of the posting keys and of the accounts.

13. What precautions you should take when you 'enable' Business Area FS?

You should only set the indicator for the ***Business Area*** field if you work with ***all*** the financial statements (by this the business area field is always ready for input irrespective of your settings of field control for posting keys/accounts). If you only work with business areas in a few financial statement areas (for example P&L), then you should not set the indicator: instead, you should make the ***Business Area*** field ready for input for the business area-relevant accounts using the *field control of the accounts / posting keys.*

14. Can you derive 'Business Area' by not assigning the same in a posting?

Yes. The **Business Area** can also be derived from other account assignments: for example, Cost Centre. But to do this, you need to define the business area in the master record of that particular Cost Centre.

15. How to post Cross-company Code Business Area postings?

By using a cross Company Code transaction, one should be able to post to different 'Business Areas' cutting across various Company Codes. Any number of 'Business Area –Company Code' combinations are possible.

16. Define 'Consolidation Business Area'?

A '**Consolidation Business Area**', identified by a 4-character ID, is an organizational unit within accounting, corresponding to a limited area of operations or responsibility (representing a central business *segment* within a business organization), from a consolidation point of view.

Companies and Consolidation Business Areas together make up the consolidation units that are the basis for business area consolidation.

Transaction Code
OCC1

17. What is a 'Credit Control Area'?

The **credit control area**, in SAP, helps in administering the credit management functions relating to the customers. This organizational unit is used both in SD and FI-AR (Accounts Receivable) modules. By definition, you can have more than one Credit Control Area in a Client and each Company Code is assigned exactly to one Credit Control Area. However, it is true that you can attach many Company Codes to the same Credit Control Area. The credit limits within the same Credit Control Area are to be defined in the same currency. Credit information is made available per customer in the Credit Control Area.

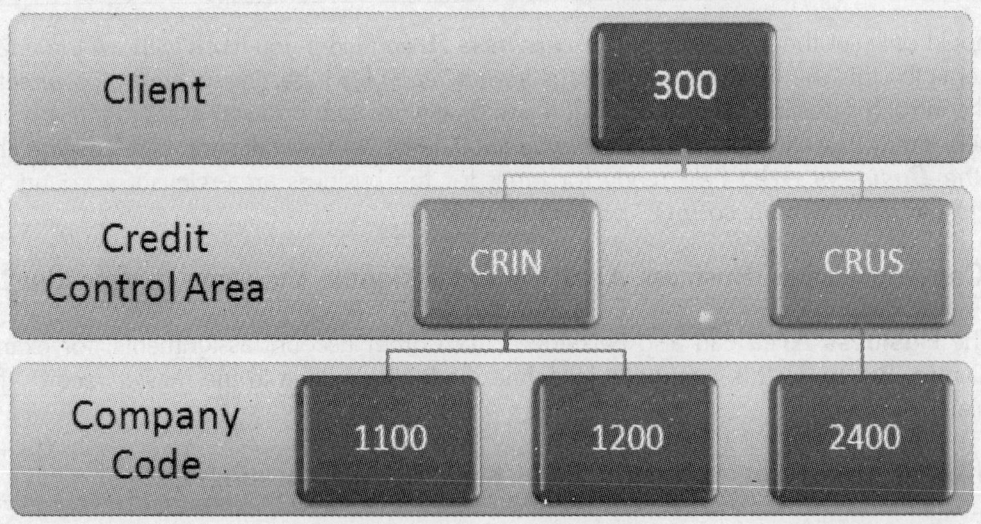

Figure 1.12: Credit Control Area: the possibilities

SAP comes delivered with the sample Credit Control Area '0001'.

Transaction Code
OB45

Cred.Contr.Area 0001 Credit Control Area 0001
Currency USD

Data for updating SD
Update
FY Variant

Default data for automatically creating new customers
Risk category
Credit limit
Rep. group

Organizational data
☐ All co. codes

Figure 1.13: Credit Control Area

18. What is a 'Functional Area'?

A '**functional area**' in SAP is an organizational unit in Accounting that is used to classify the expenses of the organization by functions like production, sales, marketing, administration etc. This classification is required for 'cost of sales accounting (COS)' (Organizations that use Funds Management do not normally use cost of sales accounting; in such cases, the Functional Area can be used as an additional account assignment).

To use the Functional Area in your organization, you must make the appropriate settings for the Functional Area in the Customizing of Financial Accounting. You also need to activate the Functional Area in the Customizing of Funds Management Government. In addition, you must make the Functional Area ready for input from when transactions are put through across application areas.

19. What Customizing settings are required for 'Functional Area'?

The settings are to be done in the *Customizing of Cost of Sales accounting*, as the functional area is also used for cost of sales accounting in Financial Accounting.

1. **Define Functional Area**

   SAP Customizing Implementation Guide > Enterprise Structure > Definition > Financial Accounting > Define Functional Area

   You may also use the following Menu Path to define the Functional Area:

   SAP Customizing Implementation Guide > Financial Accounting (New) > Financial Accounting Global Settings (New) > Ledgers > Fields > Standard Fields > Functional Area for Cost of Sales Accounting > Define Functional Area

Functional areas

Functional Area	Name
0100	Production
0300	Sales and Distribution
0400	Administration
0500	Research & Development

Figure 1.14: Functional Area

Transaction Code
OKBD

2. **Activate cost of sales accounting for preparation**

   Use the Menu Path: *SAP Customizing Implementation Guide > Financial Accounting (New) > Financial Accounting Global Settings (New) > Ledgers > Fields > Standard Fields > Functional Area for Cost of Sales Accounting > Activate Cost of Sales Accounting for Preparation*

Co...	Company Name	COS status
0001	SAP A.G.	In preparation

Figure 1.15: Activate COS accounting for Preparation

This is to make the Functional Area field ready for input in the master data for G/L accounts, cost types and some of the CO account assignment objects. Select 'In *preparation*' from the drop-down list (there will be three options: 'Inactive', 'In preparation' and 'Active'). No functional area is derived for postings in this company code.

3. **Define the derivation procedure for the Functional Area**

   SAP recommends that you select the setting FA on entry screen in order to ensure that the Functional Area can also be derived for commitments postings. The derivation of the Functional Area takes place in accordance with the rules described under Rules for deriving the Functional Area for postings. You should also be aware that you cannot define a Functional Area in the master record of a balance sheet account.

4. **Enter the Functional Area in the master data (of the specific objects)**

   If you use Funds Management integrated with Controlling, you should ensure that the Functional Area can always be derived from this master data. In this situation you should avoid using substitution.

   Use the Menu Path: *SAP Customizing Implementation Guide > Financial Accounting (New) > Financial Accounting Global Settings (New) > Ledgers > Fields > Standard Fields > Functional Area for Cost of Sales Accounting > Enter Functional Area >*

   Enter Functional Area in G/L Account Master Data

   Enter Functional Area in Cost Element Master Data

   Enter Functional Area in Cost Center Categories

   Enter Functional Area in Request Type

5. **Define a substitution for deriving the Functional Area**

   You should only execute this step if your requirements for the derivation of the Functional Area are not met by entering the Functional Area in the master data of some of the account assignment objects (You can find the steps under Set up substitution for cost of sales accounting)

6. **Activate cost of sales accounting for your company codes**

   Use the Menu Path: *SAP Customizing Implementation Guide > Financial Accounting (New) > Financial Accounting Global Settings (New) > Ledgers > Ledger > Activate Cost of Sales Accounting*

Co...	Company Name	COS status
0001	SAP A.G.	Active

Figure 1.16: COS activated

Once activated, when you post to these company codes, the Functional Areas are derived and updated.

20. What is the use of 'Financial Management (FM) Area'?

A '**financial management area**', denoted by a 4-character ID, is an organizational unit within accounting through which you can structure the business organization from the perspective of *Cash Budget Management* and Funds Management. However, to take advantage of the high degree of integration in the SAP system, you must link these FM areas with organizational units from other applications (say, if you assign a FI document to a *Funds Management* object -like a commitment item or funds center - the system has to determine an FM area, so that it can record the data in Funds Management). The FM area is taken from the company code when you assign a company code to an FM area. More than one company code can be assigned to an FM area. SAP provides you with the FM area 0001 in the standard system.

Note to define the currency for each of the FM Areas you define in the system (it is NOT necessary that this currency and the Company Code currency should be the same).

Transaction Code
OF01

FM Area 0001

Financial Management Areas

FM area text: FM area 0001

- [ ] No purc.orders
- [ ] No parked docs
- [ ] FMA ledger only
- [ ] Bank posting date
- [ ] Summarize E/R
- [ ] Clear in batch
- [ ] FI Update Off

Figure 1.17: Functional Management (FM) Area

21. What is a 'Segment'?

A '**Segment**' in SAP is a division of a company for which you can create financial statements for external reporting. The accounting principles US GAAP and IFRS require companies to perform segment reporting. US GAAP requires a virtually complete balance sheet at the segment level for segment reporting (essentially everything apart from stockholders' equity). The segment is defined as a sub-area of a company with activities that generate expenses and revenues, with an operating result that is regularly used by management for profit assessment and resource allocation purposes, and for which separate financial data is available.

Once you define a segment, it is then possible when you define the Profit Center that you can enter an associated Segment in the master record of that Profit Center. If no Segment is specified manually during posting (only possible for transactions in FI), the Segment is determined from the master record of the Profit Center which itself can be assigned manually or derived.

Note that the *Document Splitting Procedure* (made available with the introduction of New G/L) is the prerequisite for creating financial statements at any time for the Segment dimension.

Use the Menu Path: *SAP Customizing Implementation Guide > Enterprise Structure > Definition > Define Segment*, to define a Segment.

22. What differentiates a 'Business Segment' from 'Geographical Segment'?

IAS requires primary and secondary segmentation for Segment reporting, which have different reporting depth. A distinction is made between (a) Business Segment and (b) Geographical Segment.

A **business segment** is a distinguishable sub-activity of a Company that relates to the manufacturing of a product or the provision of a service and that has risks and revenues that differ from those in other business segments.

A **geographical segment**, on the other hand, is a distinguishable sub-activity of a Company that relates to the manufacturing of a product or the provision of a service within a specific field of business, with the risks and revenues of a geographical segment differ from the sub-activities in other fields of business.

23. What is a 'Profit Centre'?

A **profit center**, in SAP, is an organizational unit in accounting that reflects a management-oriented structure of the organization for the purpose of internal control through which you can analyze operating results for profit centers using either the cost-of-sales or the period accounting approach. It is also possible to use the profit center as *Investment Centre* by calculating the fixed capital.

Note that the Profit Center Accounting (PCA) at the profit center level is based on costs and revenues, which are assigned statistically by multiple parallel updating to all logistical activities and other allocations of relevance for a profit center. Every profit center is assigned to a Controlling (CO) area. This assignment is necessary because PCA displays values in G/L accounts.

Transaction Code
KE51

Use the Menu Path, *SAP Customizing Implementation Guide > Enterprise Structure > Definition > Define Profit Center.*

(In the earlier versions SAP R/3 till 4.70, profit center did not find a place in 'Definition' under 'Enterprise Structure'. But, with the introduction of mySAP ERP, this now forms a part of the 'Enterprise Structure')

Create Profit Center

Master Data

Profit Center P1000

Copy from

Profit Center

CO Area 0001

Figure 1.18: Profit Center

24. What are two pre-requisites to define a 'Profit Centre'?

The following are the two pre-requisites that you need to be aware of for defining a profit centre:

- You should have defined the **Controlling (CO) area**. The system will prompt you to enter or select the desired Controlling area before you proceed to define the profit center.
- The **Standard Hierarchy** for the Controlling area should also have been created either directly or via the enterprise organization.

25. How to ensure data consistency between 'Profit Centre' and other areas?

To ensure that your data in Profit Center Accounting (PCA) is consistent with that in other areas, you need to assign each profit center to the *Standard Hierarchy* in your Controlling (CO) area. The Standard Hierarchy is used in the information system, allocations and various planning functions. It is also possible to assign your profit centers to alternative hierarchical structures which are completely independent of the standard hierarchy. These structures are called *Profit Center Groups*.

26. Can you create a 'Profit Centre' by copying a 'Cost Center'?

Yes.

If the profit centers in your organization are closely linked to your cost centers, you can then simply copy your cost center master data to create your profit centers.

27. What is a 'Fiscal Year' and 'Fiscal Year Variant'?

A **fiscal year** is the accounting period, which normally spreads over 12 months. The financial statements are drawn for a fiscal year. The fiscal year, in SAP, is defined using a **'fiscal year variant'**.

All ***calendar year fiscal year variants***, in standard SAP, are denoted usually as K1, K2 etc.

Fiscal year variants

FV	Description	Year-depend	Calendar yr	Number of posting	No.of spe
K0	Calendar year, 0 spec. period	☐	☑	12	
K1	Calendar year, 1 spec. period	☐	☑	12	1
K2	Calendar year, 2 spec. periods	☐	☑	12	2
K3	Calendar year, 3 spec. periods	☐	☑	12	3
K4	Calendar year, 4 spec. periods	☐	☑	12	4

Figure 1.19: Fiscal Year Variant (Calendar Year)

It is also possible that the fiscal year may be shorter than 12 months, and this is called as '***shortened fiscal year***'.

Fiscal year variants

FV	Description	Year-depend	Calendar yr	Number of posting	No.of sp
R1	Shortened fisc.year Jan-Sep'09	☑	☐	9	4

Figure 1.20: Shortened Fiscal Year Variant

The fiscal year may or may not correspond to the calendar year. In the standard SAP system, the ***non-calendar fiscal year variants*** are denoted by V1, V2 etc.

Fiscal year variants					
FV	Description	Year-depend	Calendar yr	Number of posting	No.of spe
V3	Apr.- March, 4 special periods	☐	☐	12	4
V6	July - June, 4 special periods	☐	☐	12	4
V9	Oct.- Sept., 4 special periods	☐	☐	12	4

Figure 1.21: Fiscal Year Variant (Non-Calendar Year)

Transaction Code
OB29

28. How do you assign a 'Fiscal Year Variant' to Company Code?

One **fiscal year variant** can be assigned to one or more Company Codes.

CoCd	Company Name	Fiscal Year Variant	Description
0001	SAP A.G.	K4	Calendar year, 4 spec. periods
0003	SAP US (IS-HT-SW)	K4	Calendar year, 4 spec. periods

Figure 1.22: Assign Fiscal Year Variant to a Company Code

Transaction Code
OB37

29. What is a 'Posting Period'?

A fiscal year, in SAP, is divided into various **posting periods**, with a start and end date defined for each of these periods. Any document posting is possible only when the 'posting periods' are in place in the system. Normally there will be 12 posting periods. A posting period consists of a month and year.

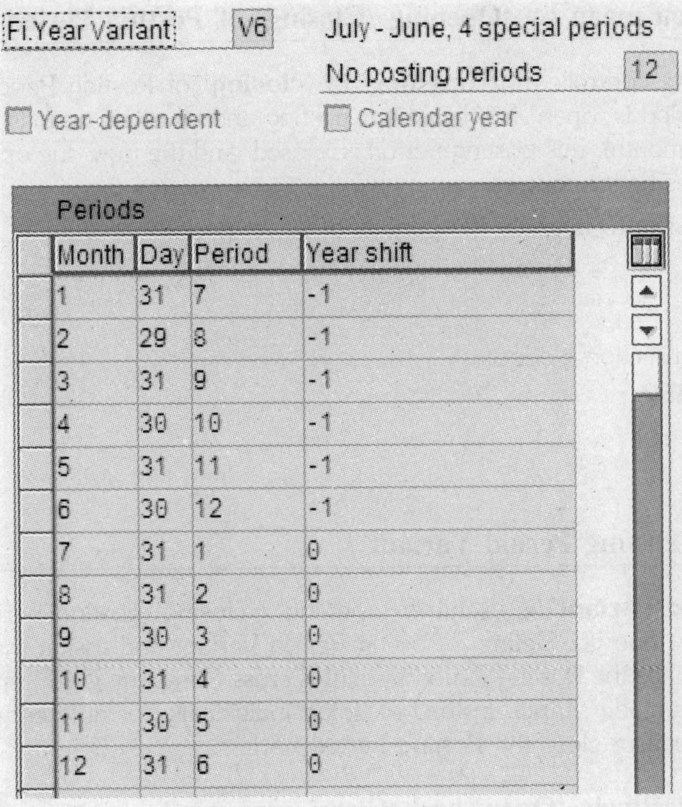

Fi.Year Variant V6 July - June, 4 special periods

No.posting periods 12

Year-dependent Calendar year

Periods

Month	Day	Period	Year shift
1	31	7	-1
2	29	8	-1
3	31	9	-1
4	30	10	-1
5	31	11	-1
6	30	12	-1
7	31	1	0
8	31	2	0
9	30	3	0
10	31	4	0
11	30	5	0
12	31	6	0

Figure 1.23: Posting Periods

30. How the system identifies a 'Posting Period'?

Based on the posting date entered into the system while posting a document, the system automatically determines the period, by looking at the document date and the year. For this, you should have properly defined the Fiscal Year Variant.

31. What happens when you post to year 2008, when you are in 2009?

First of all, to post a document relating to a previous year, say, 2008 when you are in 2009, the relevant posting period should be 'open' in the system. When such a posting is done, the system makes some adjustments on the background:

- The carry forward balances of the current year, already done, are updated in case the posting is affecting balance sheet items.
- If the posting is going to affect the Profit & Loss accounts, then the system adjusts the carried forward profit or loss balances to the Retained Earnings account(s).

32. What do you mean by 'Opening /Closing' of Posting Periods?

Postings in SAP are controlled by '**opening**' or '**closing**' of Posting Periods. Normally, the current posting period is 'open' for document posting and all other periods are closed. At the end of the period (month), this posting period is 'closed' and the new one opened for postings. This way it provides better control.

It is, however, possible to keep all the periods or select periods open.

Transaction Code
OB52

33. What is a 'Posting Period Variant'?

A '**posting period variant'** is useful in 'opening / closing' posting periods across many Company Codes, at one go. Define a Posting Period Variant and assign the same to various Company Codes. Since the Posting Period Variant is cross-Company Code, opening and closing of posting period is made simple. Instead of doing individually for different Company Codes, you just need to open or close the Posting Period Variant.

34. Can you selectively 'Open' and 'Close' accounts?

Yes.

It is possible to selectively control the 'opening' and' closing' for various types of accounts. Usually, a '+' is mentioned in the top most entry (under column 'A') indicating that all the accounts types are allowed for posting. Now, against the G/L(S) accounts specify the period which needs to be open. This ensures that all the account types are open for the current period, indicated by' +', and only the G/L accounts are open for the previous period.

Not only select account types, but also select accounts within an account type can be opened or closed for a specific period.

35. Why it is not possible to post to a customer a/c in a previously closed 'Period'?

When you want to selectively 'close' or 'open' posting period of some accounts (account range), there will be no problem with that if you are doing it for G/L accounts. But, if it is a sub-ledger account (like the customer), the same has to be achieved via opening or closing the account interval of the '***reconciliation account'*** of that account type.

36. Can you open a 'Posting Period' only for a particular user?

Yes. SAP allows you to open or close the posting period only for specific users. This can be achieved by maintaining an ***Authorization Group (AuGr).***

A	From acct	To account	Year	To period	Year	From per.2	Year	To period	Year	AuGr
+			2008	3	2009	1	2008	12	2008	
A		ZZZZZZZZZZ	2008	3	2009	1	2008	12	2008	

Figure 1.24: 'Posting' control through Authorization Group

37. What is a 'Special Period'? When you will use that?

Besides the normal posting periods, SAP allows for defining a maximum of four more posting periods, known as **special periods** as these are used for year-end closing activities. This is achieved by dividing the last posting period into more than one period. However, all the postings into these special periods should fall within the last posting period.

The special periods cannot be determined automatically by the system based on the posting date of the document: the special period need to be manually entered into the 'posting period' field in the document header.

Fiscal year variants					
FV	Description	Year-dep	Calen	Number of posti	No.of special periods
K0	Calendar year, 0 spec. period	☐	☑	12	
K1	Calendar year, 1 spec. period	☐	☑	12	1
K2	Calendar year, 2 spec. periods	☐	☑	12	2
K3	Calendar year, 3 spec. periods	☐	☑	12	3

Figure 1.25: Special Periods

38. What can be the maximum number of 'Posting Periods' in SAP?

Under G/L accounting, you can have a maximum of 16 posting periods (12 regular + 4 Special Periods). However, you can have up to a maximum of 366 posting periods in case of '***special purpose ledgers***'.

39. What is a 'Special Purpose Ledger'?

'Special Purpose Ledgers' (FI-SL) are used in reporting. These are all basically user-defined ledgers, which can be maintained either as G/L or subsidiary ones with various account assignment objects (with SAP-dimensions like cost centre, business area, profit centre etc or customer-defined dimensions like region, area etc)

Once defined, this functionality helps you to report at various levels. Ideally you collect the information, combine them and create the 'totals'. This is something like an additional reporting feature, and usage of this feature will have no effect on the regular functionalities of SAP.

40. What variations are possible in defining a 'Fiscal Year'?

- **Fiscal Year = Calendar Year**

  The fiscal year starts on Jan-1, there are 12 posting periods; the posting periods correspond to the calendar months; there is no need to define each of the posting periods (Table 1-1).

Table 1.1: Calendar Year Fiscal Year

Posting Period	Start Date	End Date
1	1-Jan	31-Jan
2	1-Feb	28/29 Feb
3	1-Mar	31-Mar
4	1-Apr	30-Apr
5	1-May	31-May
6	1-Jun	30-Jun
7	1-Jul	31-Jul
8	1-Aug	31-Aug
9	1-Sep	30-Sep
10	1-Oct	31-Oct
11	1-Nov	30-Nov
12	1-Dec	31-Dec

- **Fiscal Year is NOT the same as that of the Calendar Year**

  In this case, you need to specify (1) how many posting periods you want and (2) how the system should derive the posting period. Since the posting period does not correspond to the calendar month, the start and end date of each of the posting period need to be maintained.

41. What is known as 'Year Shift' / 'Displacement' in a Fiscal Year?

When the fiscal year is not the same as that the calendar year, we need to define a 'displacement factor' for each of the posting periods so as to correctly identify the number of the posting period.

For example, consider the fiscal year variant V3. The fiscal year starts on 1st April, ending on 31st March of the next calendar year, the displacement factor or year shift from April to December is '0, and for January to March, it will be '–1'. By defining this way, the system is able to recognize the correct posting period. A posting made on 25th Jan 2009, will then be interpreted as 10th posting period in fiscal year 2008, even though it is in the 1st calendar month of year 2009.

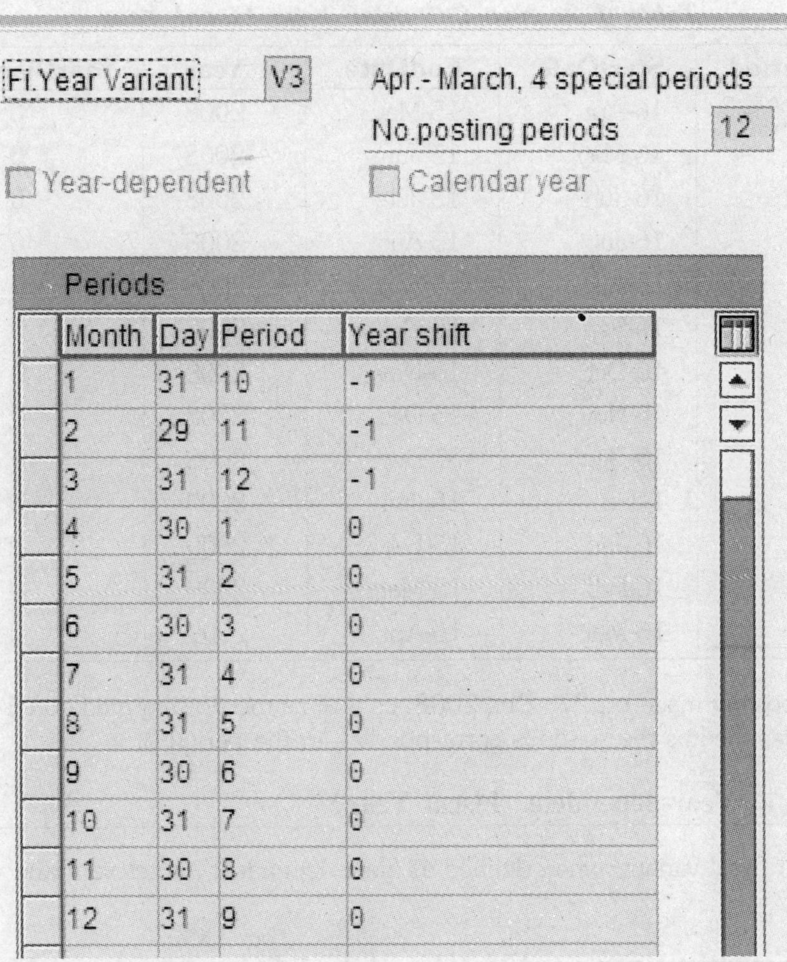

Fi.Year Variant V3 Apr.- March, 4 special periods

No.posting periods 12

Year-dependent Calendar year

Periods

Month	Day	Period	Year shift
1	31	10	-1
2	29	11	-1
3	31	12	-1
4	30	1	0
5	31	2	0
6	30	3	0
7	31	4	0
8	31	5	0
9	30	6	0
10	31	7	0
11	30	8	0
12	31	9	0

Figure 1.26: Year shift / Displacement in Fiscal Year Variant

42. Can we have 'non-Calendar' months as 'Periods' in 'non-Calendar' Fiscal Year?

Yes.

The 'non-calendar fiscal year' can either correspond to (1) calendar months or (2) non-calendar months.

In case of non-calendar months as the posting periods, you need to specify the start and end date of these posting periods. Consider a fiscal year starting on 16th April 2008 and ending on 15th April 2009. Here, the posting period-1 starts on 16th April and ends on 15th May and so on. Note that the posting period-9 will have two displacements (0 & -1) as indicated below in the Table 1-2:

Table 1.2: Non-Calendar Year Fiscal Year

Posting Period	StartDate	EndDate	Year	YearDisplacement
1	16-Apr	15-May	2008	0
2	16-May	15-Jun	2008	0
3	16-Jun	15-Jul	2008	0
4	16-Jul	15-Aug	2008	0
5	16-Aug	15-Sep	2008	0
6	16-Sep	15-Oct	2008	0
7	16-Oct	15-Nov	2008	0
8	16-Nov	15-Dec	2008	0
9	16-Dec	31-Dec	2008	0
9	1-Jan	15-Jan	2009	-1
10	16-Jan	15-Feb	2009	-1
11	16-Feb	15-Mar	2009	-1
12	16-Mar	15-Apr	2009	-1

As a result, a posting made on 27th Dec 2008, as well as the posting made on 14th Jan 2009 are correctly identified as the postings corresponding to the period-9.

43. What is a 'Year-dependent' Fiscal Year?

A calendar year fiscal variant, when defined as 'year-dependent', is relevant and valid only for that year.

44. What precautions you need to take while defining 'Shortened Fiscal Year'?

Note that the '**shortened fiscal year**' is always year-dependent. This has to be followed or preceded by a full fiscal year (12 months). Both the shortened and the full fiscal year, in this case, have to be defined using a single Fiscal Year Variant.

45. When you may require 'Shortened Fiscal Year'?

A '**shortened fiscal year**' is one containing less than 12 months. This kind of fiscal year is required (a) when you are in the process of setting up of a company, or (b) when you switch over from one fiscal year (say, calendar year) to another type of fiscal year (non-calendar).

46. How do you open a new 'Fiscal Year' in the system?

You do not need to 'open' the new fiscal year as a separate activity: once you make a posting into the new fiscal year, that fiscal year is automatically opened. Or, the new fiscal year is automatically opened when you run the '***balance carry-forward***' program.

However, you should have:

- The relevant posting period already opened in the new fiscal year
- Completed the document number range assignment if you are following year-dependent number range assignment
- Defined a new Fiscal Year Variant if you follow year-dependent fiscal year variant

47. How do you 'Carry-Forward' the account balances?

For all the G/L accounts, if you have already posted into the new fiscal year, you do not need to 'carry-forward' the balances manually. Else, use the various 'carry-forward' programs supplied by SAP for this task.

In the case of customer / vendor accounts, a posting in the new fiscal year does not 'carry-forward' the balances from the previous fiscal year: in this case, you need to manually carry forward these balances into the new fiscal year. However, any postings in the previous fiscal year(s), will update the balances carried forward into the subsequent fiscal years.

48. Explain how 'Carry-Forward' happens SAP?

- For all the Balance Sheet items, customer and vendor accounts, the balances of these accounts are just carried forward to the new fiscal year, along with account assignments if any.
- In case of Profit & Loss accounts, the system carries forward the profit or loss (in the local currency) to the Retained Earnings account, and the balances of these accounts are set to '0'. No additional account assignments are transferred.

49. Is there a pre-requisite for 'Carry-Forward' activity?

Yes, for Profit & Loss accounts, you should have defined the Retained Earnings account in the system. Additionally, you should have also specified the '***Profit & Loss Account Type***', in the master record of each of these for Profit & Loss accounts.

There are no such requirements for G/L accounts, customer and vendor accounts.

50. How SAP adjusts the 'c/f balance' in New Year when you post to previous year(s)?

When G/L balances are carried forward, at the end of a fiscal year (say, 2008) the system uses an indicator to determine whether the balance has already been carried over to the new fiscal year. That being the case, if you post values to a previous year (say, 2007) the system automatically adjusts the balance carried forward in the new fiscal year. This is very useful as you do not need to re-run the 'carry-forward' program again and again when adjustments are to be done for the previous year(s)

51. How to correct carry forward balances if you need to change a G/L classification?

If, after the balance has been carried forward into the new fiscal year, you find that a G/L account has been mistakenly classified as B/S account (instead of P & L account) in the previous fiscal year, you just need to do two things to correct the situation:

- Adjust the G/L account, in the G/L account master record (in Chart of Accounts area), as P&L account
- Re-run the balance carry-forward program

This is true if you find yourself in other situation: when a G/L account has been wrongly classified as P&L account instead of B/S account in the previous fiscal year.

52. Is it possible re-run the carry forward program for a particular G/L account?

In the case of G/L accounts, there is no option to selectively carry forward balances to the new fiscal year: you need to do this for all the G/L accounts.

However, it is possible to carry forward the balances, selectively, in the case of AP / AR accounts.

53. In what currency the balances will be carried forward?

SAP carries forward the account balances in the currencies of the ledger.

54. How many 'Retained Earnings' a/c can be defined?

You can define as many **retained earnings accounts** as you need. But normally, companies use only **one** retained earnings account (identified by 'X' in the 'profit & loss account type' field. To define more than one retained earnings account, you should use different 'profit &loss account types' and assign the P&L statement G/L accounts to these account types.

Defining more than one retained earnings account could be useful for international corporations that are required to comply with various reporting requirements when producing the profit & loss statement.

55. How to set up only one Retained Earnings account?

You need to specify the Retained Earnings account to which profits or losses are transferred, before you can include P&L statement accounts in the chart of accounts. SAP uses a special program to transfer these amounts to this account. Each P&L account is assigned to a retained earnings account via a key (normally 'X'):

In the Chart of Accounts of area of the G/L account master, select the 'P&L statement acct' option for all the P& L statement accounts if you follow *individual processing* of G/L account creation or change:

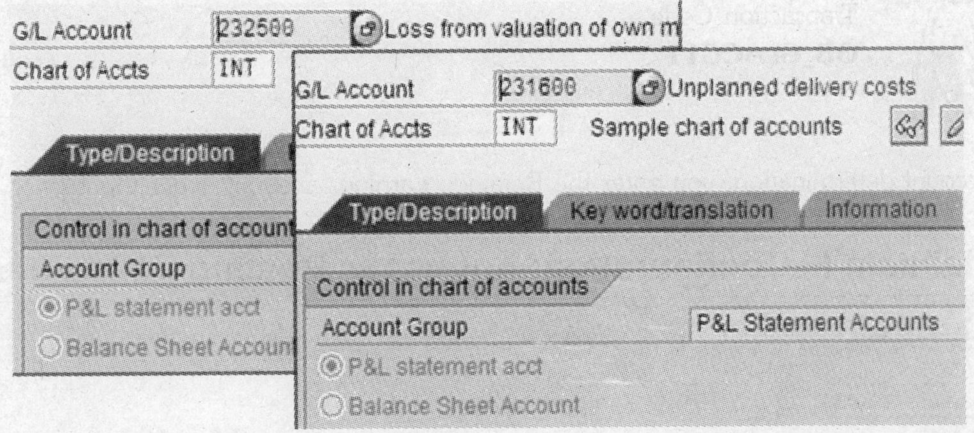

Figure 1.27: Denoting a G/L a/c as P&L statement a/c (individual processing)

Transaction Code
FSP0 (Edit Chart of Accounts Data)
FS00 (Edit G/L Account Centrally)

In the case of collective processing of G/L accounts (creation or change), put 'X' under the 'P&L Statement Acct. Type' field for all the P&L statement accounts:

Ch...	G/L Account	Short Text	Balance Sheet Ac...	P&L Statement Acct Type
INT	231000	Ext.prod.pr	☐	X
INT	231010	Loss-ML pri	☐	X
INT	231050	Acc/def ext	☐	X
INT	231080	Loss fm rev	☐	X
INT	231100	Loss-freigh	☐	X
INT	231500	Loss-own pr	☐	X
INT	231510	Loss-pr.dif	☐	X
INT	231520	Pr.dif.loss	☐	X
INT	231550	Acc/def own	☐	X

Figure 1.28: Denoting G/L accounts as P&L accounts (collective processing)

Transaction Code
OB_GLACC11

For account determination, you enter the Retained Earnings account under the key 'X'.

Maintain FI Configuration: Automatic Posting - Accounts

Posting Key

Chart of Accounts INT Sample chart of accounts
Transaction BIL Balance carried forward

Account assignment

P&L statmt	Account
X	900000

Figure 1.29: Retained Earnings Account Configuration

Transaction Code
OB53

56. How do you maintain 'Currency' in SAP?

A **currency** (the legal means of payment in a country) in SAP is denoted by a 3-character currency code, maintained as per the ISO standards.

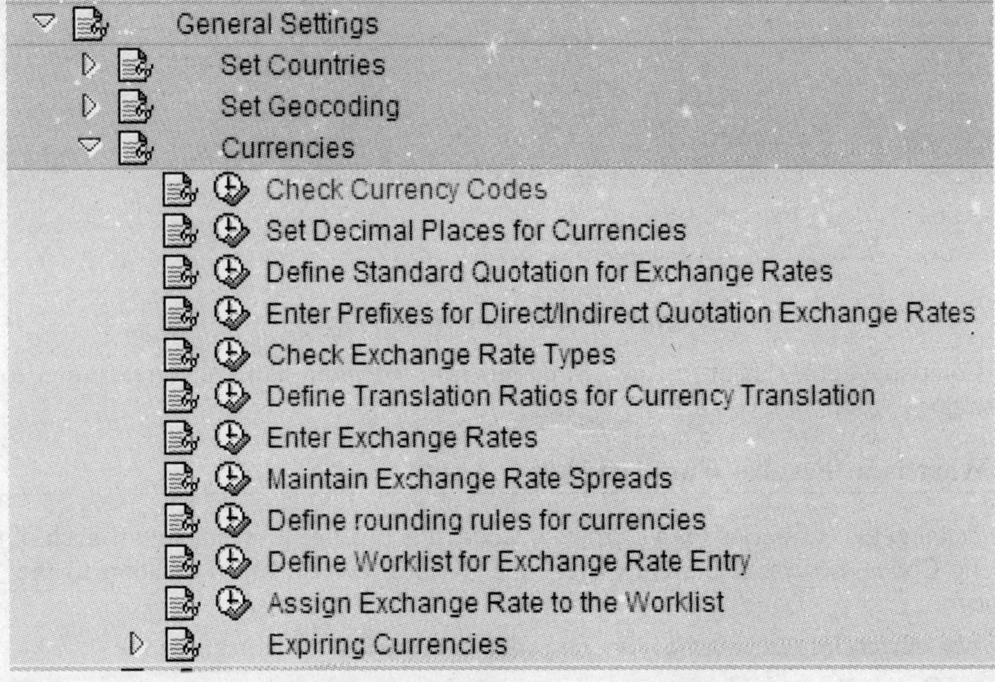

Figure 1.30: Currency settings in IMG

Example:

- USD (US Dollars)
- INR (Indian Rupee),
- GBP (Great Britain Pound)

Each currency code in the system will have a validity defined.

Transaction Code
OY03

57. What is a 'Local Currency'?

When you define a Company Code, you also need to mention in which currency you will be maintaining the accounts / leagers in financial accounting. This currency is called as the '**local currency**'. This is also known as '***company code currency***'. This is the national currency of that Company Code.

1st local currency

Crcy type	10	Company code currency	Currency	MXN
Valuation	0	Legal Valuation		
ExRateType	M	Daily Spot Rate		
Srce curr.	1	Translation taking transaction currency as a basis		
TrsDte typ	3	Translation date		

Figure 1.31: Local Currency

From Company Code's point of view, all currencies other than its local currency are 'foreign currencies'.

58. What is a 'Parallel Currency'?

When defining the currencies for a Company Code, it is possible to maintain, for each of these company Codes, two more currencies (2nd and 3rd local currencies) in addition to the 'local currency'.

These two currencies are called as the '**parallel currencies**' which can be the:

- Group Currency
- Hard Currency
- Global Company Currency
- Index-based Currency

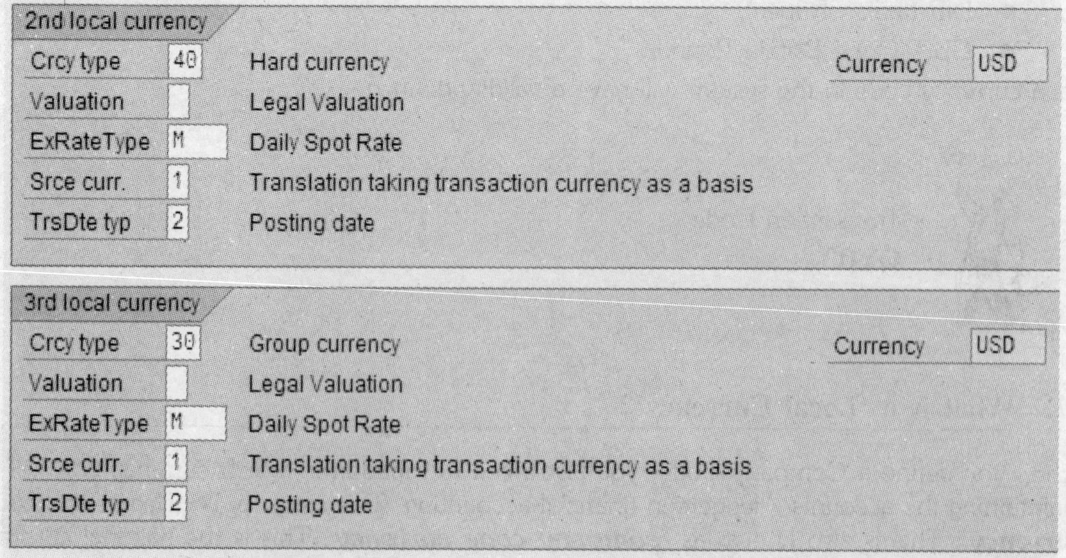

2nd local currency

Crcy type	40	Hard currency	Currency	USD
Valuation		Legal Valuation		
ExRateType	M	Daily Spot Rate		
Srce curr.	1	Translation taking transaction currency as a basis		
TrsDte typ	2	Posting date		

3rd local currency

Crcy type	30	Group currency	Currency	USD
Valuation		Legal Valuation		
ExRateType	M	Daily Spot Rate		
Srce curr.	1	Translation taking transaction currency as a basis		
TrsDte typ	2	Posting date		

Figure 1.32: Parallel Currencies (2nd and 3rd Local Currency)

To translate the values from one currency to the other, you will need to maintain ***exchange rate*** for each pair of the defined currencies in the system. For each such currency pair, you can define different exchange rates through ***exchange rate types*** (explained later in detail).

When parallel currencies are defined, the system maintains the accounting ledgers in these currencies as well, in addition to the local currency.

59. What you need to know when ledgers are maintained in 'parallel currencies'?

When you manage ledgers in parallel currencies, you need to take note of the following:

- During posting, the amounts are also saved in the parallel currencies. The amounts are translated automatically, but you can also enter them manually
- G/L account transaction figures are also updated in the parallel currencies
- Exchange rate differences also arise in the parallel currencies.
- You can also carry out a foreign currency valuation in the parallel currencies

You may define the parallel currencies in *SAP Customizing Implementation Guide: Financial Accounting Global Settings (New) > Ledgers > Define Currencies of Leading Ledger*

60. What is a 'Group Currency'?

Group currency is the currency defined at the Client level, and is used in the consolidated financial statements. Before the consolidation process can be completed, all values in the individual financial statements must be translated from the local or transaction currency into group currency.

If you have defined the group currency as the 2nd local currency, this has no additional effects. But, in all other cases, in the application component ***special purpose ledger*** you have to define an additional ledger in which transaction figures are managed

61. What is a 'Hard Currency'?

This is a country-specific 2nd currency used in countries experiencing high level of inflation.

62. What is the 'Global Company Code Currency'?

The currency defined for the Company (or the Consolidated Company) is called as the **global company code currency**.

63. What is an 'Account Currency'?

When defining the G/L accounts in the system, you are required to define a currency in which an account will be maintained, and this is called as the **account currency**. This is defined in the 'Company Code' area of the G/L master record. The concept of account currency helps to use the same chart of accounts even though the various Company Codes belonging to the corporate group can still maintain their accounts in different local currencies corresponding to the national currency of the nation where they are operating.

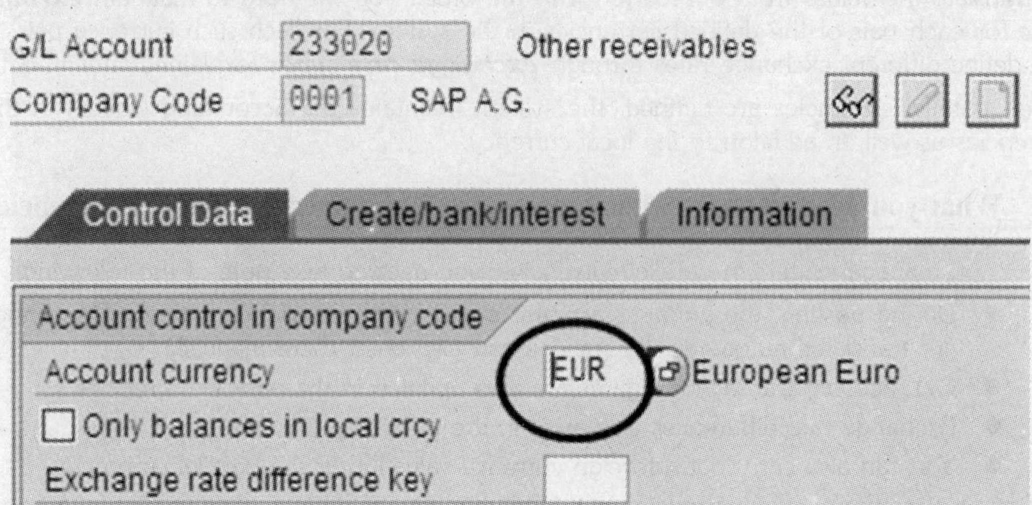

Figure 1.33: Account Currency field in G/L Account

The account currency is:

- The currency used for postings made to this account
- The currency in which transaction figures are updated and the account balance is displayed

64. What is a 'Reference Currency'?

Reference currency is the currency key used to carry out all foreign currency translations for a specific exchange rate type. If foreign currency translation is necessary between many different currencies, you can simplify the maintenance of the exchange rates by specifying a reference currency. By taking this route, you need to specify the rates of all currencies in relation to the reference currency, for this exchange rate type. All foreign currency translation is, then, carried out in two stages via the reference currency.

You can only use the reference currency for exchange rate type M (average rate), and not for buying or bank selling exchange rate types. SAP recommends defining a reference currency for the average rate and then entering exchange rate spreads for the buying and bank selling rates. This combination is particularly efficient since you only have to enter exchange rates for the individual currencies to the reference currency for the average rate exchange rate type. The system calculates all the other exchange rates.

Example:

Let USD be the reference currency. To translate from GBP to INR, the system uses the GBP/USD and INR/USD exchange rate specifications.

65. What are the two options available to setup an 'Account Currency'?

When defining the account currency, you have the following two options (Table 1-3):

Table 1.3: Options for Account Currency Setup

Option	Details
Entering the 'local currency' in the Company Code	The system automatically uses the local currency that you have defined when creating the Company Code as the default value. This allows posting to the G/L account in any currency. When you make a posting in a foreign currency, the amount is translated into the local currency. The system maintains the transaction figures: ● In the local currency (total of all the amounts posted in the local currency) ● In the individual currencies(total of all the amounts posted in various currencies)
Entering a currency other than the local currency (that is, entering a 'foreign currency')	The posting is possible only in this currency. (An exception to this is exchange rate differences resulting from valuating G/L account balances). The transaction figures and the account balance are kept in the foreign currency entered and in the local currency.

66. What are all the pre-requisites for posting in a 'Foreign Currency'?

The following are the pre-requisites that you need to take care, before posting in a foreign currency:

- Local currency already defined for the Company Code (in the global parameters)
- Foreign currency defined in the currency code Table
- Exchange rate defined for the foreign currency and the local currency
- Translation Ratio maintained for the local and foreign currency

67. How 'Exchange Rates' are maintained in SAP?

An '**exchange rate**' is defined for each pair of currencies, and for each 'exchange rate type' defined in the system. The exchange rate is defined at the document header level.

68. What is an 'Exchange Rate Type'?

The **exchange rate type** is defined according to various purposes like valuation, translation, planning, conversion etc. The standard system includes the exchange rate types for the:

- M Average rate
- G Bank buying rate
- B Bank selling rate

The system uses the exchange rate type 'M', for posting and clearing.

Transaction Code
OB07

Using exchange rate types, SAP has simplified the exchange rate maintenance: if you need to carry out currency translations between several currencies, instead of entering translation rates between every single currency, you then only need specify the translation rate between each currency and the base currency. All currency translations then take place in two steps:

- Into the base currency
- From the base currency into the target currency

Example: Consider that the base currency is USD. You want the system to have a translation from INR to GBP. At the first step INR is translated into USD. In the next step, USD is translated into GBP. However, you should have already defined, in the system, the following entries:

- Ratio for INR & USD
- Ratio for GBP & USD

Note that the system translates INR to GBP as if there is a exchange rate maintained between INR and GPB.

B	Standard translation at bk.selling rate
G	Standard translation at bank buying rate
I	Intrastat exchange rate type
INT	Internal clearing exchange rate
M	Standard translation at average rate
P	Standard translation for cost planning

Figure 1.34: Exchange Rate Types

69. What is known as the 'Translation Factor'?

The relation between a pair of currencies per 'exchange rate type' is known as **'translation factor'**. For example, the translation factor is 1 when you define the exchange rate for the currencies USD & INR:

$$\frac{\text{USD}}{\text{INR}} = \frac{1}{1}$$

You also specify whether you want to use an alternative exchange rate type for specific currency pairs. The ratios you enter here for currency translation are displayed again when maintaining the exchange rates.

Transaction Code
OBBS

70. Is there an easy way to maintain Exchange Rates, in SAP?

SAP offers a variety of tools to maintain the exchange rates, on an on-going basis. The tools include:

- Exchange Rate Spreads
- Base Currency
- Inversion

Use the SAP supplied program ***RFTBFF00***, for populating the exchange rate Table automatically form an input file, in a multi-cash format from a commercially available input file.

71. What is known as 'Exchange Rate spread'?

The difference between the 'bank-buying rate' & the 'bank selling rate' is known as the **exchange rate spread**, which remains almost constant. When you maintain the exchange rate spread, it is sufficient if you maintain the '**a*verage rate'*** for that currency in question in the system as you will be able to deduce the buying / selling rate by adding / subtracting the spread to / from the average rate.

Transaction Code
OBD6

Example:

If the average rate between GBP -> USD is 0.50805 and the spread is 0.00100, the bank buying rate derived will be 0.50705.

To make this calculation you must make the following entries configured in the system:

ExRt	From	To	Valid from	Spread	Ratio(from)	Ratio (to)
M	GBP	USD	06/26/2009	0.00100	1	1

Figure 1.35: Exchange Rate Spread

72. Explain usage of 'Direct' or 'Indirect Quotation'.

It is possible to maintain the exchange rates, in SAP, by either of these two methods. What decides the usage of a particular type of quotation is the business transaction or the market standard (of that country).

SAP adopts two prefixes to differentiate the direct and indirect quotes during entering / displaying a transaction:

- ''– Blank, no prefix. Used in Direct Quotation
- '/' – Used in Indirect Quotation

When there is no prefix entered, (blank), the quotation is construed as the 'direct quote' by the system. The possible scenarios:

- The company in question is mainly using the '***indirect quotation***'.

  Use ''(blank) as the prefix for default notation for indirect quotation. Use '*' as the prefix for the rarely used direct quotation. If some one tries entering a transaction using direct quotation, but without the '*' in the exchange rate input field, the system will issue a warning.
- The company in question is mainly using the '***direct quotation***'.

  You do not need to make any specific settings as the default is the ''(blank) prefix for the direct quotation, and '/' for the indirect quotation. So, unless you make a transaction entry with '/' prefix, the system takes all the entries as that of direct quotation.
- There could be instances of requirements where in you are required to configure in such a way that a prefix is mandatory irrespective of the type of quotation. In this case, define the direct quotation prefix as '*', and the indirect one as the system default '/' prefix. This necessitates to prefix each of the entries either by '*' or '/'. Else, the user will get a warning to correct the entry.

The exchange rate table in SAP looks like the one as displayed in the following figure:

ExRt	ValidFrom	Indir.quot		Ratio(from)	From		Dir.quot.		Ratio (to)	To
M	07/11/2007	7.81630	X	1	HKD	=		X	1	USD
M	07/10/2007	7.81650	X	1	HKD	=		X	1	USD
M	07/09/2007	7.81670	X	1	HKD	=		X	1	USD
M	07/06/2007	7.81800	X	1	HKD	=		X	1	USD
M	07/05/2007	7.81680	X	1	HKD	=		X	1	USD
M	07/03/2007	7.81320	X	1	HKD	=		X	1	USD
M	07/02/2007	7.81610	X	1	HKD	=		X	1	USD
M	06/29/2007	7.81700	X	1	HKD	=		X	1	USD
M	06/28/2007	7.81630	X	1	HKD	=		X	1	USD

Figure 1.36: Exchange Rate Table

If the field content of '*Indir. Quot*' is highlighted (usually in red), it means that you have set the 'direct quotation' method of exchange rate entry for that currency pair in customizing. Likewise, if the '*Dir.quot*' is shown in red, then it means that you have set 'indirect quotation' method of exchange rate for this currency pair in customizing.

Transaction Code
OB08

73. Explain how 'Taxes' are handled in SAP.

SAP takes care of tax calculation, tax postings, tax adjustments and tax reporting, through the three FI components namely G/L, AP and AR. The processing of the following kinds of taxes is possible:

- Tax on Sales and Purchases
  - o Input Taxes (Purchase Tax)
  - o Output Taxes (Sales Tax)
- Additional Taxes (these are country specific and in addition to the tax on sales and purchases)
- Sales Tax (Sales and Use tax as in USA)
- Withholding Tax (Income Tax in India)
  - o Classic Withholding Tax
  - o Extended Withholding Tax

74. At how many levels 'Taxes' can be handled in SAP?

SAP allows taxation at three levels:

i. National level or federal level (Europe, South Africa, Australia etc)
ii. Regional or jurisdiction level (USA)
iii. National and Regional level (India, Canada, Brazil etc)

75. How 'tax is calculation' is structured in SAP?

SAP uses a technique called '***condition method***' to calculate taxes (except Withholding Tax) in the system. The system makes use of '***tax (calculation) procedures***' defined in the system together with the ***tax codes*** for calculating the quantity of tax.

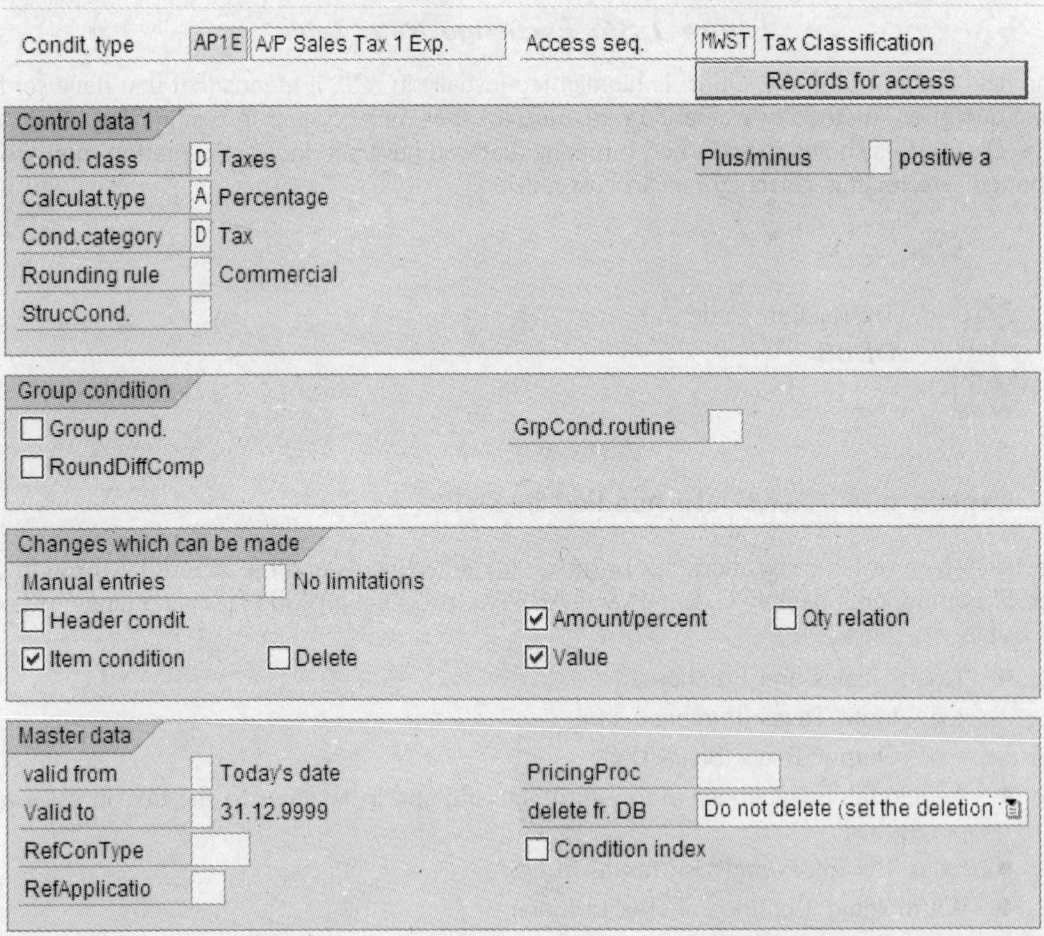

Condit. type AP1E A/P Sales Tax 1 Exp. Access seq. MWST Tax Classification
Records for access

Control data 1
Cond. class D Taxes Plus/minus positive a
Calculat.type A Percentage
Cond.category D Tax
Rounding rule Commercial
StrucCond.

Group condition
Group cond. GrpCond.routine
RoundDiffComp

Changes which can be made
Manual entries No limitations
Header condit. Amount/percent Qty relation
Item condition Delete Value

Master data
valid from Today's date PricingProc
Valid to 31.12.9999 delete fr. DB Do not delete (set the deletion
RefConType Condition index
RefApplicatio

Figure 1.37: Condition Type (Tax Processing)

i. The ***tax code*** is the starting point in the tax calculation. The tax code is *country* *specific*, with every country having a country specific *Tax Procedure* defined in the standard system, which is used as the template for defining various tax codes. The system uses the tax code to verify the following:

- Tax type
- Amount of tax calculated/entered
- G/L account for tax posting
- Calculation of additional tax portion, if any

ii. ***Tax rates*** are defined for each of the tax codes. The tax rates are then associated with ***tax types*** which are included in the tax procedures. (Because of this relationship, it is technically possible that a single tax code may have multiple tax rates for various tax types)

iii. The tax code is assigned to a ***tax procedure*** which is tagged to a G/L master record. A particular tax procedure is accessed whenever that G/L account is used in a document processing.

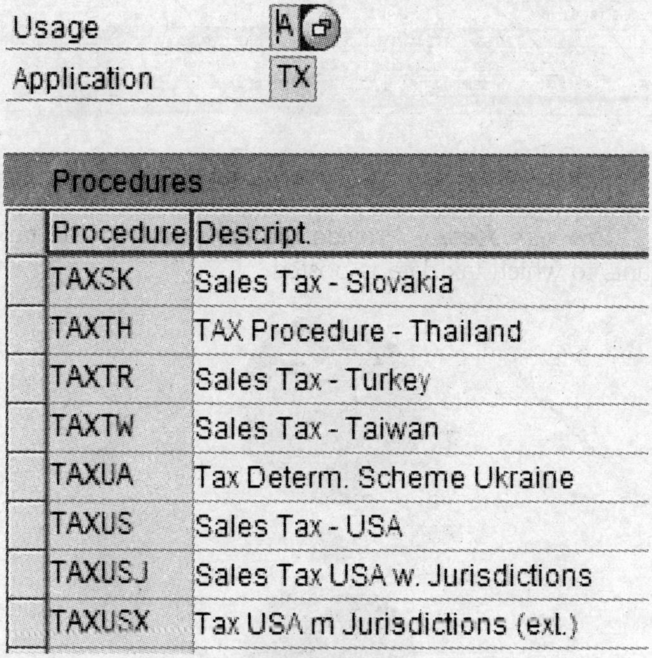

Usage A

Application TX

Procedures

Procedure	Descript.
TAXSK	Sales Tax - Slovakia
TAXTH	TAX Procedure - Thailand
TAXTR	Sales Tax - Turkey
TAXTW	Sales Tax - Taiwan
TAXUA	Tax Determ. Scheme Ukraine
TAXUS	Sales Tax - USA
TAXUSJ	Sales Tax USA w. Jurisdictions
TAXUSX	Tax USA m Jurisdictions (exl.)

Figure 1.38: Tax Procedures

76. Explain 'Tax Procedure'?

A **tax procedure** contains the following:

- ***Steps*** - To determine the sequence of lines within the procedure
- ***Condition types*** - Indicates how the tax calculation model will work (whether the

records are for fixed amount or percentages? Whether the records can be processed automatically? etc)

- ***Reference steps*** - Where from the system obtains the amount/value it uses in its calculation (for example, the base amount)

Procedure TAXUS Sales Tax - USA

Control Data

Reference Step Overview

Step	Co	CTyp	Description	Fro	To	Ma	R	Stat	P	SuTot	Reqt	CalTy	BasTy	AccK	Accru
100	0	BASB	Base Amount			☐	☐	☐							
200	0		A/P Distributed			☑	☐	☐							
210	0	AP1I	A/P Sales Tax 1 Inv.	100		☐	☐	☐						NVV	
220	0	AP2I	A/P Sales Tax 2 Inv.	100		☐	☐	☐						NVV	
230	0	AP3I	A/P Sales Tax 3 Inv.	100		☐	☐	☐						NVV	
240	0	AP4I	A/P Sales Tax 4 Inv.	100		☐	☐	☐						NVV	
300	0		A/P Undistributed			☑	☐	☐							
310	0	AP1E	A/P Sales Tax 1 Exp.	100		☐	☐	☐						VS1	
320	0	AP2E	A/P Sales Tax 2 Exp.	100		☐	☐	☐						VS2	
330	0	AP3E	A/P Sales Tax 3 Exp.	100		☐	☐	☐						VS3	
340	0	AP4E	A/P Sales Tax 4 Exp.	100		☐	☐	☐						VS4	

Position... Entry 1 of 22

Figure 1.39: Tax Procedure 'TAXUS'

- ***Account / Process Keys*** - Provide the link between the tax procedure and the G/L accounts to which tax data is posted.

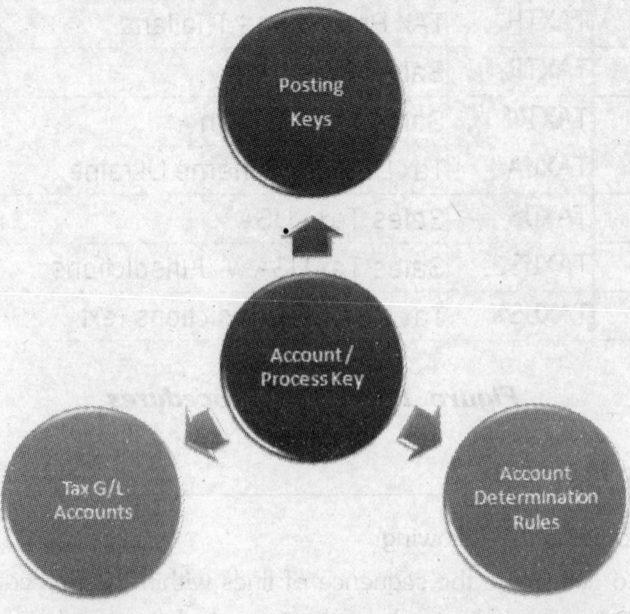

Figure 1.40: Account / Process Key for tax processing

This helps in automatic tax account assignments. To enable that these keys have necessary information for automatic assignment, you need to define the following:

- ***Posting keys*** (unless you have a specific requirement, it will be sufficient to use the G/L posting keys: Debit: 40, Credit 50)
- ***Rules*** to determine on which fields the account determination is to be based upon (like the tax code or country key)
- ***Tax accounts*** to which the postings need to be made

77. How Tax is calculated in SAP?

In SAP the tax is calculated as outlined below:

a. The ***Access sequence*** helps in identifying the sequence of Condition Tables to be used and identifying which field contents are the 'criteria' for reading the ***condition tables*** (a group of **condition types**)

Access	TAXJ	10	US Taxes with Jurisdiction
Table	53		Taxes Using Jurisdiction Code

Field Overview

Condition	I/O	Docmt Stru	Doc.field	Long field label	Spec. Val. Source	Init	ATyp
ALAND	⇐	KOMK	ALAND	Country		☐	
MWSKZ	⇐	KOMK	MWSKZ	Tax Code		☐	
TXJCD	⇐	KOMK	TXJCD	Tax Jurisdiction		☐	

Figure 1.41: Access Sequence with Fields Overview

b. The tax so calculated is normally posted to the same side as the G/L posting that contains the tax code. When exchange rate differences occur (due to tax adjustments in foreign currencies) these differences are generally posted to the specific account(s) for exchange rate differences. However, it is possible to specify (per Company Code) that the exchange rates for tax items can also be entered manually or determined by the posting or the document date, and the resulting differences posted to a special account.

c. SAP has a number of predefined account keys, and it is recommended that the standard keys be used.

78. Explain the Configurations required for Taxes in SAP.

You need to define the following in the customizing:

a. **Base amount for tax calculation**

For each Company Code you need to define whether the ***base amount*** includes the cash discount as well. If the base amount includes the discount, then the tax base is termed as '***gross***', else it is '***net***'. You may also define a similar base amount for calculating the '***cash discount***'. This is also to be maintained for each of the Company Codes.

Transaction Code
OB69

b. Tax codes

Tax code is 2-digit code specifying the percentage of tax to be calculated on the base amount. While defining the tax code, you will also specify the '***Tax type***' to classify a tax code relating to either '***input tax***' or '***output tax***'. The tax types are country specific and determine how a tax is calculated and posted.

Display Tax Code: Tax Rates

Properties | Tax accounts

Country Key	US	USA
Tax Code	S1	A/P Sales Tax
Procedure	TAXUSX	
Tax type	V	Input tax

Percentage rates

Tax Type	Acct Key	Tax Percent. Rate	Level	From Lvl	Cond. Type
Base Amount			100	0	BASB
Calculated Call			105	0	
Shared with G/L			200	0	
A/P Sales Tax 1 Inv.	NVV	100.000	210	100	XP1I
A/P Sales Tax 2 Inv.	NVV	100.000	220	100	XP2I
A/P Sales Tax 3 Inv.	NVV	100.000	230	100	XP3I
A/P Sales Tax 4 Inv.	NVV	100.000	240	100	XP4I
A/P Sales Tax 5 Inv.	NVV	100.000	250	100	XP5I
A/P Sales Tax 6 Inv.	NVV	100.000	260	100	XP6I
Expensed			300	0	
A/P Sales Tax 1 Exp.	VS1		310	100	XP1E
A/P Sales Tax 2 Exp.	VS2		320	100	XP2E

Figure 1.42: Tax Code 'S1'

Transaction Code
FTXP

c. Tax rate

Tax rate is the percentage of tax to be calculated on a base amount. You will be able to define tax rates for one or more tax types when you define a single tax code.

d. Check indicators

By making use of the check indicators, you configure the system to issue ***error / warning messages*** when the tax amount entered manually is incorrect vis-à-vis the tax amount calculated by the system using the tax code.

79. What is a (Tax) 'Jurisdiction Code'?

A **jurisdiction code**, used in countries like US, is a combination of the codes defined by tax authorities. It is possible to define up to four tax levels below federal level. The four levels can be:

- Sub-city level
- City level
- Country level
- State level

Before you can use the jurisdiction codes for tax calculation, you need to define the following:

i. Create Access Sequence (to include the country /tax code/ jurisdiction fields)

ii. Create Condition Types (which references the access sequence as defined above)

iii. Create the Jurisdiction Codes

The tax rates are defined in the tax code on a jurisdiction basis. When posting taxes with a jurisdiction code, note that the taxes may be entered per jurisdiction code or per tax level.

80. Explain 'Withholding Tax' in SAP.

Withholding tax is a tax deducted at the beginning of a payment (at source) that is 'withheld' and paid or reported to the tax authorities on behalf of the person who is subject to the tax.

For example, a customer deducts and withholds the tax for a vendor for the services provided by the vendor. In the case of income tax (a form of withholding tax) the employer deducts the tax from the employee's salary and remits it to the tax authorities on due or pre-determined dates.

To the extent that the tax has been deducted, the vendor gets a withholding certificate (income tax certificate in the case of an employee).

There are two types of withholding tax:

- Classic withholding tax
- Extended withholding tax (EWT)

81. Differentiate 'Withholding Tax' from 'Extended Withholding Tax (EWT)'.

The ***classic withholding tax*** (WT) is a procedure that has always been supported by the system which allows:

- Withholding tax for accounts payable
- Withholding tax calculation during payment
- Withholding tax code per vendor line item

With the introduction of ***extended withholding tax*** (EWT) it is now possible:

- To Assign more than one withholding tax type to a business partner
- To make Withholding tax calculation for partial payments

82. How to change over from Classic WT to Extended WT?

To change over to extended withholding tax, when you upgraded our SAP system to SAP 4.x or other ERPs, you cannot just simply activate extended withholding tax; in this case, you would not be able to carry out further processing to items already posted in the system. All relevant Customizing, master, and transaction data must be converted so that it can then be used in extended withholding tax. SAP provides a tool that supports the withholding tax changeover by automatically converting the relevant withholding tax data.

The change over needs to be carried out by completing each of the steps outlined below:

A. Preparations

- Carrying Out the Financial Accounting Comparative Analysis
- Archiving Cleared Items
- Checking the System Settings for Extended Withholding Tax
- Setting Up Authorizations for the Withholding Tax Changeover
- Blocking Users

B. Converting Data and Activating Extended Withholding Tax

- Creating and Editing a Conversion Run
- Preparing the Data Conversion
- Data Conversion
- Activating Extended Withholding Tax

C. Post-processing

- Carrying Out Post-processing of Withholding Tax Data Conversion

Withholding Tax Conversion: Conversion Run Control

Conversion 1 WHT_C_1

Preparation

Choose Company Codes

Type/Code Assignment

Analysis

Master data settings

Conversion Steps

Test run

Convert Customizing

Master Data Conversion

Document Conversion

Activation of Extended Withholding Tax

Activation

Figure 1.43: Control Screen in Transaction Code 'WTMG'

83. Explain 'Tax Reports' in SAP.

SAP comes delivered with country-specific default **tax reports** to meet your tax reporting requirements. However, it is not uncommon to use third-party software for the same purpose. As a process, it is recommended that the 'closing operations' are completed before running the tax reports. This will ensure that the system makes relevant adjustment entries (between payables and receivables, exchange rate differences etc) so that the correct tax amounts are reported.

84. What is a 'Document' in SAP?

SAP is based on the '***document principle***' meaning that a document is created out of every business transaction in the system. The **document** is the result of a posting in accounting in SAP, and is the connecting link between various business operations.

There are two types of documents:

- **Original documents**: these documents relate to origin of business transactions. Example: invoices, receipts, statement of accounts from bank etc.
- **Processing documents**: These include '***accounting documents***' generated out of postings in the system, '***reference documents***', '***sample documents***' etc. The processing documents other than the accounting ones are also known as '***special documents***' and they aid in simplification of document entry in the system.

Each document consists of:

- A *Document Header*
- Two or more *Line Items*

Before attempting to enter a document, note to call up the relevant ***document entry function*** as the system provides a variety of ready made document entry templates suited to different transactions like regular G/L entry, customer invoice posting etc. The details entered in a document can be simulated and displayed before it is actually posted in the system. You may also choose to '***park***' the document and post it later.

85. What is a 'Document Header'?

The **document header** contains information that is valid for the *whole document* such as:

- Document Date
- Document Type (Control Information)
- Document Number
- Posting Date
- Posting Period
- Company Code

Besides the above, the document header may also have information (editable, later on) like (a) trading partner, (b) document header text, (c) reference, (d) cross Company Code number etc.

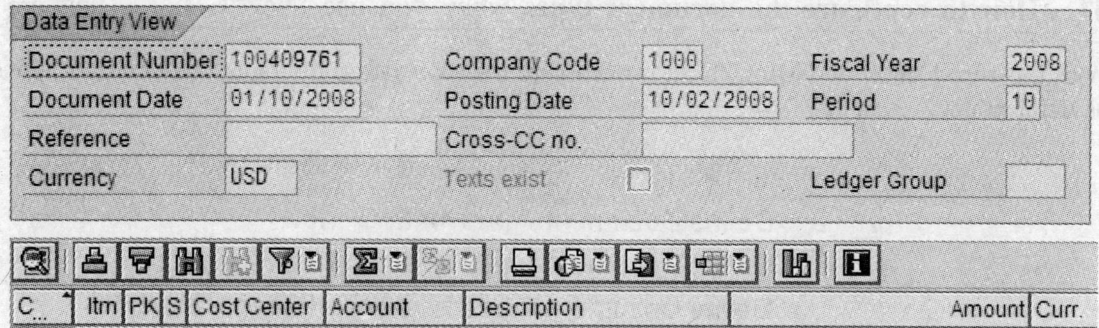

Figure 1.44: Document Header

86. What is a 'Document Type'?

SAP comes delivered with a number of **document type**s, which are used in various postings. The document type helps to classify an accounting transaction within the system, and is used to control the entire transaction determining account types a particular document type can post to. For example, the document type '**AB**' allows you to post to all the accounts, where as type '**DZ**' allows you to post only the customer payments. Each document type is assigned to a number range.

The common document types include (Table 1-4):

Table 1.4: Document Types

Doc. Type	Description	Doc. Type	Description
AA	Asset posting	KG	Vendor credit memo
AB	Accounting document	KN	Net vendors
AF	Depreciation postings	KR	Vendor invoice
DG	Customer credit memo	KZ	Vendor payment
DR	Customer invoice	KG	Vendor credit memo
DZ	Customer payment	SA	G/L accourt document
X1	Recurring entry document	X2	Sample document

Transaction Code
OBA7 (Define)
OBAB (Change)

87. How to configure the document types when you use 'New G/L'?

With the introduction of 'New G/L', it is necessary that you set up the required document types as detailed below:

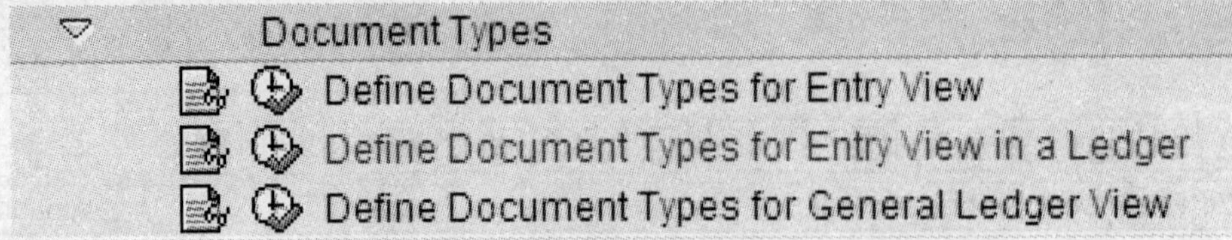

Figure 1.45: Defining Document Types with 'New G/L'

- **Define Document Types of Entry View**
  The options for configuring the document types for entry view, are outlined in Table 1-5.

Table 1.5: Document Types for Entry View

Work with only one Ledger (Leading ledger)?	Work with a leading ledger and with non-leading ledgers?	Majority of postings has the same effect in all ledgers?	What you need to do?
Yes	NA	NA	Define for all postings the document types for the documents in this entry view, and assign a number range to these document types
No	Yes	Yes	Define here all document types for the entry view for postings that affect all ledgers, and assign a number range to the document types
No	Yes	No	(a) Postings only for the leading ledger, define a separate document type for these postings in this step and assign a unique number range to this document type, and (b) for posting in non-leading ledgers make these settings under '*Define Document Types for Entry View in a Ledger*'.

- **Define Document Types for Entry view in a Ledger**
  This customizing step is used for specifying the document types (and assigning the number ranges) for postings to the non-leading ledger(s)

- **Define Document Types for General Ledger View**
  This step will be required only when the fiscal year variant of the non-leading ledger in the company code (to which the postings are made) differs from the fiscal year variant of the leading ledger in this company code. If yes, use this step to define the document types and the number ranges, for all the non-leading ledgers, for documents in G/L view.

88. How 'Account Type' is connected to 'Document Type'?

The **document type** is characterized by 2-character codes like AA, DG etc whereas an **account type** is denoted by a 1-character code like A, D etc specifying as to which are all the accounts a particular document can be posted to. The common account types include:

- **A** Assets
- **D** Customer (Debtor)
- **K** Vendor (Creditor)
- **M** Materials
- **S** G/L

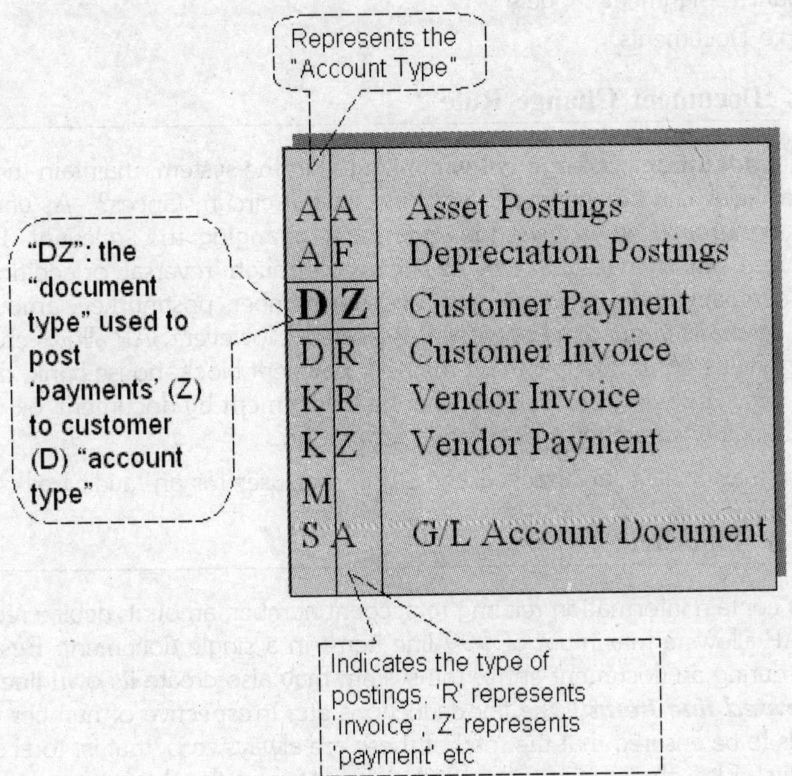

Figure 1.46: Account Type & Document Type

89. What do you mean by 'Net' Postings'?

Usually, when a transaction - say vendor invoice (document type: KR) - is posted, the system posts the 'gross' amount with the 'tax' and 'discount' included. However, SAP provides you the option of posting these items as '**net**'. In this case, the posting excludes 'tax' or 'discount'. Remember to use the special document type **KN**. (Similarly you will use the document type **DN** for 'customer invoice – net' against the normal invoice postings for the customer using the document type **DR**). For using this 'net method' of posting you should have activated the required settings in the customization.

90. Explain various 'Reference Methods'.

SAP recommends, **'reference methods'** as a *'document entry tool'* to facilitate faster and easier document entry into the system, when it is required to enter the same data time and again. Besides making the document entry process less time consuming, this also helps in error-free document entry.

The various Reference Methods used in SAP include:

- Reference Documents
- Account Assignment Models
- Sample Documents

91. What is 'Document Change Rule'?

The functionality **document change rules** configured in the system, maintain the information relating to 'what fields can be changed?' and 'under what circumstances?'. As you are already aware, SAP's ***document principle*** does not allow changing the 'relevant' fields once a document is posted; any changes can only be achieved through 'reversal' or additional postings. The fields like company code, business area, account number, posting key, amount, currency etc., can never be changed once the document is posted. However, SAP allows changing some of the fields, in the line items, like payment method, payment block, house bank, dunning level, dunning block etc. Either these can be changed document-by-document or using '***mass Change***' for changing a number a documents at one go.

The changes to 'master data' are tracked and stored per user for an 'audit trail'.

92. What is a 'Line Item'?

The **line items** contain information relating to account number, amount, debit/credit, tax code, amount etc. SAP allows a maximum of 999 line items in a single document. Besides the one entered by you during an document entry, the system may also create its own line items called '***system generated line items***', like tax deductions etc. Irrespective of number of line items entered, it needs to be ensured that the total of these are always zero (that is, total debits should equal total credits). Else, the system will not allow you to post the document.

93. Which are the business transactions for which system can generate the line items?

The following table gives you an overview of the different business transactions for which line items can be generated automatically (Table 1-6):

Table 1.6: Business Transactions for which the System generates Line Items

Business transaction	Line items
Entering a customer or vendor invoice	• Tax on sales/purchases (output tax when posting a customer invoice, input tax when posting a vendor invoice) • Payables and receivables between company codes (when posting cross-company code transactions)
Posting a customer or vendor payment and clearing open items	• Cash discount (paid and received when posting payments) • Backdated tax calculation for tax on sales/purchases (after cash discount deduction) • Gains and losses from exchange rate differences (between invoice and payment) • Unauthorized deduction of cash discount (when a payment is slightly different to the amount due) • Residual items • Bank charges
Entering special G/L transactions	• Bill of exchange charges • Tax adjustment for a down payment

94. What is a 'Document Overview'?

The first screen you see - when you change or display a document - is the **document overview** screen containing the most important information from the document header and the line items. You have a display line for each line item. You decide what data is displayed in this line by specifying the details in the **line layout variant**.

95. Describe 'Document Number Ranges' in SAP.

A **number range** refers to a number interval defined in the system so that when documents are posted, the system assigns a number form this range. You will define different number ranges for different document types. Each document in SAP is uniquely identified by the combination of (a) document number, (b) company code and (c) fiscal year.

The number range for a document type can be defined:

- Per fiscal year or
- Until a fiscal year in future.

If defined to last only one fiscal year, then this needs to be defined every year. When number ranges are defined every year, the system starts from the first number in the range for that particular year and this will help in not reaching the upper limit fast.

If you specify the fiscal year as '9999', then the document number range is valid for ever (well, almost!) and you do not have to do this exercise of maintaining number ranges every fiscal year. But, every year the system starts from the last number used up in the previous year and if a small number range is defined for a document type, you could easily run out of the number range fast.

The document numbers can either be:

- ***Internally*** assigned by the system or
- ***Externally*** input when the same is created

The number ranges can be defined in such a way that system generates the number automatically when a document is created. This is known as ***internal number assignment***. Under this, the system stores the 'last number' used for a document in the *'Current Number'* field and will bring up the next number when another document is created.

NR Object: Accounting document

Subobject: 0001

Intervals

No	Year	From number	To number	Current number	Ext
00	9999	0090000000	0099999999		☑
01	9999	0100000000	0199999999	0	☐
02	9999	0200000000	0299999999	0	☐
03	9999	0300000000	0399999999		☑
04	9999	0400000000	0499999999	0	☐
05	9999	0500000000	0599999999	0	☐
12	9999	1200000000	1299999999	0	☐
13	9999	1300000000	1399999999	0	☐

Figure 1.47: Document Number Ranges - Intervals

If ***external numbering*** is used, the user needs to input a document number every time a document is created in the system. Since user supplies the number every time, the subsequent numbering may not be sequential. Unlike internal numbering, system does not store the 'last number' in the 'Current Number' field.

The numbers in a number range can either be ***numeric*** or ***alphanumeric***. If numbers are numeric, system will prefix the number with required zeros to make the number length uniform at 10 digits. If you are using alphanumeric numbering, then the number is padded with zeros from the right. If you are following 'year-specific' numbering, it is better not to mix numeric and alphanumeric numbering for a particular document type in various fiscal years.

The system creates a minimum of one document when a transaction is created / completed. SAP recommends 'filing' of original documents (under the number of the processing document (generated in SAP)). The best practice is to enter the (external) number of the 'original document' in the *'Reference'* field of the document created in SAP system. For easy cross-reference, the SAP document number thus created needs to be noted down on the 'original document'.

The following are the activities you need to complete for configuring the number ranges properly in the system:

- Defining the number ranges
- Copying the number ranges to Company Code(s)
- Copying the number ranges to fiscal year(s)

Transaction Code
FBN1 (Define)
OBH1 (Copy to Company Code)
OAH2 (Copy to fiscal year)

With the introduction of 'New G/L' functionality, note that the configuration settings for number range assignment has been grouped separately in two areas namely (a) document entry view and (b) G/L view:

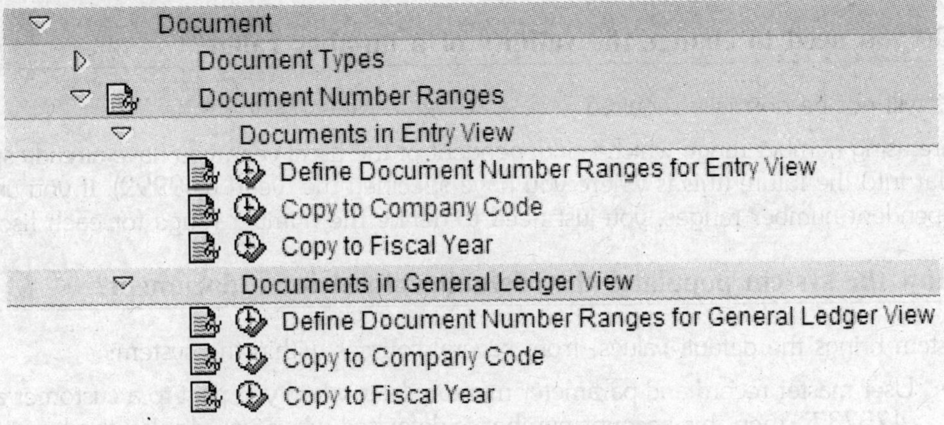

Figure 1.48: Document Number Ranges - IMG

96. What you should know about 'changing the number ranges'?

Changing a number range may be necessary if a number range originally assigned is not large enough. You can:

- Increase the upper limit of the number range or specify a new lower limit as long as another range does not already have these numbers.
- Assign a new number range to the document type

Changing number intervals
You can change the lower and upper limits for number range intervals. Changing the lower limit in a number range with internal number assignment is advisable only if a number has not been assigned yet. In changing the upper limit, make sure the new number does not fall below the current number. Of course, the system ensures that the intervals do not overlap after you change the limits.

Changing the current number level
With the internal number assignment, the current number is updated by the system automatically. Changing the current number is only permitted in special cases: this may be necessary if the system starts assigning numbers from the lower limit of the interval again and finds that a number was not released yet. In this case, you can increase the current number. The best practice, however, is that you should not change it.

97. Can you delete a number range?

You can **delete number ranges** if no numbers have not yet been assigned from that range. If numbers have already been assigned:

- The system prevents deletion, if it is a range with internal number assignment
- The system issues a 'warning' message, if the range has external number assignment

If you delete a number range, you must assign new number range to the document types affected by the deletion.

98. Do you need to change the validity of a number range?

No, this will not be normally required.

If you are using number range which is independent of the fiscal year, you have already specified a year far into the future (this is where you have specified the 'year' as 9999). If you use fiscal year-dependent number ranges, you just need to define the number range for each fiscal year.

99. How the system populates the 'default values' for a document?

The system brings the default values, from several sources within the system:

- User master record and parameter memory (say, when you post to a customer account '475737', then this account number is defaulted when you display the line items)
- System (say, the system date is defaulted as the document date)

- Account master record (say, the payment terms entered in a customer master are defaulted when you enter a document)
- Default values for accounting functions, defined in IMG (say, the posting keys and the document type associated with invoice posting transaction)

100. What are all the 'Editing Options' in document entry?

The **editing options** functionality is used for making user-specific settings for:

- Displaying data in the credit management area
- Displaying line items
- Displaying payment advice notes
- Entering documents
- Processing open items

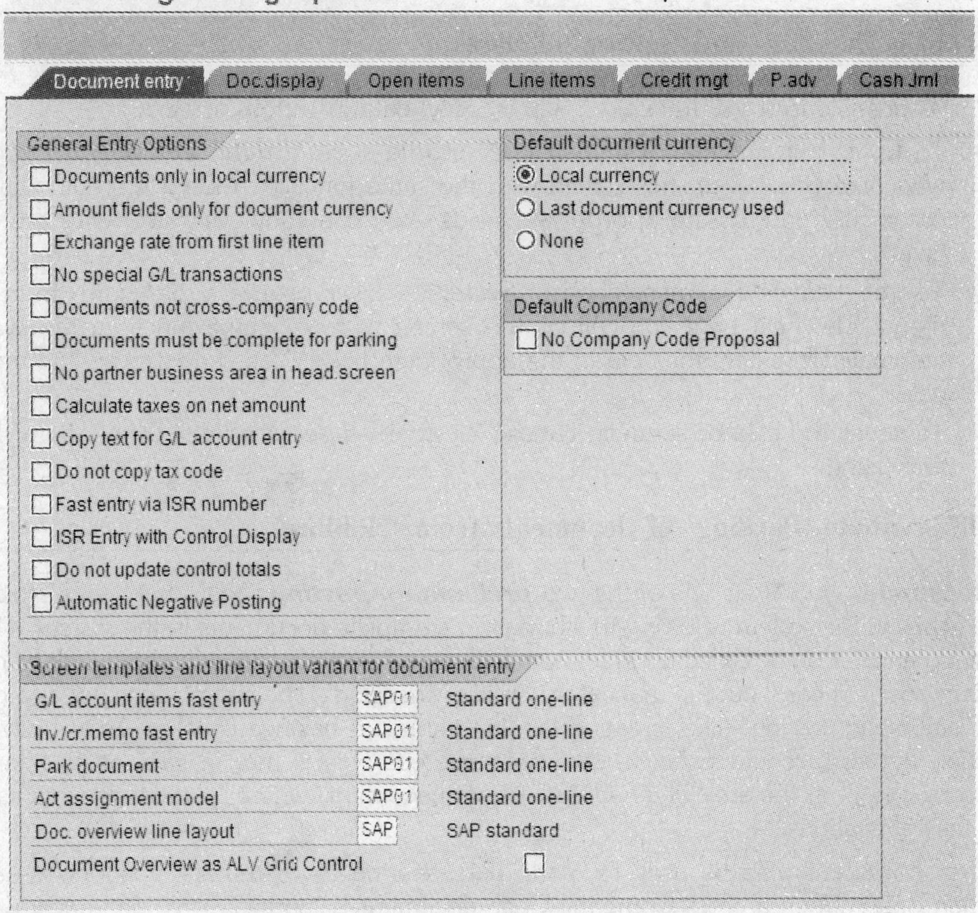

Figure 1.49: Accounting Editing Options

The ***Accounting Editing Options*** screen contains editing options for the following areas:

- Document entry
- Document display
- Open items
- Line items
- Credit management
- Payment advice notes
- Cash journal

To access editing options, from the *SAP Easy Access screen*, choose '*Accounting > Financial accounting > Accounts receivable/Accounts payable > Document entry > Others*' and then the required business transaction. On the initial screen, choose '*Settings > Editing options*'. To select or reset editing options, select or deselect them on the respective tab. To save 'editing options' in your user master record, choose '*Options > Change user master*'. The changes will take effect from the next time you log on.

101. What is 'holding' and 'setting' of data?

In SAP, it is possible to 'hold' (retain) or 'set' (specify) data in various screens.

- To **hold** data, choose '*System > User profile > Hold data*' from any menu. The next time you call up this screen with the same function, the system automatically enters the data in the appropriate fields. You can, however, overwrite the held data.
- To **set** data on a screen, choose '*System > User profile > Set data*' from any menu. The next time you call up this screen with the same function, the system automatically enters the data in the appropriate fields. You cannot overwrite the set data.
- To **reset** the held or set data, choose '*System > User profile > Delete data*' from any menu.

102. Differentiate 'Parking' of documents from 'Holding'.

Park document', in SAP, is one of the two ***preliminary postings*** (the other being 'Holding' of documents) in the system referring to storing of incomplete documents in the system. These documents can later on be called upon for completion and posting. While 'parking' a document, the system does not carry out the mandatory 'validity checking'. The system does not also carry out any automatic postings (like, creating tax line items) or 'balance checks'. As a result, the transaction figures (account balances) are not updated. This is true in case of all financial transactions <u>except</u> in the area of *TR-CM (Cash management)* where 'parked' documents will update the transactions.

Parking of documents can be used to 'park' data relating to customers, vendors or assets (acquisition only). When a cross Company Code document is 'parked', only one document is created in the initial Company Code; when this 'parked' document is posted all other documents relevant for all other Company Codes will also be created. However, it is to be noted that the ***substitution*** functionality cannot be used with document 'parking', as substitution is activated only upon transaction processing.

The added advantage is that a document 'parked' by an accounting clerk can be called upon for completion by some one else. The 'parked' documents can be displayed individually or as a list from where the required document can be selected for completion and posting. The number of the 'parked' document is transferred to the posted document. The original 'parked' document, if necessary, can be displayed even after the same has been posted to.

During a transaction when the user finds that she/he is not having a piece of information required to be entered, he/she can '**hold document**' and complete the same later. As in the case of 'parked' documents, here also the document does not update the transaction figures.

The essential differences between these two types of preliminary postings can be summarized as under:

Table 1.7: Park / Hold Documents: the differences

Attribute	'Park' document	'Hold' document
View the document in 'Account Display'?	Yes	No
Changes to the document?	Any user can access, view and/change the document	No other user, except the creator, will be able to access, view and/change the document
Document number?	System assigned	Manually entered by the user
Use of data in the document for evaluation purposes?	Possible	Not possible

103. What is known as 'Simulating' documents?

Simulating a document, before you actually post it, gives you an overview of the document items you have already entered. It helps in checking whether the entries are complete and correct. During simulation, the document goes through all the checks required for posting.

When you simulate a document, the automatically generated items, such as input tax and tax on sales and purchases, are displayed. But, to simulate, you need to have entered the document header and at least one line item.

104. Explain the 'Account Assignment Model' in SAP.

Account assignment model is a *'reference method'* used in document entry when the same distribution of amounts to several Company Codes, cost centers, accounts etc is frequently used. Instead of manually distributing the amount among accounts or Company Codes, you may use ***equivalence numbers*** for distributing both the credit and debit amounts. A cross Company Code account assignment model can also be created.

The account assignment model may contain any number of G/L accounts. The G/L account items need not be complete. The model can be used across several Company Codes, and can even include Company Codes from non-SAP systems.

Account Assignment Model: Change Line Items

Delete selected area

Acct assgnmt modelAAM-1

Currency USD

Account Assignment Model Items

PK	CoCd	G/L	Tx	Jurisdictn Code	BusA	Cost Ctr	Equiv
40	0001	100000					20
40	0001	176600					80
50	0001	110000					100

Figure 1.50: Account Assignment Model

- You can use the account assignment model while 'parking' a document (but you cannot use 'reference document' for 'parking').
- Use of account assignment model is limited to G/L accounts.

Unlike a '**sample document**' (discussed later), an account assignment model may be incomplete which can be completed during document entry, by adding or deleting or changing the data already saved in the model.

Transaction Code
FKMT

105. What is 'Recurring Entry' document'?

Recurring entry original document is used by the system as a 'reference document' for enabling posting of periodically recurring postings such as loan repayments, insurance premium payments, rent etc. Since this document is not an accounting document, the account balances are not affected. In a recurring entry original document, you will not be able to change (a) posting key, (b) account and (c) amount. The ***recurring entry documents*** are defined with a special number range (**X1**). Unlike an account assignment model, this cannot be used for cross Company Code postings.

Enter Recurring Entry: Header Data

Fast Data Entry | Account Assignment Model | Post with reference

Company Code: 0001

Recurring entry run

First run on	06/28/2009
Last run on	06/28/2010
Interval in months	1
Run date	28
Run schedule	

☐ Transfer amounts in local currency ☐ Copy texts
☐ Transfer tax amounts in local currency

Document header information

Document Type	SA	Currency/Rate	EUR
Reference		Translatn Date	06/28/2009
Document Header Text			
Trading Part.BA			

First line item

PstKy 40 Account 176600 SGL Ind TType

Figure 1.51: Recurring Entry Document

The ***recurring entry document*** *per se* does not update transaction figures but acts only as a reference and as the basis for creating accounting documents. The SAP program **SAPF120** creates the accounting documents from the recurring entry original document. There are two ways of setting the exact date when this document should be posted to:

- ***Posting frequency***: enter the day of the month and the period (in months) between two postings.
- ***Scheduled run***: configure the 'run schedule' specifying the calendar days on which the program should post these documents.

Transaction Code
FBD1

106. When you will use a 'Sample Document'?

A **sample document** is like a template, which is created and stored so that the information contained therein, can be easily copied into new documents and posted in the system. But, once a sample document is created, you will not be able to change the 'line items' already contained in that document; all you can do is to change the amounts in that sample document. But, you can over come this either (a) by defining a new sample document which can contain other line items or (b) you may add new line items to the FI document which is created by copying from the original sample document.

Sample documents have separate number ranges (**X2**).

Transaction Code
FSM1

107. What is a 'Line Layout Variant'?

Using a **line layout variant**, you can display the line item, the account number and name, and the posting amount. Using a different variant, you can display additional information such as tax information or the cost center. The standard system offers the following line layout variants:

- Account/Name
- Posting Key/Account/Business Area/Name/Tax
- Account/Assignment
- Company Code/Document

You can change these variants or add new ones in Customizing.

108. What are all the functions you can use for 'Line Item Display'?

You can use the following functions for line item display, in SAP:

- Line Layout Variants
- Selection Function
- Sort Function
- Totals Function

All these functions should support each user in this particular task. For example, an employee working with customer accounts who is responsible for customer dunning requires dunning information in the line item display. He requires a line layout with this information. On the other hand, summarized information is important for a credit controller: he will first need to look at a totals sheet to get the information that he requires.

109. Can you 'change' documents in SAP?

Though it is not recommended to change any of the documents (or the line items) that have already been posted, it is possible that you can change such documents. However, you must satisfy certain conditions to prevent any changes to documents that could result in the undesired manipulation of data, which would then make reconciliation impossible.

If you want to change the line items for an account, the account needs to be managed using line item display.

- The system prevents the data in certain fields (like, posting amount, account, posting key, fiscal year, and tax amount) of a posted document from being changed, as they have already updated certain account balances during posting.
- The system also prevents other fields from being changed in certain transactions, like with the 'net procedure' of posting, for example, you cannot change the cash discount amount when you post the payment.
- The system prevents some fields from being changed if you use certain applications (you can no longer change the account assignment to a cost center if you use Cost Center Accounting)

Whether or not you can change data in those fields which are modifiable still depends on the following factors:

- The document change rules defined.
- Which other SAP applications, such as CO (Controlling) or MM (Materials Management), are installed.
- How these other applications have been customized.

All document changes are logged. This also applies to changes to sample and recurring entry original documents, though with sample and recurring entry documents, you can change additional account assignments at any time.

SAP uses the **document change rules** to manage changing documents / line items. Though it is possible to define your own conditions in the form of company-specific rules for changing documents, SAP recommends using the standard rules.

110. What is known as 'Mass Changes to Line Items'?

The functionality '**mass changes to line items**' is used to speed up the process of making changes to customer /vendor line items: you can change a group of line items simultaneously, instead of having to change the line items of documents individually. The following data (Table 1-8) can be changed using this functionality:

Table 1.8: Mass Changes to Line Items

Payment data	Dunning data
Payment method	Dunning block
House bank	Dunning key
Payment block (vendor only)	Dunning level (vendor only)
Terms of payment	Last dunning notice

111. What is 'Clearing'?

A '**clearing**' in SAP refers to squaring-off open debit entries with that of open credit entries. Clearing is allowed in G/L accounts maintained on '*open item*' basis, and in all customer / vendor accounts.

The clearing can either be manual or automatic. In case of ***manual clearing***, you will view the open items and select the matching items for clearing. In case of ***automatic clearing***, a program determines what items need to be cleared based upon certain pre-determined open item selection criteria and proposes assignments before clearing these assigned items. In either case, system creates a ***clearing document*** with the details and enters the 'clearing number' against each the cleared open items. The ***clearing number*** is derived from the document number of the clearing document.

You will also be able to do a '***partial clearing***' when you are unable to match open items exactly: the balance amount not cleared is posted as a new open item. You may also configure ***clearing tolerance*** and also define rules on how to tackle the situation when the net amount after clearing is not zero (like, writing off, posting the difference to a separate 'clearing difference' account etc)

In case of customers who are also vendors, you will be able to clear between these two provided the same is duly configured in the relevant master data (by entering the customer number in the vendor master record, and vendor number in the customer master record).

112. Explain 'Reversal of Documents' in SAP.

In case you need to change some of the accounting information relating to an already posted document, you can only achieve the same by '**reversing**' the original document and posting a new one with correct information. However, reversal is possible only when:

- The origin of the document is in FI (not through SD or MM etc – in case of documents from SD, the same can be reversed through a credit memo, and in the case of documents from MM you need to use the appropriate functions in MM as the reversal in FI does not always reverse all the values)
- The information like business area or cost centre etc are still valid (that you have not deleted these business objects)
- The original document has no cleared items (if there are cleared items, then you need

to reset the clearing before attempting the reversal)

- The document relates only to the line items of customer / vendor / G/L
- The document contains only G/L, customer or vendor account items

While reversing, the system automatically selects the appropriate document type for the reversal, besides defaulting to the relevant posting keys. (Remember that the document type for ***reversal documents*** should have already been configured when document types were defined in the configuration)

As far as the date of the reversal document is concerned, the reversal document is normally posted in the same posting period of the original document; however, if that posting period is closed already, you may need to enter the posting date of the current open posting period.

The reversing can be made to update the transaction in either of the following ways:

- The original and reversal documents increase the credit / debit figures by the same amount
- The reversal results in an account balance as if there has not been any posting to that affected account (this type of reversal is known as 'negative' postings)

113. What is a 'Negative Posting'?

As you are aware, any reversal results in opposite postings to the credit/debit side of the original posting, leading to an increase in the account balances and the 'trial balance' is automatically inflated, on both the sides. This is against the legal requirement in some of the countries like France wherein it is required that even after 'reversal', it should not result in increased account balances. As a result, SAP came out with '**true reversal**' which overcomes this problem by '***negative postings***' to the same line item(s) during reversal. The account balance which was originally increased was restored to the actual balance, as if there has been no posting to the account at all, during the reversal (Table 1-9):

Table 1.9: Negative Postings (True Reversal): Illustration

Type of Reversal	**Type of posting**	**Account 100000**		**Account 200000**	
		Debit	**Credit**	**Debit**	**Credit**
Balance b/f		$10,000	$8,000	$15,000	$7,500
Traditional Reversal	Original Posting	$ 2,500			$ 2,500
	Reversal		$ 2,500	$ 2,500	
Balance c/f		$12,500	$10,500	$17,500	$10,000
Balance b/f		$10,000	$8,000	$15,000	$7,500
'True' Reversal or Negative posting	Original Posting	$ 2,500			$ 2,500
	Reversal	-$ 2,500			-$ 2,500
Balance c/f		$10,000	$8,000	$15,000	$7,500

114. What is 'Fast Entry'?

Instead of the regular document entry screens, SAP provides '**fast entry**' screens for facilitating a quick way of entering repetitive line items in a transaction. For achieving this, you need to define a ***fast entry screen layout*** which will specify what fields you will require for data entry, and in what order. You may configure these fast entry screen layouts for G/L account line items, credit memos and customer / vendor invoices. Each of these fast entry screen layouts will be denoted by a 5-character screen variant in the system. Fast entry screens are used in ***complex (general) postings***.

SAP's ***enjoy postings*** also meant for similar data entry screen; but the difference is that in case of 'fast entry' you will start from scratch in identifying the fields, positioning them in the line item etc. Where as in Enjoy Postings, system comes with all the fields activated and you will select the fields which you do not want to be made available for data entry.

115. What is known 'Control Totals' in SAP?

One of the control functions for entering and posting documents, the '**control totals**' is used to post documents and check whether the data has been entered correctly (for example, invoices or checks). To be able to use the control totals function, you should not select the "*Do not update control totals*" option within the 'editing options' for document entry.

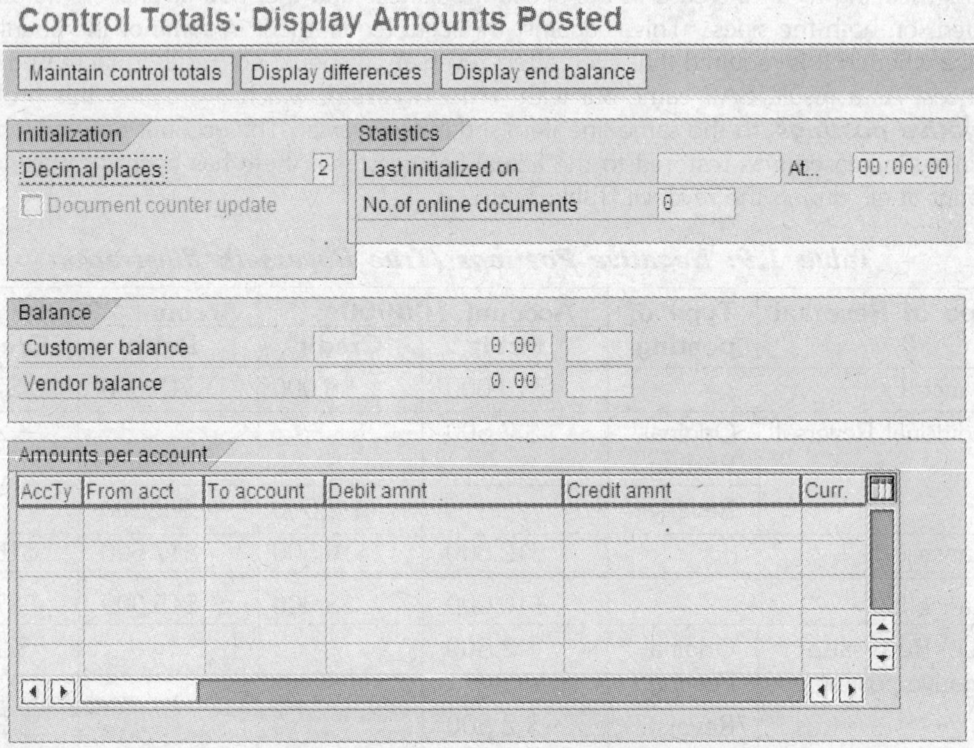

Figure 1.52: Control Totals

You can use control totals either by (a) entering the total to be posted so that the system then displays the difference after the amounts have been posted, or (b) entering an opening balance, post the amounts so that the system then displays the closing balance.

You need the following data to make use of 'control totals':

- The amount to be posted (a total that you calculate before you enter a series of documents)
- Posted amounts (the total debits and credits that the system calculates from the data you actually enter in the system)
- Difference (difference between the expected total and the sum of the amounts actually posted)
- The opening balance of an account

116. How 'Master Data' is different from 'Transaction Data'?

There are three kinds of data residing in any SAP system:

i. Table Data
ii. Transaction Data
iii. Master Data

Table data refers to the customized information for a particular Client. This includes data like payment terms, discounts, pricing, tolerance limits etc which you do not normally change on a day-to-day basis.

Transaction data is the day-to-day recording of business information like purchase orders, sales returns, invoices, payments, collections etc. This includes both the system-generated (tax, discount etc automatically calculated by the system during document posting) as well as user-generated.

Master data are the control information required to decide how transaction data gets posted into various accounts (like customers, vendors, G/L etc). The master data are usually shared across modules (example: customer master records are common both to FI and SD in SAP) obviating the need for defining the same in various application areas. The master data remain in the system for fairly a long period.

In case ***G/L Master Records***, the data is created in two areas:

1. ***Chart of Accounts Area*** (common to all Company Codes: Chart of accounts, G/L account number, account name-short & long text, B/S or P&L indicator, account group etc)
2. ***Company Code Area*** (specific to that particular Company Code: Company Code, tax code, currency, open item management, line item display, sort key etc)

In case of ***Customer / Vendor Master Record***, the data is created in two areas:

1. ***Client-specific*** (general data like account number, name, telephone, bank information etc which are common to all the Company Codes using this master)
2. ***Company Code-specific*** (valid only for the Company Code, this include: terms of payment, dunning procedure, reconciliation account, sort key, sales area, purchasing information etc)

117. Can you post an a/c document if 'Credit' is not equal to 'Debit'?

In general, unless the 'debits' are equal the 'credits' in a document; you will not be able to post the document (you may use the 'simulate' document functionality to check this). However, system allows you to post some of the documents, even if this not true in the case of '**noted items**' which will contain only a debit or credit. Since there is no updating of accounting entries, system will allow you to go ahead with the posting of these items.

118. What is a 'Posting key'?

A **posting key** in SAP is a 2-digit alphanumeric key, which controls the entry of line items. SAP comes with many posting keys for meeting the different business transaction requirements: **40** (G/L debit), **50** (G/L credit), **01** (customer invoice), **11** (customer credit memo), **21** (vendor credit memo), **31** (vendor payment) etc.

The posting key determines:

- What account can be posted to
- Which side of the account (debit or credit) to be posted to
- What is the 'layout' screen to be used for that particular transaction

It is recommended not to change any of the default posting keys.

Transaction Code
OB41

119. What is 'Schedule Manager'?

SAP's '**Schedule Manager**' helps you to organize, execute and monitor complex and repetitive business transactions (like, month end processing) from easy-to-use workspace, which resembles an all-in-one 'organizer' kind of utility containing:

- Calendar window
- Daily overview window
- Task overview window
- User notes window

The ***information window*** provides with the details of what and how you can achieve the tasks by providing useful information with hyperlinks to processes and steps within a process. This appears to the left of all other windows. Depending upon the requirement, this can be 'switched-on' or 'switched-off'.

Schedule Manager: Schedule Tasks for Task List 0-SAP-DEMO

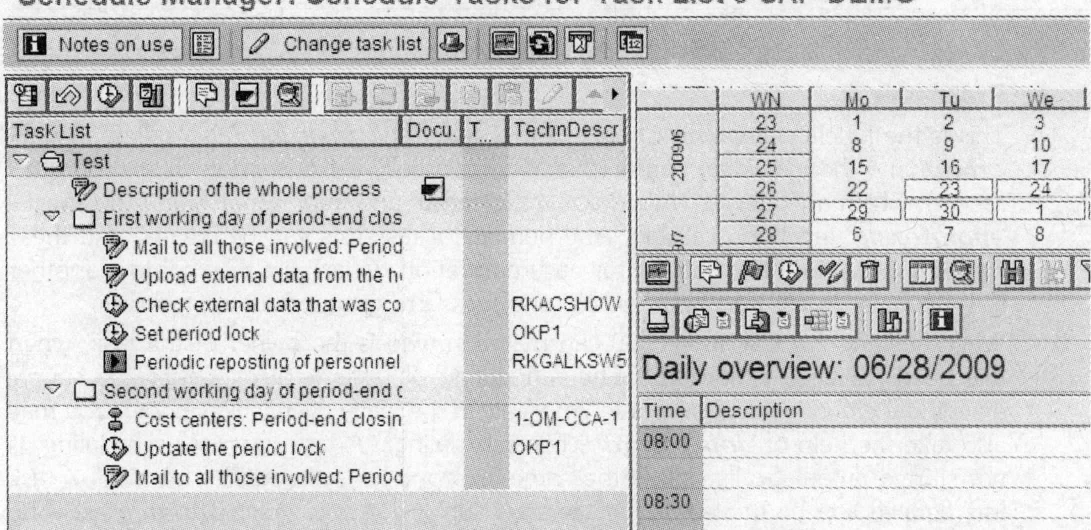

Figure 1.53: SAP Schedule Manager

The ***task overview window*** provides a complete 'drill-down' facility in a tree-structure for all tasks entered and monitored by you. The tasks are grouped into an upper level task list, which can be scheduled, released and monitored using the 'daily overview' window. Remember that the tasks maintained in the task overview window needs to be properly scheduled / released for execution: the mere listing of tasks here will not start a transaction or a program or a report.

The ***daily overview window*** is similar to an appointment column of any organizer, with fully customizable time intervals (in increments of, say, 30 minutes, 45 minutes etc). Ideally, the tasks appearing in the task list in 'task overview' window, when scheduled / released, will appear here against the appropriate time slot. By selecting a task here, you can monitor the same using the 'monitor' icon or from the menu. A look at this daily overview window, at the beginning of a day, will remind you of the tasks scheduled for that day.

The ***calendar window*** is a calendar utility to help you organized better. However, this goes beyond the regular calendar by displaying, in different colours like yellow / green, a particular date indicating that the status of tasks scheduled for that day. A 'green' background indicates that every thing is OK, but a 'yellow' indicates that there are some warnings.

Transaction Code
SCMA

120. How you can use the 'Schedule Manager' in SAP?

The Schedule Manager has the following functionalities built in:

1. Processes

This is the functionality which helps you to define the ***task list*** (also called as ***task group***) and the individual ***tasks*** (a task is essentially a *transaction* or a *program / report*), which are later on 'scheduled' / 'released' and 'monitored' using the special '***monitoring***' function available. Any number of task lists can be created and these lists are shown in a tree format for easy navigation. A task list may contain another task list or a ***chain of tasks*** within; and tasks are grouped into a task list.

While defining the task itself, you can maintain who is the owner of the task, when this needs to be executed etc. The scheduling of tasks is also possible by simply dragging them into the appropriate time slots in the 'daily overview' window. You may also take the help of '***job wizard***' while scheduling. A task, by mere scheduling, is not started automatically unless the same is properly '***released***'. The tasks / task lists defined can be moved in the hierarchy up / down or deleted form a list. The tasks can also be documented using MS-Office Word or Excel etc.

2. Scenarios

The *schedule manager* gives you ***three options*** for scheduling and monitoring:

a. ***Start transaction / program / report online and schedule the jobs (tasks) in the scheduler:*** Here, you can create or select a new task list in the scheduler, enter these in the 'daily overview' and monitor and control the tasks' execution in the 'monitor'.

b. ***Start transaction / program / report online and schedule the jobs (tasks) / job chain (task chain):*** This is similar to (a) above except that you have the option of inserting a '***job chain***' defined in '***flow definition***' into the task list.

c. ***Start transactions / reports online, schedule job or job chain, work-list:*** Here, you can also execute and monitor a complete work-list, involving several processing steps with all the step sequences. Besides scheduler, monitor, and flow definition, you can use the '***work-list monitor***', for monitoring the processing status.

3. Help Functions

Schedule Manager supplements with useful functions like:

- Runtime analysis
- Working with variables
- Releasing jobs

121. What are the advantages of 'Multilevel Worklist' in the Schedule Manager?

In the earlier releases of SAP, the period-end closing process consisted of a series of batch jobs. The sequence of the processing steps was established by the order in which the jobs were called. The objects were selected separately for each job. Through the selection criteria, it was possible to specify a unified scope of selection. This scope of selection had to be re-specified for each processing step (that is, for each individual function of period-end closing). When an object was processed, errors that occurred in previous processing steps were not taken into account. For this reason, it was necessary to check the objects with errors after completion of a job. Any errors had to be corrected and then the job restarted for the entire scope of selection. In some areas (such as the period-end close in *Product Cost by Period*), it was already possible to create a single-level worklist for the individual processing step. With this single-level worklist, the objects with errors could be called up for each processing step, and the causes of the errors determined. The processing step could then be performed again for the object after the error was corrected. This worklist did not prevent objects with errors from being processed in the subsequent processing step (that is, in the subsequent job).

The worklist of the Schedule Manager is a **multilevel worklist**. This means that the worklist is generated for a sequence of processing steps rather than for just one processing step. Thus, the worklist makes possible an efficient execution of processing step sequences. Processes such as period-end closing can be performed much more efficiently with a multilevel worklist.

The multilevel worklist has the following advantages:

- Faster processing of 'processing step sequences' (such as in period-end closing)

  Manual processing after completion of each job is no longer necessary. Manual processing is only necessary after executing a sequence of processing steps that consists of multiple jobs (for example, complete closing of an application component).
- Repeat processing steps only for objects with errors. With the multilevel worklist, the processing steps are repeated only for the objects that have errors.

  If you had an object with errors in the single-level worklist, it was often necessary to carry out the following processing steps again for the entire scope of selection.
- Decreased CPU time as the object selection only takes place once for each processing step sequence instead of for each single processing step. Objects are selected before the first processing step is executed.
- The multilevel worklist provides performance benefits particularly with complex structures in which dependencies between objects must be taken into account (such as complex project structures)
- Direct notification to (business) owners for correcting errors. Jobs are planned and monitored by members of the EDP team. In many cases they are not responsible for actually correcting the errors shown in the error logs. With the multilevel worklist, the actual employees (say, the business owners) responsible for correcting the errors can be informed directly, through workflow-triggered mail messages.

2

General Ledger (FI-G/L)

1. What is a 'Chart of Accounts'?

A '**chart of accounts**' is the list of G/L accounts used in one or more Company Codes. All the G/L accounts in a chart of accounts will have an account number, account name and some control information. The control information decides how the G/L account can be created.

2. What are all the major components of a 'Chart of Accounts'?

A '**chart of accounts**' is defined with the following items:

- Chart of account key
- Name
- Maintenance language
- Length of the G/L Account Number
- Controlling Integration
- Group chart of accounts (Consolidation)
- Block Indicator

3. What is an 'Operating Chart of Accounts'?

This is the chart of accounts, which is used for the day-to-day postings. Both FI and CO use this chart. It is mandatory that this chart of accounts be assigned to the Company Code. This is also known as '**operative**' or '**standard**' chart of accounts.

4. How 'Group Chart of Accounts' differs from 'Operating Chart of Accounts'?

The **group chart of accounts**, also known as ***corporate chart of accounts***, is used for consolidating all Company Codes (with dissimilar *operating chart of accounts*) belonging to the same Company. This is the 'universe' of all-inclusive G/L accounts from where the *operating chart of accounts* is derived. It is <u>not</u> mandatory that this has to be assigned to a Company Code.

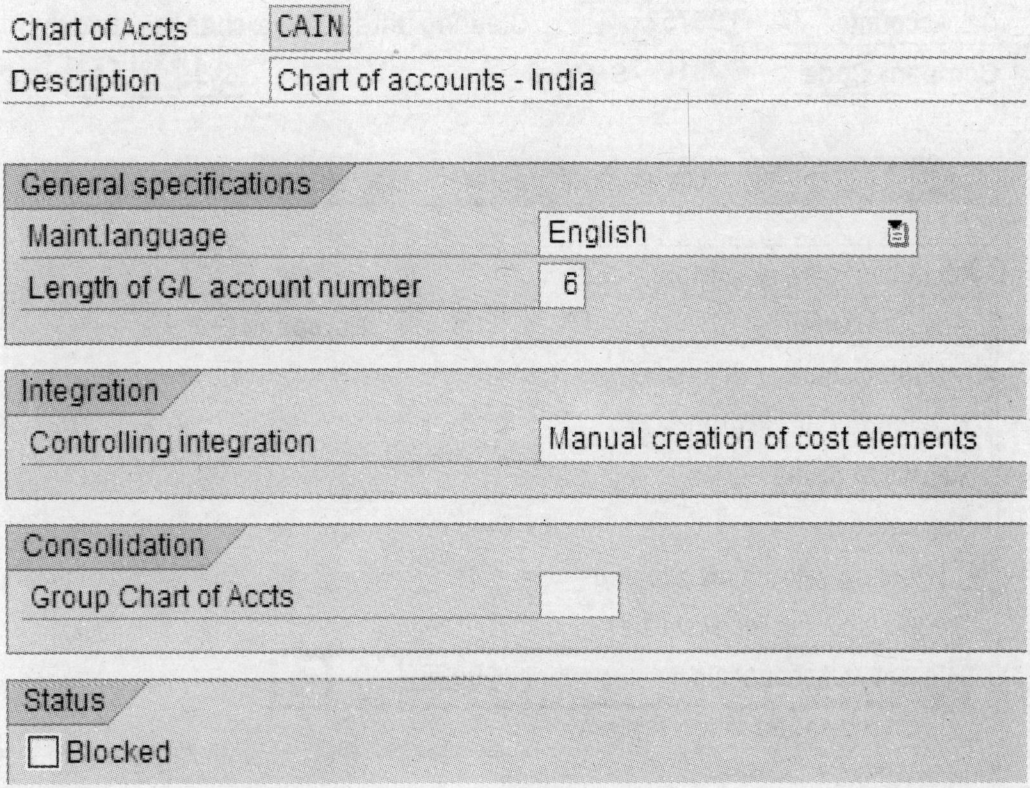

Chart of Accts: CAIN
Description: Chart of accounts - India

General specifications
Maint.language: English
Length of G/L account number: 6

Integration
Controlling integration: Manual creation of cost elements

Consolidation
Group Chart of Accts:

Status
☐ Blocked

Figure 2.1: Chart of Accounts

5. What is a 'Country Chart of Accounts'? Why you need this?

This chart of accounts, also known as **alternate chart of accounts**, contains the G/L accounts to meet the specific statutory / legal requirements of a company from where a Company Code operates. The assignment of this chart of accounts to a Company Code is also optional. It is possible that both the operating and the country chart of accounts are one and the same. In that case, you will not need two different charts of accounts.

In cases, where the operating and country chart of accounts are different, the link needs to be established by entering the G/L account number from the 'country chart of accounts', in the G/L master record (under the Company Code section) of the 'operating chart of accounts' in the field '*Alternative Account Number*' in the 'control data' tab.

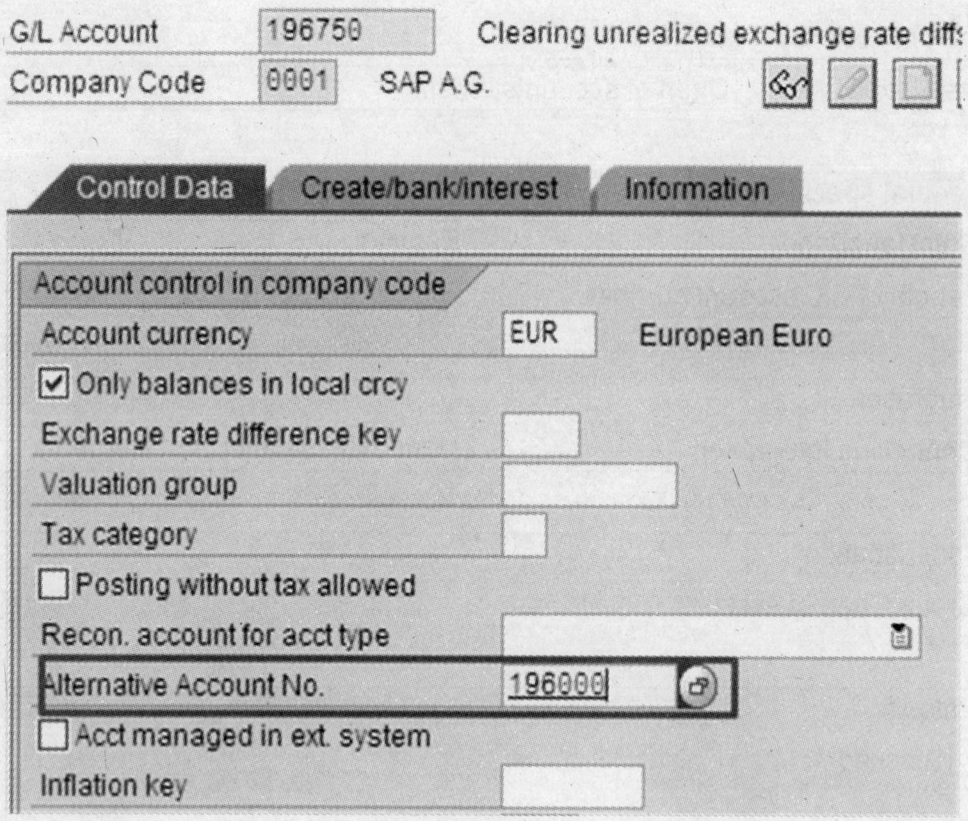

G/L Account 196750 Clearing unrealized exchange rate diffs

Company Code 0001 SAP A.G.

Control Data | Create/bank/interest | Information

Account control in company code

Account currency EUR European Euro

☑ Only balances in local crcy

Exchange rate difference key

Valuation group

Tax category

☐ Posting without tax allowed

Recon. account for acct type

Alternative Account No. 196000

☐ Acct managed in ext. system

Inflation key

Figure 2.1a: Mapping Country & Operating Charts of Accounts

6. Can one 'Chart of Accounts' is assigned to several Company Codes?

Yes.

One chart of accounts can be assigned to several Company Codes. However, the reverse is not possible i.e., you will not be able assign more than one chart of accounts to a single Company Code.

7. How to create a 'G/L Account Master Data'?

The **G/L account master data** can be created by any one of the following methods:

- Manual creation
- Creating with reference
- Through Data Transfer Workbench
- Copying from existing G/L accounts

The **manual creation** of G/L account master records is both laborious and time consuming. You will resort to do this only when you can't create master records using any of the other methods listed above.

You will follow the second method, **creating with reference**, when you are already in SAP and have an existing Company Code (*Reference Company Code*) from which you can copy these records to a new Company Code (*Target Company Code*).

You will be able to do this by accessing the Menu: '*SAP Customizing Implementation Guide > Financial Accounting (New) > General Ledger Accounting (New) > Master Data >* G/L Accounts > *G/L Account Creation and Processing > Create G/L Accounts with Reference*'.

Transaction Code
OB_GLACC01

While doing this, you can copy the '***account assignments***' as well ensuring that the integration of G/L with other applications is intact. SAP facilitates that you can (i) limit the number of G/L records thus copied to the target Company Code, (ii) create new records if necessary, and (iii) change the account number / name.

When you have G/L accounts in a non-SAP system and you feel that these accounts will meet your requirement you will then use '**data transfer workbench**' of SAP to transfer these records into SAP, and change the same to suit SAP environment. Since this will not have 'account assignment' logic as required in SAP, you need to be careful in defining these assignments.

You will resort to the last option of **copying from existing G/L accounts** only when you feel that there is a *chart of accounts* in the system which entirely meets your requirement; else, follow the second method described above.

You will be able to do this by accessing the Menu: '*SAP Customizing Implementation Guide > Financial Accounting (New) > General Ledger Accounting (New) > Master Data >* G/L Accounts > *G/L Account Creation and Processing >* Alternative Methods > *Copy G/L Accounts > Copy Chart of Accounts / Copy Company Code.*

8. What is 'Collective Processing' of G/L accounts?

The **collective processing** helps you to make systematic changes to a number of G/L accounts in a single step. For example, you have used '***creating with reference***' method to create G/L accounts in a new Company Code and you want to change the account names as well as the 'G/L account type' (P&L or B/S). Then you will use this ***mass processing (collective processing) method*** to achieve the same. You can make changes to:

- Chart of accounts data
- Company Code data

Use Menu Path: '*Accounting > Financial accounting > General Ledger > Master Records > G/ L Accounts > Collective processing > Chart of Accounts Data / Company Code Data / Descriptions*'. You can also use the IMG Menu Path: '*SAP Customizing Implementation*

Guide > Financial Accounting (New) > General Ledger Accounting (New) > Master Data > G/L Accounts > *G/L Account Creation and Processing > Change G/L Accounts Collectively > Change Chart of Accounts Data > Change Company Code Data > Change Account Name*'.

Remember that the 'collective processing' helps only to edit and you can not use this method to create new master records.

9. What is 'Individual Processing' of G/L accounts?

Against the 'collective processing' of G/L accounts where you edit a number of accounts in a single step, **individual processing** helps to edit or create G/L account master records one at a time. Here you can edit (including display, change, block, unblock and delete) or create a New G/L account in three different ways:

i. ***Centrally***: You will be editing or creating a G/L account master record in both chart of accounts area and Company Code area in one go. This is also known as '**one-Step' G/L creation**.

Transaction Code
FS00

ii. ***In Chart of accounts area***: you first edit or create the record here before doing the same in the Company Code area.

Transaction Code
FSPO

iii. ***In Company Code area***: you edit or create the record here after the same has been done in the chart of accounts area.

Transaction Code
FSSO

Put together, steps-2 & 3 relate to 'step-by-step' creation of G/L account master records.

10. Is it possible to change an existing balance sheet G/L a/c to P&L type?

Technically, you will be able to change all the fields, except the account number, of a G/L account in the chart of accounts area. However, in this particular instance when you change the '*G/L account type*' from 'B/S' to 'P&L', make sure that you again run the '*balance carry forward*' program after saving the changes so that the system corrects the account balances suitably.

11. Why system does not allow changing 'Tax Category' in a G/L master?

You will be able to change the 'Company Code' related fields like tax category, currency etc provided that there has not been any posting to these accounts. Pay attention to the following:

- If you need to denote an existing G/L account to henceforth be managed on 'open item basis' or vice versa, then make sure that the account balance is zero in either case.
- If you are trying to change an existing 'reconciliation account' (to a regular G/L), then make sure that the account has not been posted to.
- If you are attempting to denote an existing ordinary G/L account into a 'reconciliation account', ensure that the account has zero balance.

12. What is an 'Account Group'?

The **account group** (or **G/L account group**) - a 4-character alphanumeric key - controls how G/L account master records are created in the system. This helps to 'group' G/L accounts according to the '*functional areas*' to which they must belong. The account group is mandatory for creating a master record. The same account groups can be used by more than one Company Code if they all use the same chart of accounts. However, each G/L account is assigned to only one account group.

The account group determines:

- What ***number interval*** is to be used while creating the master record?
- What ***screen layout*** is to be used while creating the master record in the Company Code area?

While defining the account groups in the system, you also need to define the corresponding ***field status*** for each of these groups. Else, you will not be able to see any fields as all these would be hidden by default.

SAP comes delivered with a number of '*account groups*' like:

- **SAKO** G/L accounts general
- **MAT.** Materials Management accounts
- **FIN.** Liquid Funds accounts

Chrt/Accts	Acct Group	Name	From acct	To account
INT	AS	Fixed assets accounts		999999
INT	CASH	Liquid funds accounts		999999
INT	GL	General G/L accounts		999999
INT	MAT	Materials management accounts		999999
INT	PL	P&L Statement Accounts		999999
INT	RECN	Recon.account ready for input		999999

Figure 2.2: G/L Account Groups

In most of the situations, you will not require additional groups other than the ones already available in the standard system. However, if you need to create a new one, it is easier to copy an existing one and make modifications to the same instead of creating from scratch.

Transaction Code
OBD4

13. What is a 'Screen Layout'?

The 'account group' determines which **screen layout** should be used while creating a G/L account master record. For each of the account groups, you can define different screen layouts, which essentially determines the '***field status***' of a field.

The field status refers whether the field is:

- **Suppress** (field is invisible, hidden from display)
- **Req. entry** (display on, entry required)
- **Opt. entry** (display on, entry not mandatory)
- **Display** (display only)

All the above four are shown as 'radio buttons' against each of the fields in the screen layout, and you should select any one to set the status to that field; by default all the fields are 'suppress'.

There are two levels of controls of field status, to decide which takes the priority, while deciding the screen layout:

- Field status at the **account group** level
- Field status at the activity (creat change/ display) level i.e. at the ***transaction*** level.

Maintain Field Status Group: Document entry

Field check

Page 1

General Data

Chart of accounts INT Group AS

Fixed assets accounts

Document entry

	Suppress	Req. Entry	Opt. entry	Display
Reconcil.acct ready for input	◉	○	○	○
Field status group	○	◉	○	○

Figure 2.3: Field Status

You may also have field status defined for posting keys (40-debit & 50-credit for the G/L account postings. Also remember to define the field status for 'reconciliation accounts' as you will not be able to define any such status in the sub-ledger accounts (for example: customer or vendor).

SAP has in-built rules to link, called ***link rules***, these two levels and to decide the final status of a field in the 'screen layout'. The link rules also help to over come the field-status settings differences arising out of different settings at (1) Client level (field status for posting keys), (2) Company Code level(field status settings at the account group level).

14. What is a 'Field Status Group'?

Field status variant 0001 Field status for 0001

Field status group	Text
CH67	Reconciliation Accts with Contract Ref.
G001	General (with text, assignment)
G003	Material consumption accounts
G004	Cost accounts
G005	Bank accounts (obligatory value date)
G006	Material accounts
G007	Asset accts (w/o accumulated depreciatn)

Figure 2.4: Field Status Variant / Field Status Group

The 'field status' of an individual field or a group of fields is marked into a **field status group**, which is then assigned to individual G/L account master records. You may attach field status groups to a ***field status variant*** so that the same 'field status groups' are used in various Company Codes.

Transaction Code
OBC4

The **field status variant** is named similar to the Company Code. For example, if your Company Code is 1000, the field status variant is also named as 1000, and the same is assigned to the Company Code.

CoCd	Company Name	City	Fld stat.var.
0001	SAP A.G.	Walldorf	0001

Figure 2.5: Assign Field Status Variant to Company Codes

Transaction Code
OBC5

15. What do you mean by 'Balances in Local Currency' only?

When you create G/L account master records, it is necessary to decide whether you want an account to have the transactions updated only in local currency. Then you will set this indicator accordingly in the 'Company Code area' of the master record. Pay attention to set this indicator for the ***clearing accounts*** like:

- Cash discount clearing accounts
- GR /IR clearing accounts

You should not set this indicator for reconciliation accounts for customers or vendors. Setting it in all other instances is optional. It is usually set for particular balance sheet accounts including:

- Accounts which are not managed on an open item basis and not kept in foreign currencies.
- Accounts which are managed on an open item basis and have the same types of items posted in different currencies, but always allow clearing to be made if the local currency amounts correspond.

G/L Account 196750 Clearing unrealized exchange ra
Company Code 0001 SAP A.G.
Control Data | Create/bank/interest | Information
Account control in company code
Account currency EUR European Euro
Only balances in local crcy
Exchange rate difference key
Valuation group

Figure 2.6: 'Balances in Local Currency' Indicator in G/L Account

Example:
Consider an invoice for USD 1,000, which on that day of posting translates into an amount of INR 45,000 with an exchange rate of I USD = INR 45. Imagine that when the goods are received, the exchange rate was 1 USD = INR 44.

- If the indicator is set, the system ignores the exchange rate as if the line items have been maintained only in the local currency (INR), and the items are cleared.
- If the indicator is NOT set, the system makes a posting for the 'exchange rate difference' (INR 1, 000) before clearing the two line items.

16. What is 'Line Item Display'?

To display line items of an account, you need to set the indicator '**line item display**' to 'on' in 'account management in company code' block of the "control data" tab of that account's master record. This is mandatory for customer and vendor accounts.

Account management in company code
Open Item Management
Line item display
Sort key 037 Currency key
Authorization Group
Accounting clerk

Figure 2.7: 'Line Item Display' Indicator in Account Master

For each line item, an entry is saved in an index table, which contains the connection between the line item and the account. The line items can be displayed using (a) classical display or (b) SAP List Viewer (ALV). And, you can use several '***display variants***' to suit your need to display various fields when you feel that the *Standard Variant* is not meeting your requirements.

In the New G/L, the line item display is always possible for the general ledger view. You need to set this indicator if you (a) also want to see the line items in the entry view, and (b) want open item management.

17. What is 'Archiving'? How it differs from 'Deletion'?

Archiving refers to deleting data from the documents from the database and storing the same in a file, which can be transferred to an 'archiving system' later on. Archiving does not physically delete the documents.

Deletion actually removes the documents from the database. To proceed with archiving and deletion you need to consider the following:

i. ***Block*** posting to these archived master records.

ii. ***Mark*** (the master records) ***for deletion***

Mark for deletion at the 'chart of accounts area' to delete the records from all the Company Codes. However, if you do not want to delete from all the Company Codes, but only from one or more Company Codes then do the same in the 'Company Code area' of the master record(s).

iii. ***Archive*** all the transaction figures from the relevant documents.

iv. Call up a special program to '***delete***' the records:

The program will check whether that particular document could be deleted: if yes, it will proceed to 'archive' and then to 'deletion'.

18. When to 'Block' an account?

You may use '**blocking**' to:

- Block an account from further postings
- Block creation of account itself (at the Company Code level or chart of accounts area

19. Explain 'Intercompany Postings' in SAP.

Intercompany postings arise when a Company Code in a centralized procurement, for example, pays for itself and on behalf of other Company Codes. When posted, the transaction results in three documents for:

- Paying Company Code (say, 1111) in its books
- Other Company Codes (say, 2222 & 4444)
- Intercompany transaction itself

Before making intercompany transactions, you need to configure both 'intercompany payables' and 'intercompany receivables'. For each combination of these Company Codes, you will be required to maintain a 'clearing account' which must be referenced to in each of these Company Codes. You will also be able to configure whether you manually input the transaction number or allow the system to automatically assign the numbers. In case of system generated transaction numbers, this 16 digit number consists of (1) 10 digit document number (1222222222) of the paying Company Code , followed by (2) 4 digits representing this paying Company Code(1111) and (3) 2 digits representing the last two digits of the financial year (07) (Example: 1222222222**1111**07).

20. Can you manually 'clear' the 'Open Items'? When?

Under **manual clearing**, you will select the open items, based on the incoming payment so that the selected 'open items' are 'cleared' (knocked-off). In cases like refunds from a vendor or transactions involving bank sub-accounts, clearing accounts etc., you will resort to manual clearing.

When cleared, the system flags these line items as 'cleared', creates a ***clearing document*** and enters the ***clearing document number*** and clearing date in these open items. Besides the clearing document, the system may also generate 'additional documents' in cases like ***partial*** or ***residual processing***, and for posting the loss / gain to the assigned G/L account.

While doing this, if there is a ***payment difference***, the same can be treated the way it is configured in the system:

- If the difference is with in the ***tolerance limit***, defined in the system using the ***tolerance groups*** (defined at the Company Code level), the ***cash discount*** is adjusted or the system automatically posts the difference to a gain/loss G/L account.
- When the payment difference exceeds the limits of defined tolerance, then the incoming amount may be processed as a ***partial payment*** (the original open item is not cleared, but the incoming payment is posted with a reference to that invoice) or the difference is posted as the ***residual item*** (the original open item is cleared and a new open item created by the system for the difference amount) in the system.

21. How do you perform 'Period Closing' in SAP?

You do a **(period) closing** in SAP, in three steps:

- Completing the pre-closing activities
- Financial Closing
- Managerial Closing

22. What is 'Pre-closing'?

You need to ensure the following as **pre-closing** activities:

- Post all the recurring entries for expenses and accruals.
- Ensure that all the interfaced programs have been run so that the required data have been transferred to system.
- Post all the depreciation, material receipts, invoices, salaries etc. In short, ensure that

all the transactions for the period in question have been duly recorded and posted into the system.

23. Explain 'Financial Closing'.

If you have not yet migrated to SAP ERP or if you are not using the new G/L functionality, then you may follow the following activities step-by step to complete the financial closing (if you use New G/L functionality, then you will use the Closing Cockpit to accomplish closing, easier and faster – Closing Cockpit functionality is explained in 2.1 General Ledger Accounting (New))

i. Revaluate / Regroup

- ***Revalue*** *balance sheet* items managed in foreign currencies – use the report ***RFSBEW00*** to valuate G/L balance sheet accounts managed in a foreign currency.(The report generates a *batch input* session to post the revenue or expense resulting from any exchange rate differences)
- ***Clear*** *receivable* or *payable* with 'exchange rate difference'
- ***Valuate*** all the *open items* using the report ***SAPF100***. This is used to valuate all the open receivables and payables, using the period-end exchange rates. Here also, the report generates a *batch input* session to post the entries resulting from any exchange rate differences.
- ***Regroup*** GR/IR using the program ***RFWERE00*** to allocate the net balance (depending on whether the balance is a net debit or credit) in the GR/IR account to one of two G/L accounts (created to actually depict the net effect of the balance in the GR/IR account)

ii. Ensure accounting accuracy

Use the program ***SAPF190***, to compare the totals created by the system in the (1) indexes (customers, vendors and G/L) and documents(customers, vendors and G/L) with that of the (2) account balances (customers, vendors and G/L) to ensure the transaction accuracy.

iii. Run required reports

Generate the ***financial statements*** (balance sheet and profit & loss account), using the ***financial statement versions***. You may also generate the key figure/ratio reports (use the G/L account information system).

24. What is a 'Financial Statement Version'?

Financial statement version helps to define the *financial statements* (both the ***Balance Sheet*** and ***Profit & Loss statements***). When you copy the settings from an existing Company Code to a new one, you will also be copying the financial statement version defined for the 'source' Company Code.

Fin.Stmt.versi...	Financial Statement Version Name
BACO	Financial Statement - Colombia
BACZ	Financial Statement (Czech Republic)
BAES	Financial Statement (Spain)
BAFI	Financial Statement (Finland)
BAFR	Financial Statement (France)
BAGB	Financial Statement (Great Briain)
BAHK	Financial Statement (Hongkong)
BAHU	Financial Statement Hungary
BAIN	Financial Statement Version - India
BAJP	Financial Statement (Japan)

Figure 2.8: Financial Statement Version

You can define a new financial statement version and build the financial statements from scratch. You may create the financial statements both for (1) external reporting (Company Code financial statements) and (2) internal reporting (business area financial statements).

You may also create the balance sheets for a group of Company Codes using *FI-SL (Special Purpose Ledgers)*. The financial statements may be defined to provide information from (1) period accounting point of view (G/L account groups wise) or (2) cost of sales point of view (Functional Area financial statements).

All the above statements can be configured and defined to provide different levels of details: a financial statement version can have a maximum of 10 hierarchy levels, with each level assigned with an item (*account category*). As you go down the hierarchy, you define the account categories in more detail, with the lowest level being represented by the G/L accounts. The system displays the relevant amount for each of these items.

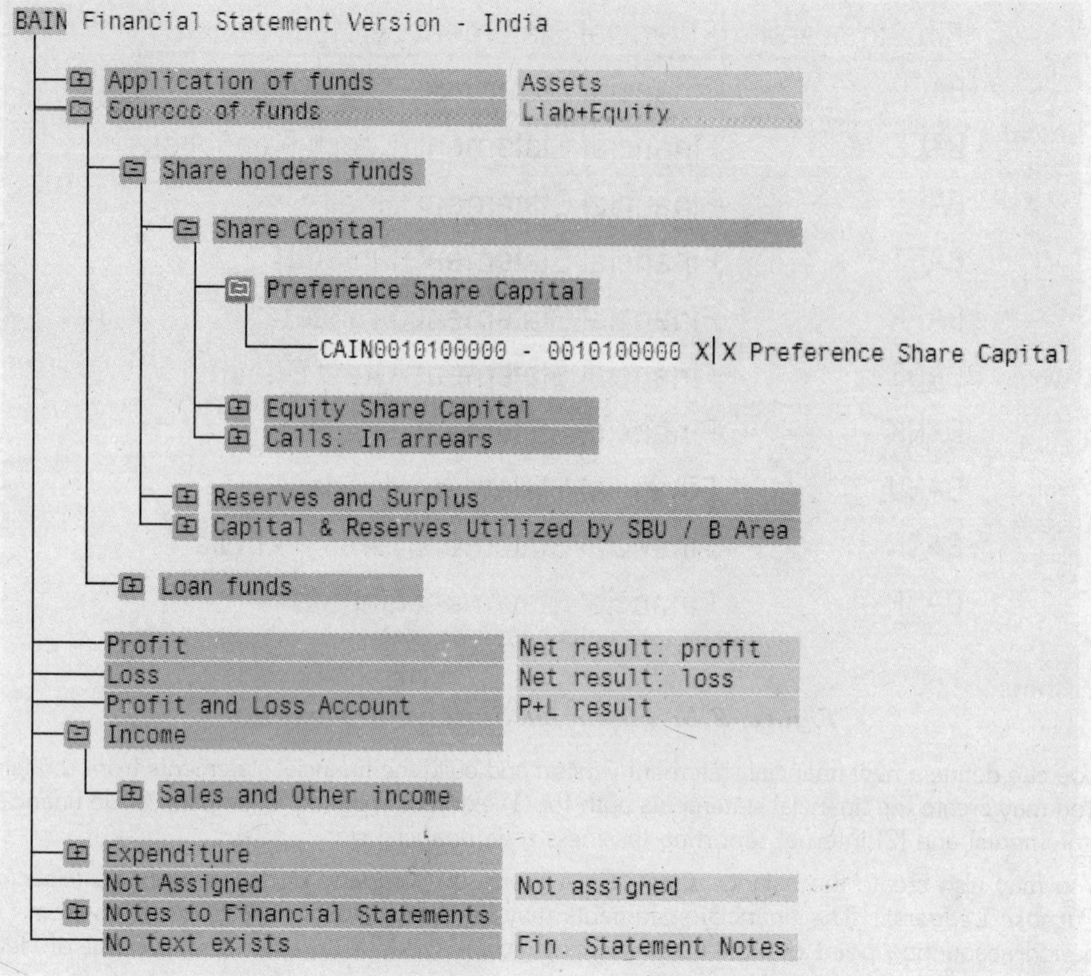

Figure 2.9: Items in a Financial Statement Version

25. What are the minimum items in a 'Financial Statement Version'?

Irrespective of the details you require in a **financial statement version**, it is mandatory that you have, at least, the following items defined:

a. Assets

b. Liabilities
   - Net Result: Profit
   - Net Result: Loss

c. ***P /L result*** (during annual closing, when you run the program **RFBILA00**, the system calculates the profit or loss by subtracting the 'total liabilities' from 'total assets' and updates the relevant Net Result item - Profit or Loss)

d. ***Not assigned*** (posted amounts but not yet assigned to any of the account groups)

26. How to ensure that 'correct' balances in 'Financial Statement Version'?

In order to have a balanced statement (*Profit & Loss* and *Balance Sheet*) you need to ensure that the accounts are correctly and completely assigned to the nodes of the ***financial statement version***. You may do this by necessary assignments at the (1) account balance level or (2) node balance level.

At the ***account balance level***, you need to ensure that the account is shown in two different nodes, but you will turn "ON" the 'debit indicator' of the account on one node and turn "ON" the 'credit indicator' on the other node. Imagine that you have a bank current account 10001000. When you turn "ON" the debit indicator, this account shows the only the debit balances and is construed as the asset. On the other hand, when the credit indicator is turned "ON", the balances on this node now indicates that you owe to the bank (overdraft).

You may also use the ***node level assignment***. In this case, the system uses the 'debit/credit shift' and shows only the 'effective' balance at the node and not at the individual account level.

27. How to perform 'Annual Closing' in SAP?

Annual closing is also like any other 'period closing' and you will be performing all the activities which are required for a period-end-close. Besides, you will also be completing the following:

- Carry forward Vendor and Customer accounts
- Carry forward the G/L account balances of all the Balance Sheet items
- Close the Profit & Loss Accounts and carry forward the balance (profit or loss) to the retained earnings account(s)

For G/L account 'carry forward', use the program SAPF011.

It will be faster and easier to use the Closing Cockpit to accomplish this if you use the New G/L.

28. Explain 'Managerial Closing'.

The **managerial closing** involves completion of the following:

- Do a preliminary Controlling period closing
- Settle/re-allocate costs across Controlling organization
- Draw and review internal reports
- Re-open the Controlling period
- Correct and adjust the accounting data, if required
- Reconcile FI and CO by running the FICO *Reconciliation Ledger*
- Run re-adjustment programs to ensure that the *Business Areas* and the *Profit Centres* are balanced
- Draw reports and analyze

2.1 General Ledger Accounting (New)

29. Why SAP brought out General Ledger Accounting (New)?

Before the advent of my SAP ERP / ECC versions, various releases of SAP R/3 including SAP R/3 Enterprise (4.70), companies had to handle G/L accounting by using different SAP applications. Depending on specific company or industry requirements, or local accounting principles, one had to implement application components or functions that sometimes had their own user interfaces. For example, you might use Special Purpose Ledger (FI-SL) to meet certain reporting requirements like having totals in additional table fields. Likewise, SAP Profit Center Accounting (PCA) resided in a separate application. The software for both the FI-SL and Profit Center Accounting offered certain functions that were not automatically reconciled with functions in the G/L accounting software. This had resulted in closing activities involving additional reconciliation effort, and delays.

The New G/L, starting with mySAP ERP 2005, covers all these functions and requirements, but retains the familiar accounting interface – such as, currency translation – and continues to provide functions that support postings. Upstream software for S&D and MM works with the New G/L in exactly the same way as before. The familiar and well-tested tables (BSEG: document table, BSIS: open items for New G/L accounts and BSAS: cleared items for G/L accounts) are still part of the New G/L and form the database for many standard and customer-specific reports. New G/L functions for financial allocation or statistical key figures, for example, share the same interface design as functions for controlling.

If you are familiar with SAP R/3, then you will be comfortable using the New G/L as the user interface is almost similar and intuitive.

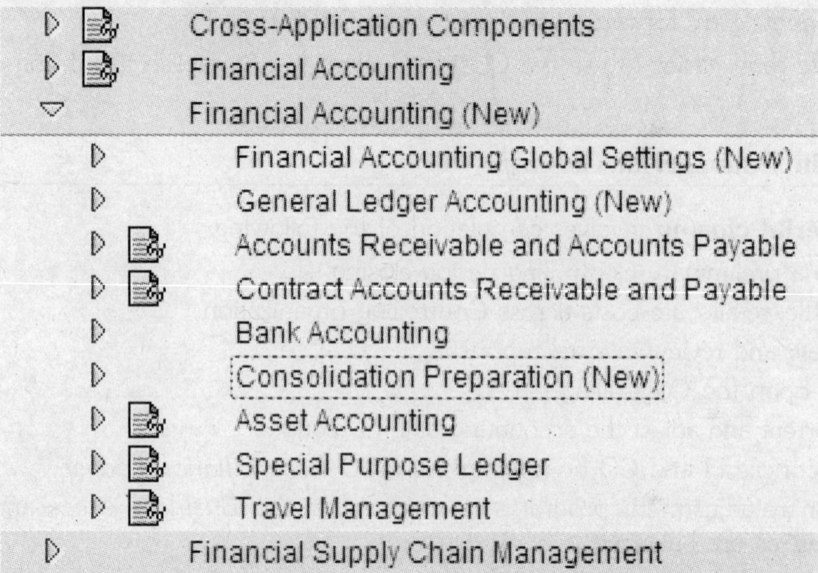

Figure 2.1.1: New G/L Functionality in IMG

30. What are the technical advantages of using New G/L?

The following are some of the major technical advantages of New G/L:

- The New G/L does away the need for separate ledgers like Cost-of-Sales ledger, Special Purpose Ledger, Reconciliation Ledger, or Profit Center ledger, with the introduction and portrayal of business models occurring within a single solution.
- Users already familiar with SAP R/3 require very little training as the user-interface is similar as that of the Classical G/L.
- New G/L stores all the data in a single totals table, eliminating data redundancy, and you just need to input data only once.
- No need for additional reconciliation activities during closing, as the data is always automatically reconciled with other applications.
- Inclusion of additional fields, standard SAP fields or customer defined fields, for flexible reporting has been made easier.

31. What are business advantages of using New G/L?

The following are some of the major business advantages of using New G/L:

- Easy and flexible international business reporting
- Fast Close
- Financial and management accounting integrated in a single interface
- More transparency with improved audit trails
- Parallel accounting possibility
- Reduced TCO (Total Cost of Operations)
- Usage of customer fields

32. What are all the features of 'New G/L'?

The traditional or '***Classic G/L accounting***' in FI has been focused towards providing a comprehensive external reporting, by recording all business transactions in the system. However, to meet the modern day requirements, this has now been enhanced and the **New G/L**' provides the following:

- ***Parallel accounting***: Maintaining several parallel ledgers to meet different accounting principles
- ***Integrated legal and management reporting***: Unlike the traditional G/L, the 'New G/L' enables you to perform internal management reporting along with the legal reporting. So, you are in a position to generate *Financial Statements* for any dimension (say, profit centre) in the business.
- ***Segment reporting***: With the introduction of Segment dimension, SAP now enables you to produce Segment Reports based on ***IFRS*** *(International Financial Reporting Standards)* and the ***US GAAP*** *(Generally Accepted Accounting Principles)* accounting principles.

- ***Cost of Sales accounting***: Now it is possible to perform Cost of Sales accounting in the 'new FI-G/L'.

33. Explain the 'Ledger' concept in New G/L.

The New G/L uses the Special Purpose Ledger (FI-SL) technique to save total values in the tables, many of which are preconfigured upon delivery. In the New G/L, a ledger or ledger group can portray one or more valuation views. All Company Codes are assigned to a '**leading ledger**' for each client. This ledger contains the group-valuation view. You can add **additional ledgers (non-leading ledgers)** for each company code: by assigning different characteristic values and fiscal-year definitions, you can use these additional ledgers for different purposes – such as parallel accounting or management reporting.

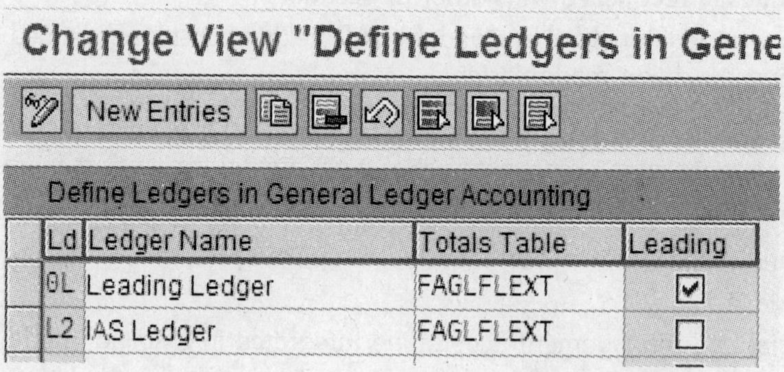

Change View "Define Ledgers in Gene

New Entries

Define Ledgers in General Ledger Accounting

Ld	Ledger Name	Totals Table	Leading
0L	Leading Ledger	FAGLFLEXT	☑
L2	IAS Ledger	FAGLFLEXT	☐

Figure 2.1.2: 'Ledgers' in New G/L

With the focus of New G/L on how data is updated rather than changes to the interface, it is now possible to directly perform postings that previously required several different components. This is also true with the transfer postings between Profit Centers or other characteristics (such as Segments) that were previously stored in FI-SL: you can now use a G/L account posting that specifies the corresponding Profit Center. The advantage of this kind of posting is that the system always reconciles the Profit Centers and G/L account instantaneously, as all the data are stored in the same table. The document numbers by document type are still based on the number range object from the G/L component of SAP R/3 (RF_BELEG); however, in cases involving a posting to a ledger with a fiscal year that differs from that of the leading ledger, the system issues document numbers from a different number range object (FAGL_DOCNR).

You can handle **parallel accounting** using the ledger approach as an alternative to the account approach. To provide different valuation views for period-end closing, you can either perform automatic postings using the valuation programs (such as foreign-currency valuation) or use manual postings to a specific ledger.

For postings related to daily operations, the software normally updates all ledgers assigned to the Company Code as the leading ledger exists in all company codes (across all clients). You can, however, define additional ledgers for each company code, possibly with different fiscal-year variants. An incoming invoice, such as a payment on account, always updates all ledgers related to the respective Company Code. The period check is always performed for the leading or representative ledger. If a ledger group does not contain the leading ledger, one of the ledgers in the group becomes the representative ledger. This approach means that postings are made only if the period of the leading or representative ledger allows. SAP ERP does not validate any other fiscal-year definitions that exist in other ledgers of the ledger group. The software updates the other ledgers in every case, which does not prevent completion of the posting. Note that you cannot make postings specific to ledgers or to ledger groups to accounts managed on an open-item basis.

34. Explain the 'Leading Ledger' in New G/L.

The standard SAP system comes delivered with '0L' as the **leading ledger** together with the 'totals' table 'FAGLFLEXT'. The leading ledger is the principal ledger which uses the fiscal year variant and posting period variant, among other control parameters, from the Company Code. The leading ledger manages all the local currencies of the Company Code. Only the values from the leading ledger are posted to Controlling (in the standard system). Note that there will be only one 'leading ledger'.

35. What are the two 'Views' in New G/L?

With New G/L, users can switch between (1) **entry view** (regular view or data entry view) and the (2) **G/L view**. A user can enter/display/change documents in exactly the same way as before (that of Classic G/L) using the 'entry view'. This is the view most of the users will be working with.

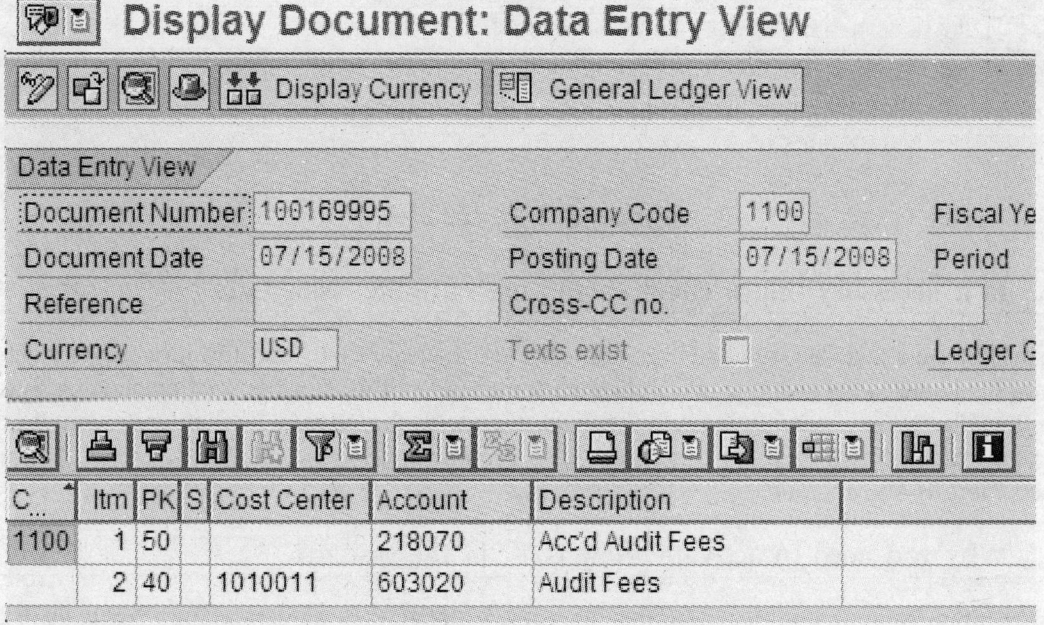

Figure 2.1.3: Entry View

However, one can easily toggle to the 'G/L view' which is always specific to a ledger. Depending on the system setting, you can also display one or more G/L views. That is why in certain ledger views, it might be useful to derive specific characteristics or set a zero balance for all the segments involved in each document.

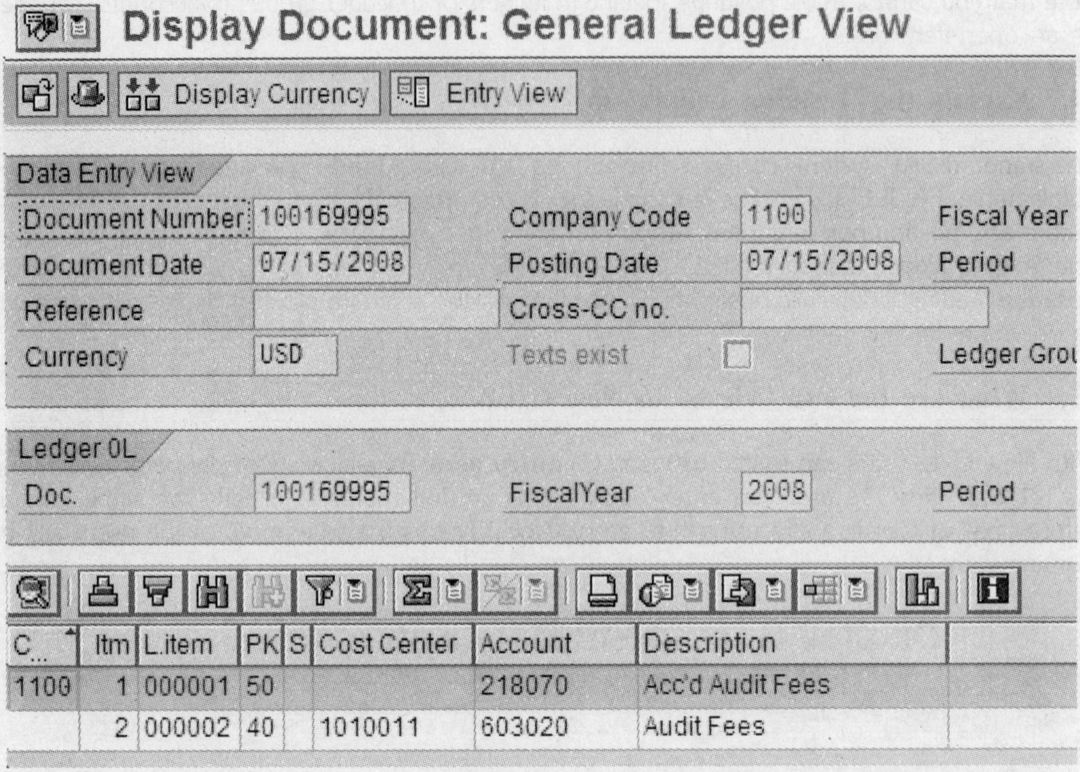

Display Document: General Ledger View

Display Currency | Entry View

Data Entry View

Document Number 100169995 | Company Code 1100 | Fiscal Year
Document Date 07/15/2008 | Posting Date 07/15/2008 | Period
Reference | Cross-CC no.
Currency USD | Texts exist | Ledger Grou

Ledger 0L

Doc. 100169995 | FiscalYear 2008 | Period

C...	Itm	L.item	PK	S	Cost Center	Account	Description
1100	1	000001	50			218070	Acc'd Audit Fees
	2	000002	40		1010011	603020	Audit Fees

Figure 2.1.4: G/L View

36. Is it necessary that a client should use only the 'New G/L'?

For all the new installations, SAP recommends use of New G/L, and the functionality will be active by default. However, for an existing customer use of this is optional: they can continue to use the 'Classic G/L' accounting and they can migrate to the New G/L when they want it (after they migrated to SAP ERP). You should also remember that the New G/L will be activated when there is an 'upgrade'.

37. Why you need to activate 'New G/L' in the system?

By activating New G/L accounting, the functions for New G/L accounting are made available.

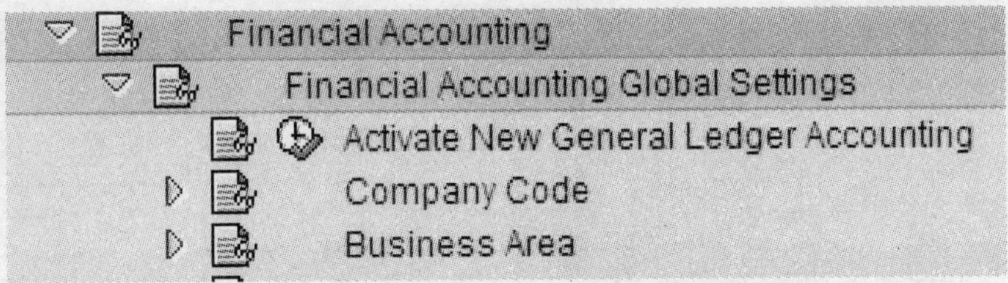

Figure 2.1.5: Activate New G/L Accounting in IMG

Once the New G/L functionality is activated, in the *SAP Reference IMG*, the previous financial accounting menu is replaced by the '*Financial Accounting (New)*' menu. Under '*Financial Accounting Global Settings (New)*' and '*General Ledger (New)*', you can make the settings for New G/L accounting. You activate the tables of New G/L accounting so that your posting data is written to them.

Financial Accounting (New)
Financial Accounting Global Settings (New)
General Ledger Accounting (New)

Figure 2.1.6: New G/L Accounting Menu in IMG

If you already use 'Classic G/L' accounting in your production system, you need to perform migration of data before you activate New G/L accounting. Migration is only possible as part of a project. In the standard system, the tables from '*Classic G/L accounting*' (**GLTO**) are updated as well as the tables in 'New G/L' during the activation. This enables you to perform a 'ledger comparison' during the implementation of 'New G/L' to ensure that your 'New G/L accounting' has the correct settings and is working correctly.

38. When you will deactivate updates to 'Classic G/L' in the system?

It is recommended that you 'deactivate' the update of tables for 'classic G/L accounting' once you have established that 'New G/L' is working correctly. To do this, in Customizing choose *Financial Accounting Global Settings (New) > Tools > Deactivate 'Update of Classic General Ledger'*.

Remember that when you 'activated' New G/L accounting, not only are the tables of New G/L accounting updated in the standard system, but also the balances in the tables of Classic G/L accounting (Table GLT0). This default setting is maintained to enable you to use comparison reports during the implementation phase of New G/L to ensure that New G/L accounting delivers correct results. Once you have established that New G/L accounting is set up correctly and is operating correctly, you can 'deactivate' the updates from Classic G/L accounting. To do this, 'deselect' the indicator '*Write Classic General Ledger (GLT0')*.

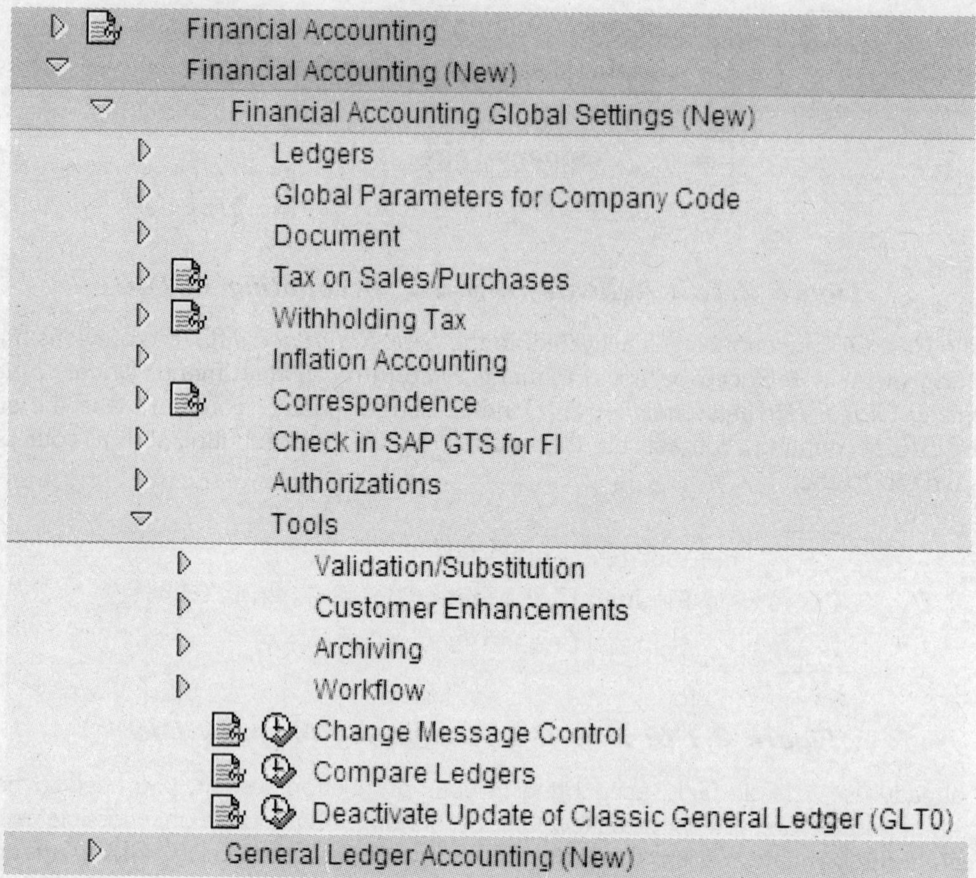

Figure 2.1.7: Deactivating update of Classic G/L - IMG

Change View "Update/Read Classic General Ledger": Details

Update/Read Classic General Ledger

☐ Write Classic General Ledger (GLT0)

☐ Read Classic General Ledger (GLT0)

Figure 2.1.8: Deactivating Update of Classic G/L

In the standard system, reading data from the tables of Classic G/L is deactivated, meaning that the programs of Classic G/L accounting (such as classic financial statement) read the balances from the tables of New G/L accounting. If you want the programs of Classic G/L accounting to read the tables of Classic G/L accounting, select the indicator '*Read Classic General Ledger (GLT0)*'. Note to select this indicator only if the indicator '*Write Classic General Ledger (GLT0)*' is also selected

39. Explain the new Tables included in New G/L.

The two important tables of Classic G/L - BSEG & BKPF - remain in the New G/L also, with all the documents relevant for the Leading Ledger updated in these tables. However, you have some additional fields like LDGRP, RLDNR etc in BSEG (Document Header) and fields like SEGMENT in BKPF (Document Line Items).

SAP has introduced three new tables in New G/L to (a) handle totals, (b) store G/L specific line items and (c) calculate valuations for year-end closing in parallel ledgers.

a. New totals table

In addition to using the new totals table in the standard software, you can define your own table, using a new table (FAGLFLEXT) as a template. When you define new totals tables, ensure that you do write the necessary programs to include the data from these tables. This step is important because the report writer software or drill-down tools do not recognize new totals tables that you create. The new totals table contains additional standard fields for storing totals. With the standard table, you can easily activate support for many scenarios by customizing the software. The table thus supports activities like:

- Business Area updating
- Cost Center updating (Field: RCNTR)
- Cost-of-sales accounting
- Functional Area (Field: RFAREA)
- Preparation for consolidation
- Profit Center updating (Field: PRCTR)
- Segment reporting (Field: SEGMENT)

You can add other fields (standard fields like 'plant' supplied ready made by SAP or your own fields – known as customer fields - in the totals table with minimum effort. A mere extension of these fields to the new table is not sufficient; you need to activate all such fields as 'enhancements' for each of the ledgers. The new totals table can contain several ledgers that store period totals to combine characteristics. You can now create totals for fields like Profit Center, Segment, and partner – in addition to fields for general-ledger account, company code, and fiscal year.

b. Storing ledger-specific line items

Two new tables (FAGLFLEXA and FAGLFLEXP) store the ledger-specific line items (actual and planned) and contain additional information for use in the 'entry view'. These tables let you update different characteristics and document-splitting information, different period shifts, and different currencies in specific ledgers for individual documents. These let you perform reporting tasks for specific dimensions at the line-item level and select data from fields that are not found in the single-item indexes

(BSIS and BSAS) from the G/L in SAP R/3.

c. **Valuations for year-end closing in selected parallel ledgers**

A third table (BSEG_ADD) contains documents that are posted in connection with valuations for year-end closing in selected parallel ledgers. If you do not portray parallel accounting or you use the account approach to portray parallel accounting, these documents are inapplicable. This ledger will not have any split information. If you do not use additional ledgers then this table will not be updated.

40. What is the major difference between FAGLFLEXA & FAGLFLEXT?

While the table FAGLFLEXT is used to store the ledger-specific line items in split form, the other table FAGLFLEXA is used to store the split totals. The table FAGLFLEXA replaces the table GLT0 of Classic G/L.

41. Explain the mapping of tables between Classic and New G/L?

The illustration in Table 2.1-1 explains how the various tables of Classic G/L have been mapped to new tables in the New G/L accounting:

Table 2.1.1: Classic & New G/L: Table Mapping

New G/L		**Classic G/L**	
Table Name	**Used to Store**	**Table Name**	**Used to Store**
FAGLFLEXT	Totals	GLT0, GLFUNCT, GLPCTSPL LDG	Totals
FAGLFLEXP	Plan line items	GLPCP	Plan line items
FAGLFLEXA	Actual line items	GLPCA, SPL LDG	Actual line items
		BSEG	Document line items
FAGL_SPLINFO FAGL_SPLINFO_ VAL	Splitting data	BFOD_A, BFOK_A	Adjustment tables for Business Area , Profit Centres
		BSIS/BSAS BSIK/ BSAK BSID/BSAD	Index tables

42. Explain the 'Segments' in the New G/L accounting?

With the New G/L accounting, SAP has used the 'Segment' field as a standard account assignment object. These segments are used to replace the account assignment objects (like, Business Area, Profit Center and Profitability Segment) used earlier. Now, the usage of 'Segment Reporting' (below the Company Code level) gives a detailed look at the different activity areas of a company, such as Business divisions, Products and Markets as these segments can be defined in addition to Company Codes, Controlling Areas, Profit Centers, Functional Areas, Business Areas, etc.

Similar to business area and functional area, segments are not assigned to any Controlling area or Company code and are technically defined at the client level.

Once the New G/L is activated, a 'Segment' field appears in the profit center master record.

43. How many Segments you can have in Table FAGLFLEXT?

In Classic G/L scenario, in the Special Purpose Ledger (FI-SL) there are 45 object number tables each with 15 key fields. The FI-SL totals table can contain maximum of 45 key fields. These 45 key fields do also contain some fixed standard fields as company code, G/L account, profit centre, and segment. However, in the New G/L, fields as company code, account, profit centre, segment are standard in the table key. In addition to that, two customer includes are available where the customer can include additional 15 fields (other SAP standard fields as the plant or customer defined fields). It is important note that more additional fields can result in large amount of data volume causing performance problems in processes as reporting, foreign currency valuation, allocation.

44. Comment on BW data source as 'FAGLXX' replaces 'GLT0' in 'New G/L'.

The only data source for the New G/L which has been delivered by SAP is 0FI_G/L_10 which only extracts data from the leading ledger. If data from the non-leading ledger are requested then you need to create the data source. With the change in the table logic, with the table FAGLXX (New G/L) replacing GLT0 (Classic G/L), create the data sources using the Transaction Code FAGLBW03. Replace 'xx' in the place-holder "3FI_G/L_xx_TT" with the ledger description: say for a ledger 'LL' the data source then will be '3FI_G/L_LL_TT'. In some cases an extract structure is required to create a data source. This structure has to be generated using transaction FAGLBW01. This has to be done if the ledger for which the data source needed is not based on the delivered standard totals table FAGLFLEXT.

Transaction Code
FAGLBW03

Assign DataSource to a General Ledger

Ledger	Description	Table	Totals Record-DataSource
0L	Leading Ledger	FAGLFLEXT	
L2	IAS Ledger	FAGLFLEXT	

Figure 2.1.9: Assigning Data Source to a G/L

45. Can a 'Totals' table, be used to manage both line items & totals?

No, there is no provision to manage both the line items and the totals in one table. The line items on totals need to be managed in different tables.

46. How to enhance and bring in additional fields to a Totals table?

SAP allows you to bring in additional fields by:

- Adding a ***standard field*** (like material number): these fields can easily be added using the Customizing function
- Adding a ***customer field:*** these fields are inserted using a 'include' function in COBL

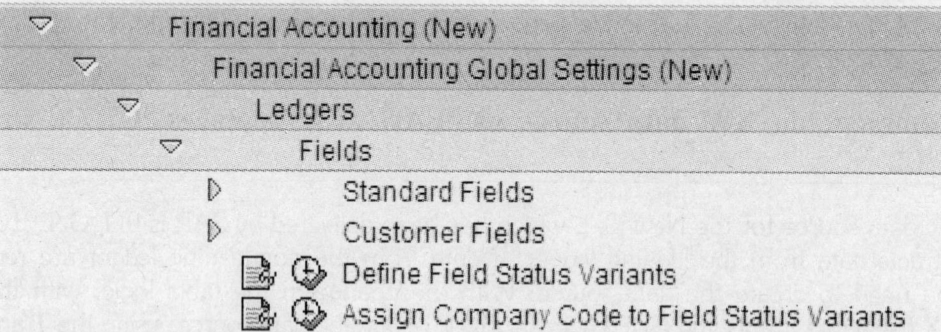

Figure 2.1.10: Standard & Customer Fields in New G/L setup

47. Comment on 'Customer Field' enhancement in New G/L.

Though SAP does not restrict or recommend on how many customer dimensions you need to have, note that this needs to be decided by implementation considerations as performance could be impacted by having too many customer fields. It is possible that you will be able to work with a few different ledgers each even with one characteristic. There is not much difference on extending the customer fields: if you have enhanced BSEG using COBL, technically you can do the same but in the New G/L the new fields need to be inserted using an 'include' called 'CI_COBL' in COBL.

All such customer defined fields are extended within the line item structures and are available within the entry view for general inquiry/reporting. Fields can also be customized for inclusion in the totals table, making them available in the ledger view.

Note that only fields included in the totals table have balances carried forward.

48. What is 'Document Splitting' in New G/L?

The '**document splitting**' functionality in New G/L is an appropriate tool for determining missing account assignments according to cause in common accounting processes (invoices, payments, or clearing). For each FI document, document splitting applies account-assignment information to non-assigned accounts according to assignment rules set in the customizing area.

The document-splitting functionality is based on the following model:

Accounting documents contain accounts with assignments, such as revenues or expenses. Such accounts provide dependent accounts (accounts payables, accounts receivables, and taxes, for example) with account assignments based on context (such as invoice or payment). The model is process oriented: account assignments from original processes are projected into the subsequent processes, thereby enabling account assignments according to cause in the subsequent processes.

Consider the example of a vendor invoice: you can assign Profit Centers to expense accounts manually, derive the assignment automatically, or make the assignment using a substitute Cost Center. Document splitting places these Profit Centers in the payables accounts of the invoice document.

This functionality can help you create balance sheets for entities that extend beyond the scope of the Company Code. Typical examples include balance sheets at the Segment or Profit Center level or balance sheets based on company-specific or industry-specific entities. There are also mechanisms to determine all account assignments outside of document splitting – in the delivering component itself. This determination would include postings from SAP human capital management or materials management application area.

49. What are the two types of 'Document Splitting' in New G/L?

The '**document splitting**' is built at two technical points:

a. Document Creation

b. Accounting Interface

50. Explain 'Document Splitting' during 'Document Creation' in New G/L.

A classic example of **document splitting during document creation** is the 'clearing transaction' wherein cash discount and realized exchange rate differences are split according to source (according to the proportions of the account assignments in the expense or revenue lines of the original document, such as an invoice). What is special here is the specific reference to the original transaction or line item. Controlling functions in the software are updated accordingly and reconciled with the G/L accounting functions.

Another example of item-related document splitting is foreign-currency valuation of open items: this function transfers exchange-rate differences to the controlling software. It is important to note that the balance-valuation function has no reference to items or transactions. Here, the dimension-specific balance of the account (such as the balance for each segment) is used as the basic value.

51. Explain 'Document Splitting' at 'Accounting Interface'.

Technically, this process of **document splitting at accounting interface** has two levels of details:

i. The **standard account-assignment** projection, which results from customized settings. Account assignments are projected from the base rows to the target rows. To minimize the effort required for implementation, SAP ERP provides a number of preconfigured methods. You can activate only one method per client. With method '0000000012', the solution delivers settings that support most standard processes (such as invoice, payment, or payment on account).

Method	Text
0000000001	Splitting: Customer, Vendor, Tax
0000000002	Splitting: Customer, Vendor, Tax, Money, Co.Code Clearing
0000000012	Splitting: Same as 0000000002 (Follow-Up Costs Online)
0000000101	Splitting for US Fund Accounting
0000000111	Splitting for US Fund Accounting (Follow-Up Costs Online)

Figure 2.1.11: Document Splitting Methods

ii. The **inheritance** by subsequent processes of business transactions, such as the clearing of vendor and customer invoices.

With this variant, the solution transfers the original account assignments of the invoice to the clearing lines. This variant is a fixed feature in the program and cannot be altered. After the clearing transaction, the original item (such as the payables or receivables line) and the clearing item for the respective account assignment are balanced to zero.

Activate Document Splitting

☑ Document Splitting

Method 0000000012

Level of Detail

☑ Inheritance

☑ Standard A/C Assgnmt Constant

Figure 2.1.12: Document Splitting: Levels of Details

52. How 'Document Splitting' in New G/L is different from split in SAP R/3 FI-SL?

The document split function in New G/L has been enhanced as follows:

- Additional functions from SAPF181, such as post-capitalization of assets and the splitting of follow-up costs (discount, currency differences, and so on).
- The split information is also available for the closing activity in FI (foreign currency valuation, regrouping, and so on, and therefore also at the segment level).
- CO-relevant valuation postings (for example, expense from exchange rate differences) can be transferred to CO in split form.

53. How Profit Center / Segment splitting occurs for 'B/S only entries'?

The value for profit center/segment must be entered or derived in order to produce an offsetting split or zero-balancing transaction item in the G/L-view of the document. The splitting rules can be configured to assist with this; provided the process is clearly defined and appropriate accounts/document types are consistently used.

54. Explain 'Document splitting' considerations for 'Residual Postings'.

You should pay attention to some of the considerations/cautions of document splitting on residual postings. For example, have you considered what happens if the profit center or segment is changed in the system prior to a residual posting being completely cleared?

All clearing postings utilize a ***passive split***, whereby the original split information about the item is used as the basis for the clearing update.

55. What if you activate/define 'Define Splitting Characteristics for CO' in IMG?

This depends on the characteristics supplied by SAP and the characteristics of the customer. The characteristics that are stored here can be transferred in split from CO in connection with the determination of the follow up cost (like foreign currency valuation, realized exchange rate difference, discount etc). The only pre-condition is that the G/L account should have been created as a Cost Element.

56. Can Segment assignment (via Profit Center) be over-ridden on a FI posting?

Yes.

During data entry it is possible to over-type/over-ride (manual entry) the segment relationship. However, note that this may not be desirable. Instead you should go in for a substitution routine to enforce the relationship so that the manual over-riding is not allowed.

57. What is 'Zero Balance' switch in Document Splitting?

When you 'set' this indicator in customizing the characteristics for Document Splitting, the system will check to see if the balance is zero for that characteristic. If the balance is not zero, then the system creates additional clearing lines on clearing accounts so as to produce a zero balance. This check-box needs to be 'selected' only when you need to report balance on that particular characteristic (say; Profit Center).

Document Splitting Characteristic for General Ledgers			
Field	Zero balance	Partner field	Mandatory Field
Business Area	☐	PARGB	☐
Profit Center	☑	PPRCTR	☐
Segment	☑	PSEGMENT	☑

Figure 2.1.13: Document Splitting Characteristics for G/L

58. What is the use of 'Mandatory Field' switch in Document Splitting?

When you 'set' this indicator in customizing the characteristics for document splitting, then all the postings - for which no value is set after the Document Split for that specified field – are rejected by an error message. You should not select this if you want these postings to take place despite there is no value set after the splitting. But, you need to be aware that the complete balance of that dimension is at risk.

59. Can you selectively deactivate Document Splitting in a few Company Codes?

Yes.

The activation of document splitting, by default, applies to the entire client. However, you can exclude Company Codes for which you do not need this splitting functionality. But, note that once you exclude certain Company Codes from document splitting then you will no longer be able to create any cross-Company Code transactions with the splitting functionality.

Change View "Deactivation per Company Code": Overview

New Entries

Dialog Structure
- Activate Document Splitting
- Deactivation per Company Code

Deactivation per Company Code		
Company Code	Company Name	Inactive
0001	SAP A.G.	☐
0003	SAP US (IS-HT-SW)	☑

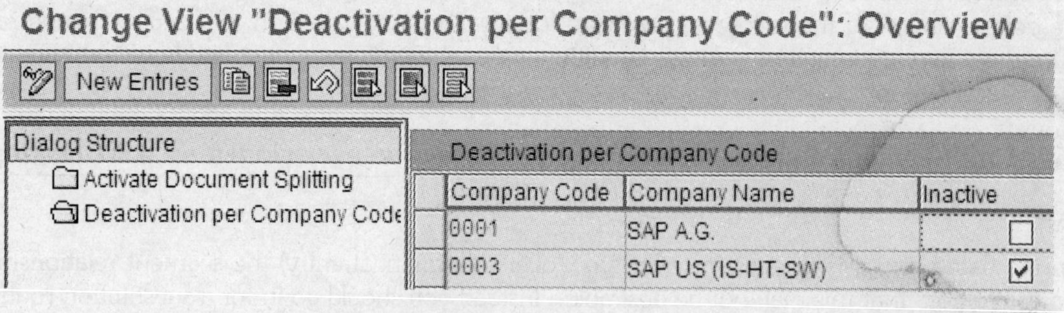

Figure 2.1.14: Document Splitting: Deactivate for Select Company Codes

60. How Profit Centre Accounting has been mapped to New G/L?

You need to (a) define the update of the characteristics 'profit center' and 'partner profit center' in the ledger by selecting the scenario 'Profit Center update' (FIN_PCA), (b) define the field '*profit center*' as a splitting characteristic in the document splitting. Now to create balance sheet on the profit centre, you just need to set the 'zero balance' indicator. The last thing required is to activate the required entry field to ensure that the 'profit centre' is set in all postings.

61. What is known as 'Extended Document Splitting'?

SAP provides you with the standard document functionality with default splitting rules / methods. In case, the standard functionality is not sufficient, you create your own rules / methods appropriate to and make necessary settings so that the system applies the rules / methods you defined and not the standard ones. When you use your own document splitting rules / methods, then this is known as **extended document splitting**. It is important to note that you will not be able to switch between the standard rules, and your own rules.

62. Explain the various methods to achieve 'Fast Closing'.

Most of the closing tasks are organization-specific. Depending on your SAP implementation and your requirements you can use some or all of the following methods to achieve **fast closing** in your organization:

- Elimination of reconciliation ledger postings by enabling **real-time CO to FI integration**
- Elimination of profit and loss (P&L) and balance sheet adjustments with **online splitting functionality**
- Elimination of transfer payables/ receivables to Profit Center Accounting (PCA) by using **segment reporting in the New G/L**
- Elimination of PCA allocation by using New G/L allocations
- Use of a **Closing Cockpit** to obtain a simplified overview of the entire closing process
- Use of cross-system intercompany reconciliation to speed up intra-group reconciliation processes.

63. How to eliminate Reconciliation Ledger Postings?

It is now possible to completely eliminate reconciliation ledger postings by enabling the **real-time CO-to-FI integration**, using the New G/L functionality, in SAP ERP.

Though real-time integration from FI to CO has been available since SAP R/2, when a posting involved cross-Company Codes (or business areas), this information was stored initially in CO and then transferred to FI at period close. The reconciliation ledger - maintained in the CO module - was used for CO reconciliation with FI. Typically, you would execute the transaction **KALC** (reconciliation ledger posting) at each period end, there by creating FI documents to reconcile CO with FI. The drawback was that the reconciliation postings were not created on the cost-object level and it was difficult to match the FI reconciliation posting with the corresponding CO transaction postings.

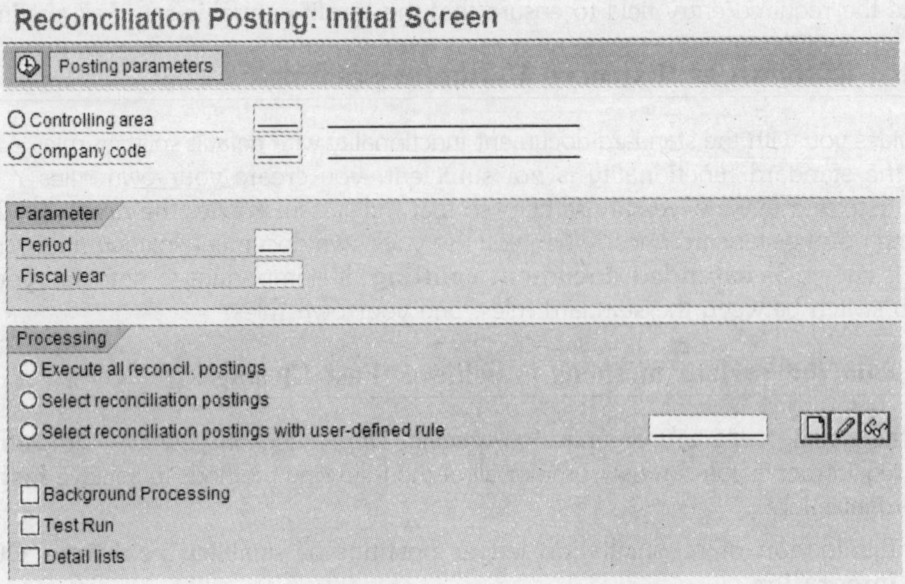

Reconciliation Posting: Initial Screen

Posting parameters

Controlling area

Company code

Parameter

Period

Fiscal year

Processing

Execute all reconcil. postings

Select reconciliation postings

Select reconciliation postings with user-defined rule

Background Processing

Test Run

Detail lists

Figure 2.1.15: Reconciliation Posting using Transaction Code KALC

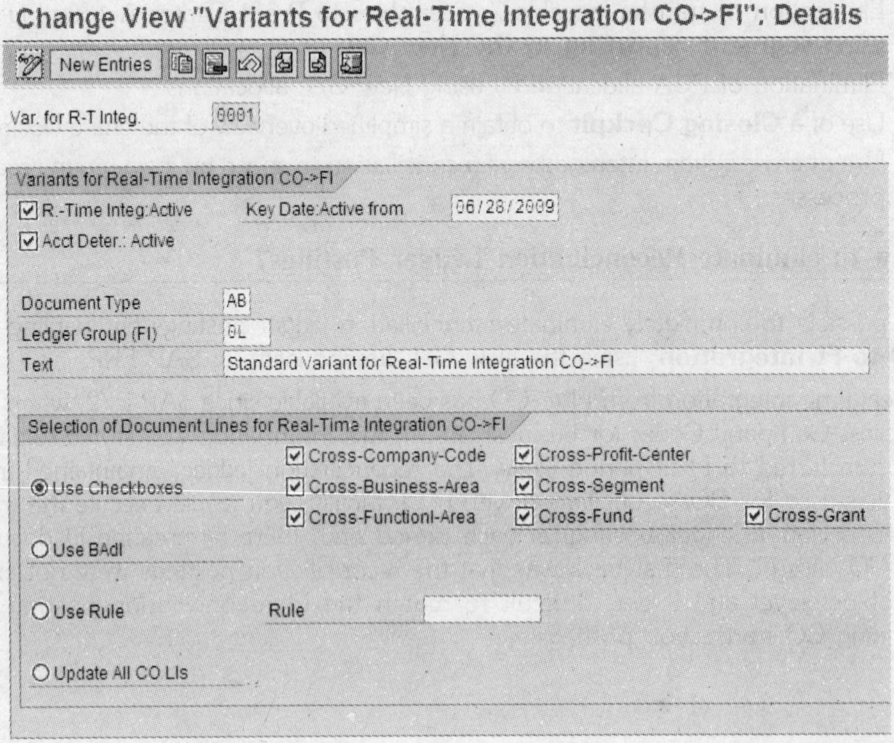

Change View "Variants for Real-Time Integration CO->FI": Details

New Entries

Var. for R-T Integ. 0001

Variants for Real-Time Integration CO->FI

R.-Time Integ:Active — Key Date:Active from 06/28/2009

Acct Deter.: Active

Document Type AB

Ledger Group (FI) 0L

Text Standard Variant for Real-Time Integration CO->FI

Selection of Document Lines for Real-Time Integration CO->FI

Use Checkboxes — Cross-Company-Code, Cross-Profit-Center, Cross-Business-Area, Cross-Segment, Cross-Functionl-Area, Cross-Fund, Cross-Grant

Use BAdI

Use Rule — Rule

Update All CO LIs

Figure 2.1.16: Variant for CO-to-FI Real-time Integration

In New G/L scenario, using of reconciliation ledger is not recommended, as it is not possible to have segment or profit center details in the reconciliation posting, which may cause problems for reconciliation and segment reporting. So, you need to d*eactivate* the reconciliation ledger before the CO postings are updated online in the reconciliation ledger, and enable real-time integration CO and FI.

To enable real-time CO-FI integration, you need to define **variants** which control the integration. These variants define the cases in which CO transactions create financial documents. For example, you can set up a variant so that any cross-company, cross-profit center, cross-segment, and functional area CO postings create FI follow-up documents. Define the variants, by following Menu Path '*SAP Customizing Implementation* Guide > *Financial Accounting (New) > Financial Accounting Global Settings (New) > Ledgers > Real-Time Integration of Controlling with Financial Accounting > Define Variants for Real-Time Integration*'.
Once the variants are defined, you need to assign them to the Company Codes, define rules for selecting CO line items, and set up the account determination (to transfer secondary cost element postings to FI, as they are not defined as G/L accounts) for the integration.

64. How to transfer CO documents retrospectively?

When you enable real-time CO-to-FI integration, you always specify a date known as '*Key Date: Active from*'. Then, the integration happens for all the postings on or after this key date, but not before.

Transfer CO Documents into External Accounting

General Selection Criteria

Controlling Area	1000		
Document Number		to	
Fiscal Year	2009	to	
Business Transaction		to	
Posting Period		to	
Posting Date	01/01/2009	to	06/28/2009
User Name		to	
Created on		to	
Time of Entry	00:00:00	to	00:00:00

Control Parameters

☑ Test Run

Figure 2.1.17: Retrospective Transfer of CO Documents to FI

SAP provides functionality for transferring documents retrospectively (in a situation where your New G/L was active, say, from 1/Jan/2009, but this real-time CO-to-FI integration was activated only on 28/Jun/2009).

Transaction Code
FAGLCOFITRNSFRCODOCS

You may also use the Menu Path *'SAP Customizing Implementation* Guide > *Financial Accounting (New)* > *Financial Accounting Global Settings (New)* > *Ledgers* > *Real-Time Integration of Controlling with Financial Accounting* > *Transfer CO Documents Retrospectively'*.

65. How to eliminate P &L / Balance Sheet adjustments by 'Online Splitting'?

Before the New G/L, at period end programs SAP F180 (balance sheet adjustment) and SAP F181 (P&L adjustment) populated the cost objects details in the offsetting lines based on the original cost objects in PCA. It was time consuming to verify, reconcile, and explain the adjustment postings. With the profit centre accounting (PCA) now integrated into the New G/L accounting with SAP ERP, the online splitting and zero balancing functions enable you to create balance sheets not only for company codes but also for entities such as the profit center and segment. As a result, it is no longer necessary to execute a periodic adjustment posting for balance sheet and P&L statements, as all information is already available on the document level in the New G/L. The elimination of these programs significantly speeds up the closing process.

66. How to eliminate transfer payables/receivables to PCA by Segment Reporting?

You can, now, eliminate the transfer of payables/ receivables to PCA using segment reporting in the New G/L. With the New G/L segment reporting functionality, profit center/segment details are updated in the G/L in real time, so you do not need to update PCA to get segment reporting. These reports are now available in the New G/L. It is no longer necessary to transfer balance sheet items to PCA periodically for segment reporting. In other words, you can eliminate transferring balance sheet items to profit center accounting from the period closing process. Although PCA is integrated into the New G/L, it does not mean that you have to turn off PCA. You can still use PCA parallel to the New G/L and continue to use the adjustment programs.

Transaction Code
1KEK

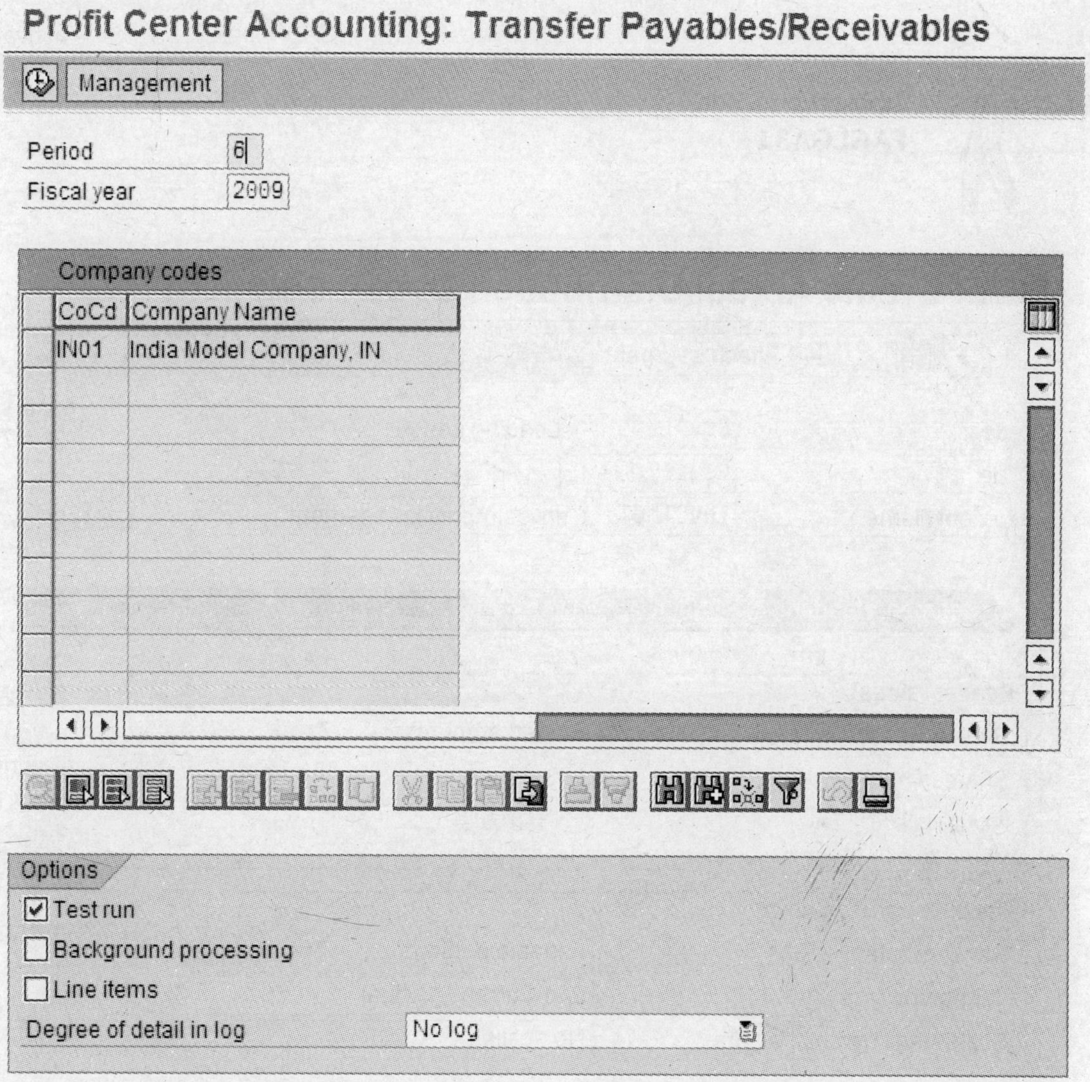

Profit Center Accounting: Transfer Payables/Receivables

Management

Period 6

Fiscal year 2009

Company codes

CoCd	Company Name
IN01	India Model Company, IN

Options

☑ Test run

☐ Background processing

☐ Line items

Degree of detail in log: No log

Figure 2.1.18: Transfer Payables/Receivables Elimination

67. Describe elimination of PCA allocations by using New G/L allocations

The distribution and assessment functionality from profit centre accounting (PCA) and FI-SL are available within the New G/L. This enables criteria-based amount distributions on the cost-object (segment, profit center) level in the G/L. Define the cost allocations in the SAP Easy Access Menu Path: '*Accounting > Financial Accounting > General Ledger > Periodic Processing > Closing > Allocation > Actual Distribution*'. It uses cycle and segment methods to define distribution and assessment rules.

Transaction Code
FAGLGA31

G/L: Create Actual Distribution Cycle: Segment

Attach segment

Ledger	0L	Leading Ledger
Cycle	CL-1	
Segment Name	INVSTMGT	Investment Management ☐ Lock i

Segment Header | Senders/Receivers | Sender Values | Receiver Tracing Fa

Sender values

Sender rule	Posted amounts
Share in %	100.00 %
◉ Act. vals	○ Plan vals

Receiver tracing factor

Receiver rule	Variable portions
Var.portion type	2nd Currency: Actual
Scale Neg. Tracing Factors	No scaling

Figure 2.1.19: Eliminating PCA Allocations through New G/L Allocations

Other functions from FI-SL, such as rollup and planning, are also part of the New G/L. You can execute these tasks directly in the New G/L. You have a unified data structure instead of multiple related databases, which gives you the advantage of eliminating reconciliation tasks.

Even though the cost allocations in the profit center and the New G/L both depend on the same logic, you need to take note of the following:

- Actual cycles should always be assigned to version-1 because the system updates actual postings in the New G/L in version-1. To manage various planning scenarios you can create planning versions in customizing. To maintain planning versions in the New G/L use the Transaction Code **GCVP**.

- Assessment accounts should be created in the New G/L and should be different from the secondary cost elements.
- Both distribution and assessment create FI postings.

And, you also need to be aware of the fact that the cost center allocations are still in CO and should be performed in cost center accounting.

68. What is 'Closing Cockpit'?

An extension of the Schedule Manager functionality, the '**Closing Cockpit**' is a new concept in SAP ERP, which you can use it for scheduling the tasks you execute on a regular basis. Using the same logic as that of the Schedule Manager, it provides a simplified overview of the entire closing process, and you can define all your closing tasks on a single screen.

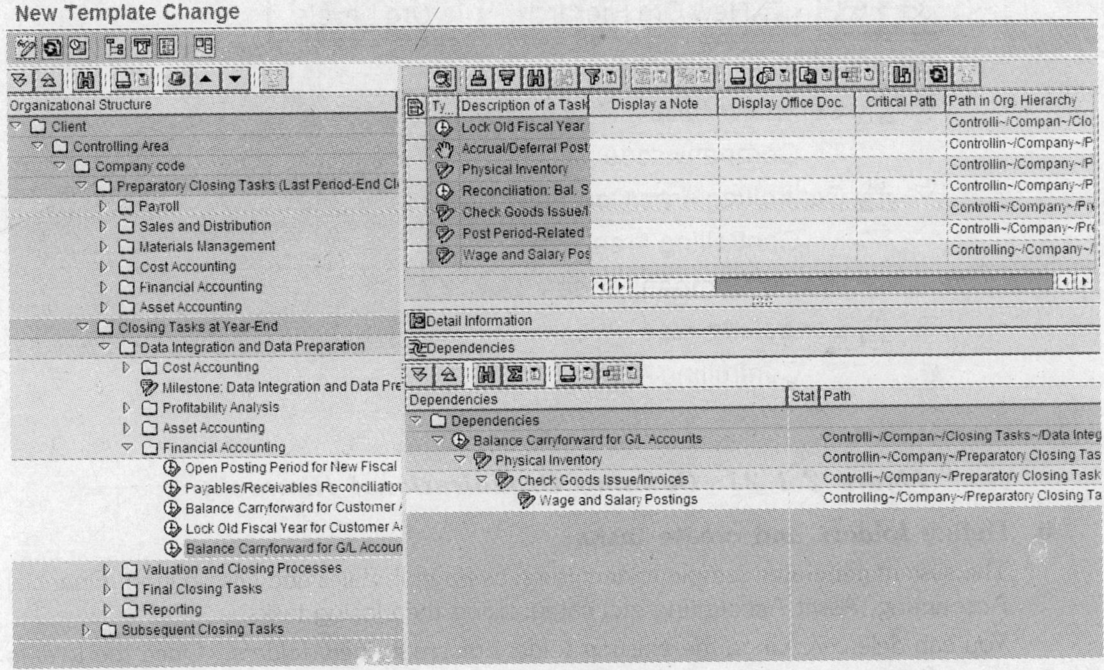

Figure 2.1.20: Closing Cockpit

With the Closing Cockpit, the closing process becomes more transparent and you can find errors easily, as you will be able to schedule, execute, and monitor your tasks for a selected organizational level.

Transaction Code
CLOCOC

69. How to make use of the 'Closing Cockpit'?

To make effective use of the Closing Cockpit, you just need to follow the following four steps:

i. Define organizational hierarchies and template

Define your organizational hierarchy (for example, Company Code) so that the system executes the closing process for the defined organizational structure(s). From Closing Cockpit, select '*Template/Task List*' on the menu bar and then select '*Organizational Hierarchies*' to define /select the hierarchy for the template (the system generates a proposal for a task list template according to the selected hierarchies and organizational objects available in the system).

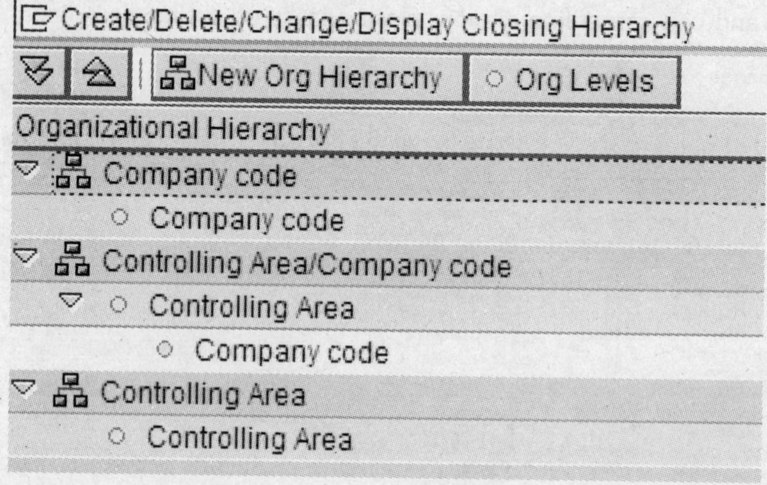

Figure 2.1.21: Defining Organizational Hierarchy

ii. Define folders and create tasks

The system generates sample folders (such as Payroll, Sales and Distribution, Financial Accounting, Asset Accounting etc) categorizing the closing tasks.

You can delete /change the existing folders or create new folders. Once the folders are defined, create the *closing tasks* in the folders (by right-clicking on the relevant folder or by copying / changing an existing task).

Note that SAP delivers templates in the standard business context for month-end closing ('*1-FC-MONTH*') and year-end closing ('*1-FC-YEAR*') that you can map to your own organization.

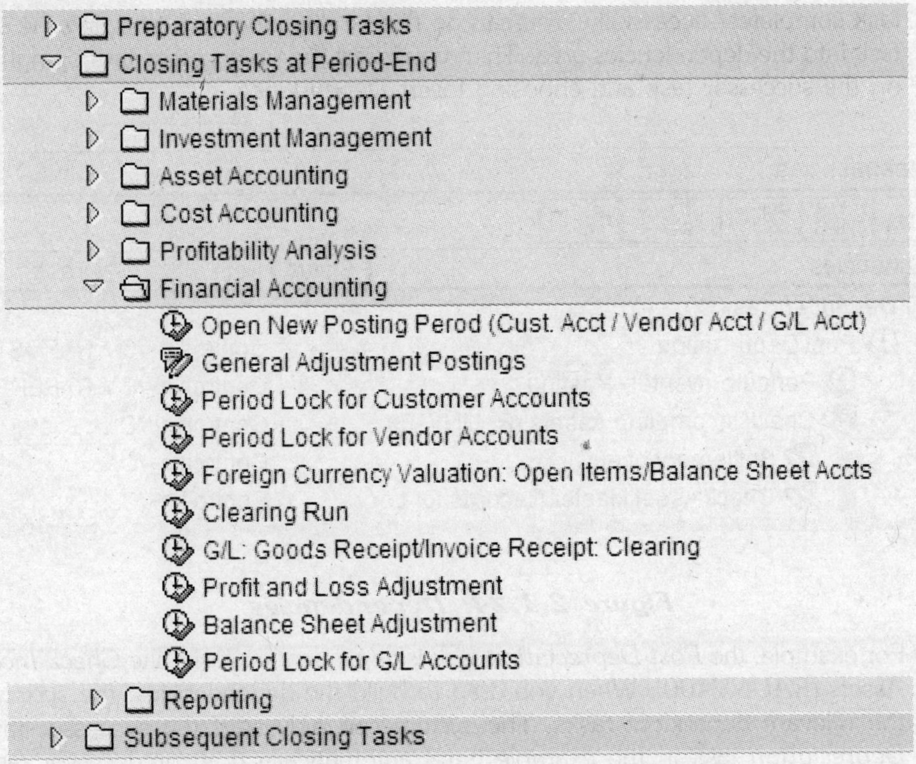

- Preparatory Closing Tasks
- Closing Tasks at Period-End
  - Materials Management
  - Investment Management
  - Asset Accounting
  - Cost Accounting
  - Profitability Analysis
  - Financial Accounting
    - Open New Posting Perod (Cust. Acct / Vendor Acct / G/L Acct)
    - General Adjustment Postings
    - Period Lock for Customer Accounts
    - Period Lock for Vendor Accounts
    - Foreign Currency Valuation: Open Items/Balance Sheet Accts
    - Clearing Run
    - G/L: Goods Receipt/Invoice Receipt: Clearing
    - Profit and Loss Adjustment
    - Balance Sheet Adjustment
    - Period Lock for G/L Accounts
  - Reporting
- Subsequent Closing Tasks

Figure 2.1.22: Folders and Tasks

It is possible to define all the steps in the overall process in the task list template as a note, transaction, program (with or without a variant), or a flow definition.

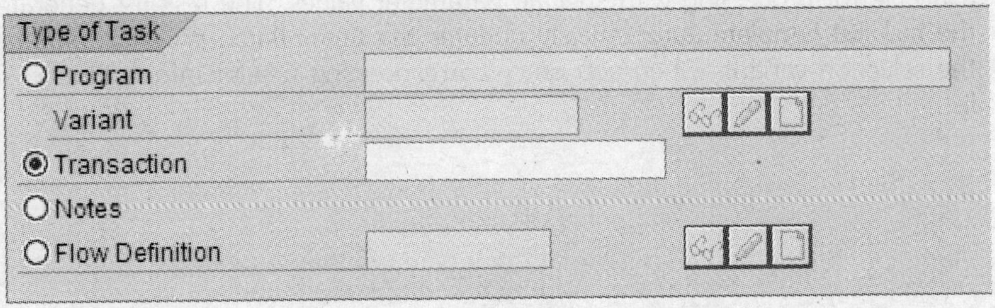

Type of Task

- Program
- Variant
- Transaction
- Notes
- Flow Definition

Figure 2.1.23: Type of Task

iii. Define dependencies

Programs and transactions included in the task list template are frequently dependent on each other due to business-related or system-related factors. You can define a finish-to-start dependency so that the dependent tasks do not start until the prerequisite task completes successfully. You can do this by dragging and dropping the successor task into the dependencies area. Then you insert the predecessor task by right-clicking on the successor task and choosing Insert *Dependency*.

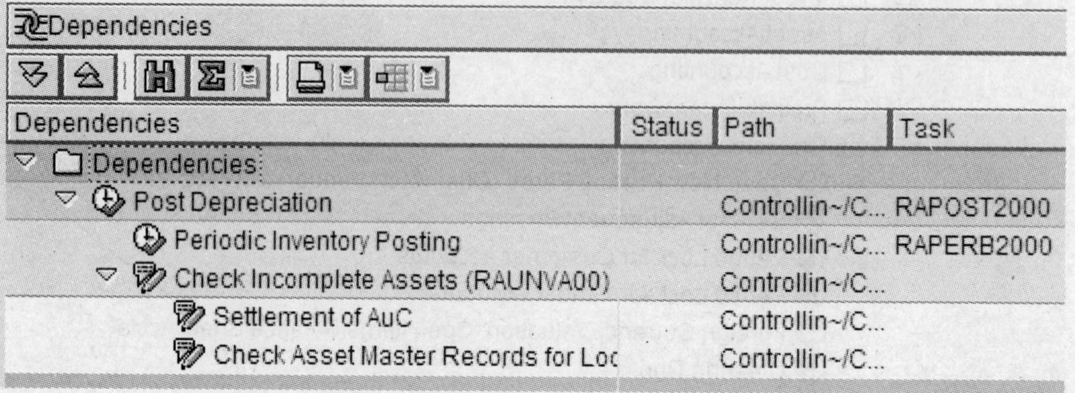

Figure 2.1.24: Dependencies

For example, the *Post Depreciation* task is dependent on tasks like *Check Incomplete Assets (RAUNVA00)*. When you drag to build the dependencies, the system inserts the relevant dependent tasks. The system can only start the successor task (*Post Depreciation* task in the example here) automatically if all predecessor tasks have the processing status terminated without errors.

iv. Create and release the task list

To perform tasks included in a task list, you need to create *variant parameters*. With the separation of the task list template from the task list, you can define the structured process flow as a generic template (*task list template*) and then make a task list available for processing with specific parameter values. The task list generated from the task list template automatically updates the time-related program parameters of the selection variants when you enter corresponding header information in the task list.

3

Accounts Payable (FI-A/P) / Accounts Receivable (FI-A/R)

1. Who is a 'Customer'?

A **customer**, in SAP, is known as a *business partner* from whom receivables are due as a result of services rendered viz., goods delivered, services performed, rights transferred etc. A customer in SAP is represented by a master record.

2. Explain 'Customer / Vendor Master Records'.

There are three categories of data maintained in a typical master record for a customer:

- General Data
- Company Code Data
- Sales Area Data (for customers) / Purchasing Organization Data(for vendors)

The **general data** include general information like account number, name, telephone, bank information, trading partner, vendor (if the customer is also a vendor), group key, bank key, bank account, alternate payee etc that are common to all the Company Codes using this master.

The **company code data** comprises of terms of payment, payment methods, tolerance group, clearing with vendor, dunning data (dunning procedure, dunning recipient, dunning block, dunning clerk etc), reconciliation account, sort key, sales area (purchasing organization in the case of vendor master), head office etc. Except the sales (purchasing for a vendor) related information, all other details are usually maintained by the accounting people who can also access the sales data/purchasing data when the master is maintained '*centrally*'.

The **sales area data** in the Company Code area of a customer master record contains the following:

- Billing data (payment terms if different from the payment terms maintained at the Company Code level, account assignment group etc)
- Order related (sales district, sales office, sales group, customer group etc)

- Price related (pricing group, pricing procedure etc)
- Shipping data (shipping strategy, delivery priority etc)

General data

- Address
- Control
- Payment transactions
- Contact Persons

Company code data

- Accounting info
- Payment transactions
- Correspondence
- Withholding tax

Purchasing organization data

- Purchasing data
- Partner functions

Figure 3.1: Vendor Master Record – Various Data

Transaction Code

Activity	In Accounting		Centrally	
	Customer	**Vendor**	**Customer**	**Vendor**
Create	**FD01**	**FK01**	**XD01**	**XK01**
Change	**FD02**	**FK02**	**XD02**	**XK02**
Display	**FD03**	**FK03**	**XD03**	**XK03**
Block / Unblock	**FD05**	**FK05**	**XD05**	**XK05**
Mark for Deletion	**FD06**	**FK06**	**XD06**	**XK06**

The **purchasing organization data** in the Company Code area of a Vendor master record contains the following:

- Conditions (order currency, payment terms, Incoterms, minimum order value etc)
- Sales data (A/c with Vendor)
- Control data (as in the screen shot below)

Create Vendor: Purchasing data

Alternative data | Sub-ranges | Interchangeability

Conditions

Order currency: USD
Terms of paymnt: 0001
Incoterms
Minimum order value
Schema Group, Vendor — Standard schema vendor
Pricing Date Control — No Control
Order optim.rest.

Sales data

Acc. with vendor

Control data

☐ GR-Based Inv. Verif.	ABC indicator
☐ AutoEvalGRSetmt Del.	ModeOfTrnsprt-Border
☐ AutoEvalGRSetmt Ret	Office of entry
☐ Acknowledgment Reqd	Sort criterion
☑ Automatic purchase order	PROACT control prof.
☐ Subsequent settlement	☐ Revaluation allowed
☐ Subseq. sett. index	☐ Grant discount in kind
☐ B.vol.comp./ag.nec.	☐ Relevant for price determ. (del.hierar
☐ Doc. index active	☐ Relevant for agency business
☐ Returns vendor	
☐ Srv.-Based Inv. Ver.	Shipping Conditions

Default data material

Figure 3.2: Vendor Master Record: Purchasing Data

During creation of a master record, the system checks for 'duplicates' for the same customer / vender which is achieved by the system through the 'Search-Id' (*Match Code*) configured on the customer's / vendor's address information.

As in the case of G/L account master record, the creation of customer / vendor master record is also controlled by the '*Account Group*' which is called as '*customer account group / vendor account group*' *(CPD / CPDL / KREDI / LIEF)* which controls the numbering for customer / vendor master records, field status, whether an account is a regular one or *'One-Time' account* etc.

3. Outline 'One-time Accounts'.

When you face a situation that you have customers whom you only supply once or rarely, you can create a special customer master record for these '**one-time accounts**'. As against the regular master records, no data specific to a single customer is stored in the one-time master record, since this account is used for more than one customer: all the customer-specific data (like address, bank details etc) are not entered until the document for the transaction is entered into the system. When you post to a one-time account, the system automatically goes to a master data screen: here you will enter the specific master data for the customer, which is stored separately in the document. Except this, you can process the master record for a one-time account in the same way as you process all other customer master records, you can dun open items from it with the dunning program or pay items using the payment program etc. However, you cannot clear amounts with a vendor.

As the customer master records for one-time accounts are created with their own account groups, the customer-specific fields (such as name, address and bank details) are hidden from display when you enter the customer master record. In the case of reconciliation accounts for one-time customers, it is possible to have two different reconciliation accounts for domestic and foreign receivables: for this you need to create two one-time master records.

4. Who is an 'Alternate Payee'?

A customer who pays on behalf of another customer is known as '**alternate payee**' (or **alternate payer**). Though the alternate payee pays on behalf of another, the system maintains all the transaction details in the account of the original customer. Designating 'alternate payee' does not absolve the customer of his / her obligation for payment.

The 'alternate payee' can be maintained in (a) Client specific data or (b) Company Code area. When maintained in Company Code area you can use that payer only in that Company Code; if defined at the Client level you can use the same across all Company Codes.

There are three ways of 'selecting 'the alternate payee when an invoice is processed:

i. The alternate payee (say, 1000) entered in the customer master record is the one selected by the system as default.

ii. When there is more than one alternate payer (say, 1000, 1900, 2100 etc) defined for a single customer in the master record (you will do this by clicking on the '***allowed payer'*** button and create more than one payer), you may select a payer (say, 2100) (other than the default, 1000) while processing the invoice. Now the system will ignore the alternate payer (1000) coming from the master record.

iii. If you have put a 'tick' mark in the *'individual entries'* check-box in '*alternate payer in document*' section in the customer master record, then this will allow you to propose a new alternate payer, say, 3000 (other than those already defined in the system). Now, after defining this alternate payer you can use the same in processing the invoice. In this case, this alternate payer (3000) takes precedence over the payers (1000 & 2100) in step 1 & 2 above.

5. What is the use of 'Trading Partner'?

The concept of **trading partner** is used to settle and reconcile 'inter-company transactions': both sales and purchases. This is generally achieved by entering the Company-ID (Not the Company Code) to which a customer belongs in the 'trading partner' field under the tab '*Account Control*' in the customer master record. You can do a similar entry in the vendor master record.

6. Explain 'Blocking a Customer Account'.

A customer can be blocked centrally or for posting only. It is possible to block a customer in all the company codes or in only one company code. You can **block a customer account** for a variety of reasons:

- You may block a customer account so that postings are no longer made to that account.
- You will block a customer account before 'marking' a customer master record for deletion.
- It may also be necessary to block a customer that you use only as an alternative dunning recipient, so that nobody can post to that customer by mistake.
- You block customer for payment: when blocked for payment, the payment program still processes the open items in the account during the payment run, but it does not pay any open items from the blocked accounts. However, you can display a list of customers blocked for the payment program.
- You block a customer for dunning: when blocked an account for dunning, the dunning program still analyzes the open items in the account during the dunning run, but no dunning notice is created.

When you have also implemented the Sales and Distribution (SD) application component, the following 'blocks' are possible for a customer:

- Posting block
- Order block
- Delivery block
- Invoicing block

Since you will not be able clear any open item, it is recommended that you block a customer account only when there are no open items in that account. Of course, you can cancel a block at any time, by simply removing the relevant block indicator.

7. Can you 'Archive' a customer master record immediately?

It is possible to **archive customer master records** that are no longer required. When archived, the data is extracted from the SAP database, deleted, and placed in a file so that you can then transfer this file to an archive system. However, you will not be able to archive a customer account immediately because the system first has to check the following:

- *Is there a transaction figure for that account in the system?*

  The account must not contain any transaction figures in the system. Transaction figures from previous years that have not been archived will also prevent the system from deleting the account master record.
- *Is the account 'marked for deletion'?*

  The account must be marked for deletion (using the *deletion flag*) in its master record. But, remember to *block an account* for posting before you mark it for deletion.

Note that when you mark a customer master record for deletion, you can set the deletion flag for all company codes or just for one specific company code. Even after the deletion flag has been set for a customer account, you can still cancel the deletion flag at any time as long as the master record has not yet been physically deleted from the system.

8. Can you Post to a Customer account which is 'Marked for Deletion'?

You can still post to an account which has already marked for deletion. Because, you might still need to clear open items. When you post to such an account which is marked for deletion, the system just issues a warning that you are posting to an account that is marked for deletion. It does not prevent you from posting to that account.

9. Can you assign a customer / vendor master record to a business area? Explain.

It is not possible to assign customer / vendor master records to a business area: the business area is usually determined from the business area(s) assigned to the related G/L account posting(s) and therefore, you do not have to carry out the account assignment manually.

In an *invoice*, the customer/vendor item takes the business area(s) of the expense or revenue posting: if the business area is unique in the document (the system checks that any business area entered in the customer/vendor item is the same as that in the offsetting G/L account item and issues an error message if this is not the case), it is copied into the line item automatically. If there is more than one business area, no value is entered in the customer/vendor item and a transfer posting to the receivables/payables account is carried out subsequently.

The *taxes* are always posted without a business area. The system then, at a later date, makes a transfer posting from the tax account to the business areas for the revenue or expense accounts.

During *payments*, customer/vendor items in payment documents take the business area from the invoice. The cash discount and exchange rate difference postings take their business area from the customer/vendor item they originated from: if posted without a business area, and the business area is only determined subsequently by means of a transfer posting to the GL; note that you need to carry out this subsequent step for the cash discount and exchange rate postings.

The system cannot automatically derive the business area that triggers the *down payments* since the invoice that belongs to the down payment is not entered until later. The business area in the customer/vendor item is therefore either not assigned, or is assigned manually.

Like taxes, the *bank item* is posted without a business area (unless one is assigned manually).

10. Explain 'Tolerance' in transaction processing.

Tolerances are defined in the system to facilitate dealing with the differences arising out of accounting transactions and to instruct the system how to proceed further. Normally, you define tolerances (either in 'absolute terms' or in 'percentage') beyond which the system will not allow you to post a document should there be difference.

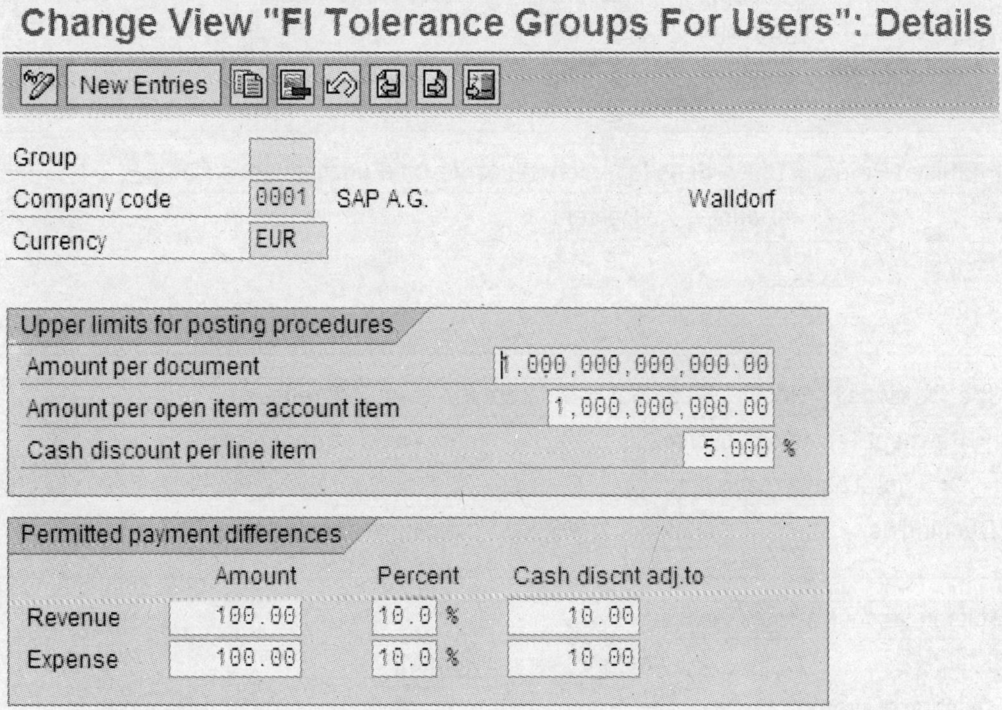

Change View "FI Tolerance Groups For Users": Details

New Entries

Group
Company code 0001 SAP A.G. Walldorf
Currency EUR

Upper limits for posting procedures
Amount per document 1,000,000,000,000.00
Amount per open item account item 1,000,000,000.00
Cash discount per line item 5.000 %

Permitted payment differences

	Amount	Percent	Cash discnt adj.to
Revenue	100.00	10.0 %	10.00
Expense	100.00	10.0 %	10.00

Figure 3.3: FI Tolerance Group (Employee Tolerance)

In SAP, tolerances are defined per Company Code and there are several types:

- Employee tolerance

- Customer / vendor tolerance
- G/L account clearing tolerance

Change View "Customer/Vendor Tolerances": Details

New Entries

Company Code	0001	SAP A.G. Walldorf
Currency	EUR	
Tolerance group	DEB1	

Specifications for Clearing Transactions

Grace days due date	1	Cash Discount Terms Displayed	
Arrears Base Date			

Permitted Payment Differences

	Amount	Percent	Adjust Discount By
Gain	999.00	10.0 %	1.00
Loss	5.00	2.5 %	1.00

Permitted Payment Differences for Automatic Write-Off (Function Code AD)

	Amount	Percent
Rev.		%
Expense		%

Specifications for Posting Residual Items from Payment Differences

- [x] Payment Term from Invoice — Fixed payment term
- [x] Only grant partial cash disc

Dunning key 2 Triggers maximum dunning level 2

Tolerances for Payment Advices

	Amount	Percent
Outst.receiv.from		%
Outst.payable from		%

Figure 3.4: Customer / Vendor Tolerances

You will define an '***employee tolerance groups***' in the system and assign the employees to these groups. While defining the tolerance group you will specify:

1. Upper limits for various posting procedures

- Amount per document
- Amount per open account item
- Cash discount, in percentage

2. Permitted payment differences

How much over or under payment an employee is allowed to process. This is defined both in absolute value and in percentage.

Besides defining the above two, at the Company Code level, you will also define similar tolerances for ***customer / vendor tolerance group*** (say, DEB1). Once defined, each of the customers (vendors) is assigned to one of these groups. Here also, you define the '***permitted payment differences***'.

While processing, the system compares the tolerance of an employee against the customer tolerance (or vendor tolerance or the G/L) and applies the most restrictive of the two.

11. What is 'Dual Control' in master records?

Dual control helps to prevent unauthorized changes, to the important and 'sensitive' fields, in the master records in the system. (All such sensitive fields are defined in the Table **T055F** during customizing the application. And, these fields are defined per Company Code and per Client) Consider, for example, a sensitive field like '***payment block***' in a vendor master record. When a user changes this field's content, the system requires another user (usually of higher authority) to approve this change and an ***audit trail*** is maintained of all such changes. Unless the change is approved, in this example, this particular master is blocked by the system for considering the same in the next '***payment run***'.

Transaction Code

Activity	Customer	Vendor
Display changes (accounting area)	**FD04**	**FK04**
Display changes (centrally)	**XD04**	**XK04**
Confirm changes, individually	**FD08**	**FK08**
Confirm changes, in a list	**FD09**	**FK09**

12. Explain 'Sales Cycle' as in SAP.

The **sales cycle** comprises of all activities starting from quotation / inquiry, sales order, delivery, billing and collection. The various Processes within SAP to complete a sales cycle are shown in Figure 3-5.

Typically the following are the documents created during a sales cycle:

- Inquiry
- Quotation
- Sales Order
- Delivery Note
- Goods Issue
- Order Invoice
- Credit / Debit Note

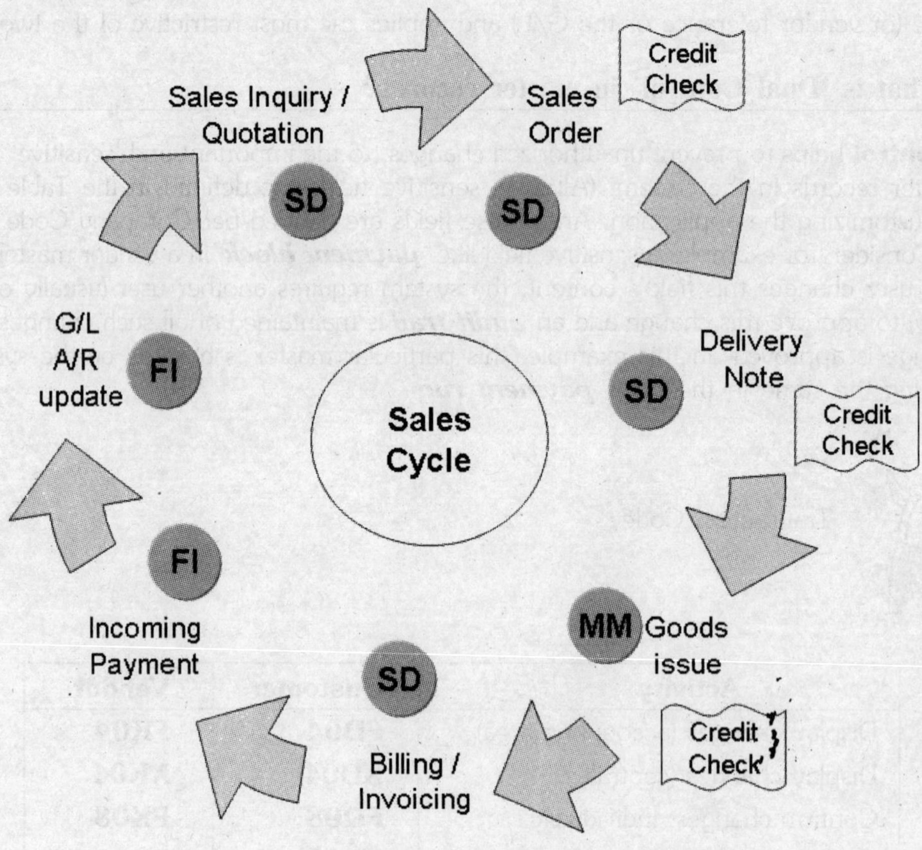

Figure 3.5: Sales Cycle

13. Explain 'Automatic Account Assignment' in SD.

During goods issue in the sales cycle, the system is usually configured to update the relevant G/L accounts automatically and to create the relevant accounting documents. This customization in IMG is also called as ***material account assignment*** and is achieved through a number of steps as detailed below:

1. Determine '*valuation level*' (company code or plant).
2. Activate '*valuation grouping code*' and link the same with '*chart of accounts*' for each '*valuation area*'.
3. Link '*valuation class*' with '*material type*' (FERT, HAWA, HALB etc) with '*account category reference*' (combination of valuation classes).
4. Maintain '*account modification codes*' for '*movement types*'.
5. Link '*account modification codes*' with '*process keys*' (*transaction / event keys*)
6. Maintain a *G/L account* for a given combination of *chart of accounts + valuation grouping code + account modification code + valuation classes.*

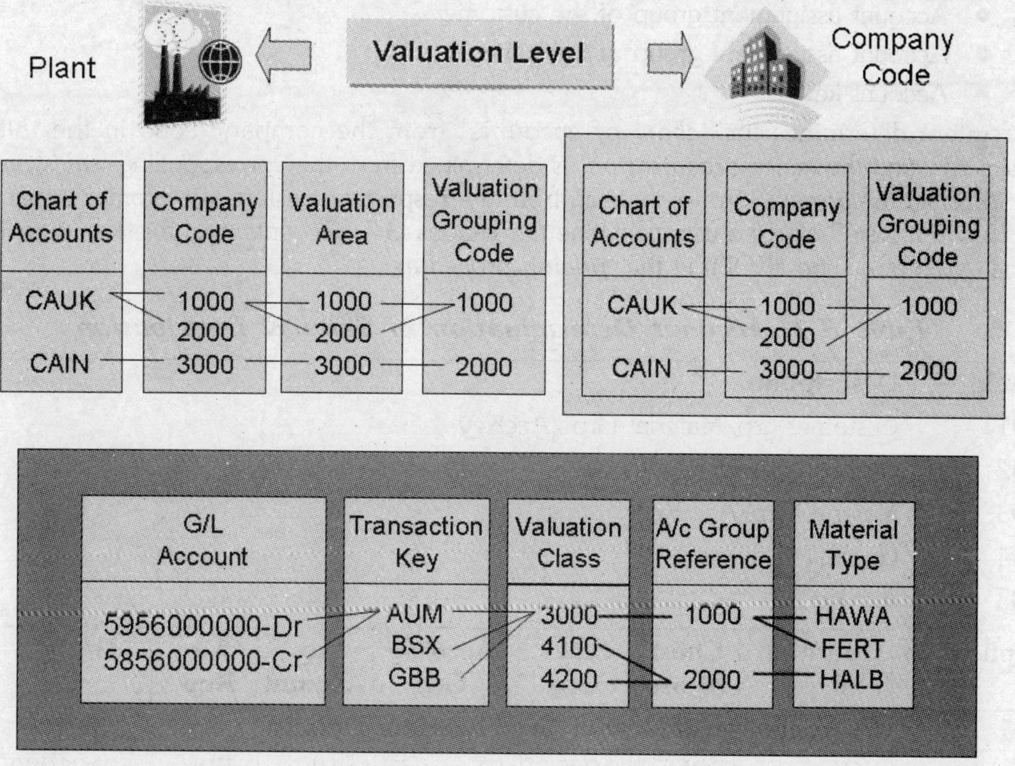

Figure 3.6: Automatic Account Determination in SD

The process of **automatic account determination** is as follows:

1. Depending upon the '*plant*', entered during goods issue (GI), the '*Company Code*'

is determined by the system which in turn determines the relevant '*chart of accounts*'.

2. The *plant* thus entered in goods issue, determines the '*valuation class*' and then the '*valuation grouping code*'.
3. The '*valuation class*' is determined from the '*material master*'.
4. Since the '*account modification code*' is assigned to a '*process key*' which is already linked to a '*movement type*', the '*transaction key*' (DIF, GBB, AUM, BSX etc) determines the '*G/L account*' as posting transactions are predefined in for each '*movement type*' in 'inventory management'.

14. Explain 'Account Determination' in SD.

The billing documents created during the sales cycle results in automatic postings to G/L accounts on the FI side. In general, **account determination** is based on the following five factors:

- Chart of accounts
- Sales organization
- Account assignment group of the customer
- Account assignment group of the material
- Account key

The system determines the '*chart of accounts*' from the company code in the '*billing document*', and the '*sales organization*' is determined from the corresponding '*sales order*'. The '*account assignment group*' is taken from the respective masters of customer / material. The '*account key*' helps the user to define the various G/L accounts, and this key is assigned to the '*condition type*' (KOFI) in the '*pricing procedure*'.

Table 3.1: Account Determination in Sales & Distribution

Table	**Description**
001	Customer grp/Material Grp./AccKey
002	Cust. Grp/AccKey
003	Material Grp/Acc Key
004	General
005	Acc Key

Application	**Condtion Type**	**Chart of a/c**	**Sales Org**	**AcctAsg Grp**	**Acc Asgmnt**	**A/c Key**	**G/L a/c**
001	**Customer grp/Material Grp./AccKey: Details**						
V	KOFI	COMP	1000	01	10	ERL	5012100000
V	KOFI	COMP	1000	01	10	ERS	5012100000
V	KOFI	COMP	1000	02	10	ERL	5012200000
V	KOFI	COMP	1000	02	10	ERS	5012200000

V	KOFI	COMP	2000	01	20	ERL	5013100000
V	KOFI	COMP	2000	01	20	ERS	5013100000
V	KOFI	COMP	2000	02	20	ERL	5013200000
V	KOFI	COMP	2000	02	20	ERS	5013200000
005	**Acc Key: Details**						
V	KOFI	COMP	1000		MWS		2470000000
V	KOFI	COMP	2000		MWS		2470000000

These *G/L accounts* are automatically (Table 3-1) determined when you make the following configuration in the system:

i. Assigning an '*account determination procedure*' to a '*billing document type*'
ii. Assigning this '*account determination procedure*' to a '*condition type*'
iii. Assigning this '*condition type*' to an '*access sequence*'
iv. Configuring the '*condition tables*'

15. Outline 'Credit Management' in SAP.

Credit management helps in determining credit limits of customers, aids in creation of '***credit check***' policies besides helping the companies in monitoring and evaluating their customers. This is a cross-functional responsibility in SAP, covering both the Sales & Distribution and Financial Accounting modules.

As in case of any automated process like dunning, payment etc, credit management in SAP requires certain pre-requisites to be defined before hand:

i. ***Customer master data*** is created both in SD & FI
ii. ***Credit control area*** has been defined and assigned to Company Code

SAP makes use of the concept '***credit control area***' for credit management. As explained elsewhere, credit control area is an organizational element defined to which one or more Company Codes are attached. In case of customers defined under more than one Company Code, they may fall under different credit control areas. But, note that:

- A Client can have more than one credit control area.
- A credit control area can be assigned to more than one Company Code. But the converse is not true: one Company Code can not be assigned to more than one Credit Control Area.

While defining the credit limit for a customer:

- You will define a maximum limit per Credit Control Area (Example: credit control area AAAA -> USD 500, 000, Credit Control Area BBBB -> USD 200,000)
- You will define a global maximum limit for all credit control areas put together (USD 600, 0000)

iii. ***Credit data*** (per Credit Control Area 'maximum limit' as well as the 'total' for all areas, in the control data screen) for the customer has been created
iv. ***Risk categories*** have been defined and assigned to customers
v. ***Credit groups*** (document credit group) for document types have been defined. Document credit groups combine order types and delivery types for credit control
vi. Defined, in SD, at what of time (when order is received or when a delivery is made etc) the ***credit check*** should happen

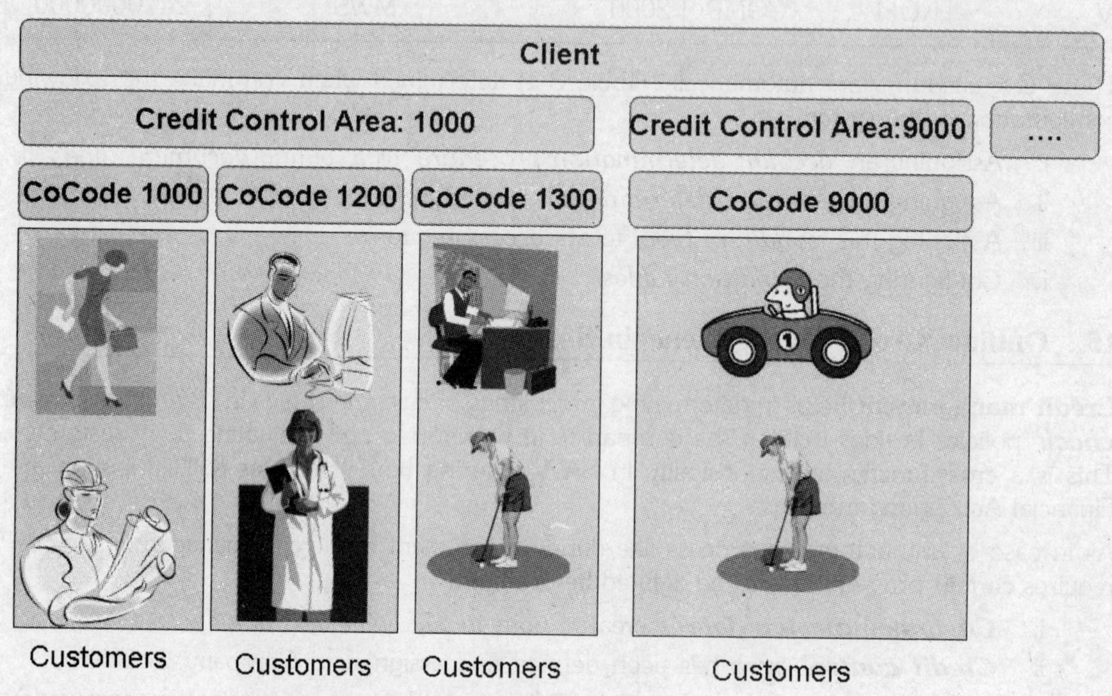

Figure 3.7: Client-Credit Control Area-Company Code-Customer

16. Explain the 'Credit Management Process' in SAP.

The ***credit management process*** starts when a sales order is entered in SD. Imagine this leads to exceeding the credit limit defined for the customer. Now:

a. System creates three ***comparison totals*** considering (1) open receivables, (2) sales order values, value of goods to be delivered, and billing document value from SD and (3) special G/L transactions (e.g. 'down payments' and 'bills of exchange').
b. Based on (a) above the system throws an (1) error message, and prevents from saving the order or (2) warning message, and the system does not prevent saving, but order is 'blocked'.
c. ***Credit representative***, using the ***information functions*** (SD information system, FI information system, credit overview, credit master list, early warning list,

oldest open item, last payment, customer master, account analysis etc), process this blocked order either (1) from the 'blocked SD documents list' or (2) the mail box, and releases the order, if necessary.

d. Delivery is created, billing document generated and posted, A/R updated

e. Customer pays the invoice, A/R is posted

17. What is a 'Credit Check'?

Credit check is defined for any valid combination of the following:

- Credit Control Area
- Risk category
- Document credit group

18. Differentiate 'Static Credit Check' from 'Dynamic Check'.

Under **static credit check**, the system calculates the credit exposure of a particular customer as the total of:

a. Open order (delivery not yet done)

b. Open delivery (value of deliveries yet to be invoiced)

c. Open billing documents (not transferred to accounting)

d. Open items (AR item not yet settled by the customer)

Customer's credit exposure is not to exceed the established credit limit.

The **dynamic credit check** is split into two parts:

- **Static limit**: Total of open items, open billing, and open delivery values
- **Dynamic limit** (Open Order Value): The value of all un-delivered and partial delivered orders totalled and stored on a time-scale in future (10 days, 1 wk etc) known as 'horizon date'.

During the 'dynamic credit check', the system will ignore all orders beyond the 'horizon date'. The sum total of 'static' and 'dynamic limits' should not exceed the credit limit established for the customer.

19. List the Reports in 'Credit Management'.

SAP provides you with the following **reports in credit management**:

- RFDKLI10 Customers with missing Credit Data
- RFDKLI20 Re-organization of Credit Limit for Customers
- RFDKLI30 Short Overview of Credit Limit
- RFDKLI40 Overview of Credit Limit
- RFDKLI41 Credit Master Sheet
- RFDKLI42 Early Warning List (of Critical Customers)
- RFDKLI43 Master Data List

- RFDKLI50 Mass change of Credit Limit Data
- RVKRED06 Checking Blocked Credit Documents
- RVKRED08 Checking Credit Documents which reach the Credit Horizon
- RVKRED09 Checking the Credit Documents from Credit View
- RVKRED77 Re-organization of SD Credit Data

20. How 'Partial Payment' differs from 'Residual Payment'?

When processing the '***incoming payment***' to apply to one or more of the 'open items' of a customer, there may be a situation wherein the incoming payment is more than the '***tolerances***' allowed. In this case, you can still go ahead and process the payment by resorting either to (1) Partial Payment or (2) Residual payment.

Partial payment results in posting a credit to the customer's 'open item', but leaves the original item intact. As a result, no open item is cleared. During partial payment, the system updates the '***invoice reference***' and '***allocation***' fields.

As against the partial payment, the **residual payment** clears the particular 'open item' against which the payment is applied. However, since there are not enough amounts to clear the entire open item, the system creates a new open item being the difference between the original invoice item and the payment applied. Note that the new invoice/open item created by the system will have the new document date and new baseline date though you can change these dates.

21. What is a 'Payment Advice'?

A **payment advice** helps in automatic searching of 'open items' during the 'clearing' process to match an 'incoming payment'. This is possible because of you can use the 'payment advice' number instead of specifying parameters in '***selection screen***'. A typical payment advice may contain details like: document number, amount, currency, reason for under payment etc. The payment advices are of various categories; the first 2 digits of the payment advice number helps to differentiate one payment advice from another:

- Bank advice
- EDI advice
- Lockbox advice (created during clearing process, available in the system whether clearing was successful or not)
- Manual advice
- Advice from a bank statement

Most of the payment advices are deleted as soon as the clearing is successful in the system.

22. How can 'Reason Codes' help in incoming payment processing?

Reason codes configured in the system help to handle the 'payment differences' of individual open items in an invoice (either using payment or advice or in the normal course). To each of the reason codes, you will define the 'posting rules' and the G/L accounts in the IMG.

Once done, when there is a payment difference against a particular open item, the system looks for the reason code:

- When '***charge-off indicator***' has been set for that reason code, then the system posts the payment difference to a G/L account. When this indicator is not set, then a new open item is created for the payment difference.
- When '***disputed item indicator***' has been set, then the system ignores these line items from counting for customer's credit limit.

23. What is 'Dunning' in SAP?

The SAP System allows you to 'dun' (remind) business partners automatically. The system duns the open items from business partner accounts. The ***dunning program*** selects the overdue open items, determines the ***dunning level*** of the account in question, and creates ***dunning notices***. It then saves the ***dunning data*** determined for the items and accounts affected. You can use the dunning program to dun both customers and vendors. It may be necessary to dun a vendor in case of debit balance as a result of a credit memo.

Dunning is administered through a *Dunning Program*, which uses ***dunning key*** (to limit the dunning level per item), ***dunning procedure*** and ***dunning area*** (if dunning is not done at Company Code level).

Change View "Dunning Keys": Overview

New Entries

Dunn.Key	Max.level	Print sep	Text
1	1	☐	Triggers maximum dunning level 1
2	2	☐	Triggers maximum dunning level 2
3	3	☐	Triggers maximum dunning level 3
Z		☑	Payment has been made, separate item display

Figure 3.8: Dunning Key

Transaction Code
F150

24. What is a 'Dunning Procedure'?

SAP comes delivered with a number of **dunning procedures** which you can copy and create your own.

Transaction Code
FBMP

Maintain Dunning Procedure: List

Choose | New procedure

Procedure	Name
0001	Four-level dunning notice, every two weeks
0003	Payment reminder, every two weeks
0005	Four-level dunning notice, every two weeks, RE forms

Figure 3.9: Dunning Procedure List

Maintain Dunning Procedure: Overview

Dunning levels | Charges | Minimum amounts | Dunning texts | Sp. G/L indicator

Dunn.Procedure 0001
Name Four-level dunning notice, every two weeks

General data

Dunning Interval in Days	1
No.of dunning levels	4
Total due items from dunning level	
Min.days in arrears (acct)	6
Line item grace periods	1
Interest indicator	
Public hol.cal.ID	

☑ Standard transaction dunning
☑ Dun special G/L transactions
☐ Dunning Even for Credit Account Balance

Reference data

Ref.Dunning Procedure for Texts 0001 Four-level dunning notice, every two weeks

Figure 3.10: Dunning Procedure Overview

A **dunning procedure** controls:

- ***Dunning interval*** / frequency
- ***Grace days*** / minimum days in arrear
- Number of ***dunning levels*** (at least one level)
- Transactions to be dunned
- Interest to be calculated on the overdue items
- Known or negotiated leave, if any, which needs to be considered in selecting the overdue items
- Company Code data like (a) Is dunning per 'dunning area'? (b) Is dunning per 'dunning level'? (c) Reference Company Code (d) Dunning Company Code etc
- Dunning forms / media to be selected for the dunning run

25. What is a 'Dunning Area'?

Dunning area is optional, and is required only if dunning is not done at Company Code level. The Dunning area can correspond to a sales division, sales organization etc. The individual dunning areas can use different procedures or the same dunning procedure.

The dunning areas with the required dunning procedures are to be entered into the customer or vendor master record if you use different dunning procedures. Otherwise, the system uses the standard dunning procedure. The dunning area is then entered in the line item. The system enters the dunning area into the master record automatically with the corresponding data.

Transaction Code
OB61

26. Describe the 'Dunning' process.

The **dunning process** involves three major steps:

1. **Maintaining dunning parameter**

   As the first step in dunning, you need to maintain certain parameters, which identify the current dunning run. Entering the date of execution and the dunning run identifier is the starting point, after which you will continue to maintain other parameters like:

   - Dunning date to be printed on the notice
   - Document posted up to
   - Company Code
   - Account restrictions (optional)

   Now, you can save the parameters and display the log generated (to see if there were any errors), dunning list (list of accounts and items) and some dunning statistics (blocked accounts / items etc).

2. Creating dunning proposal

Once scheduled, the 'dunning program' prepares the 'dunning proposal' as described below:

a. ***Dunning program*** determines which accounts to dun:

   i. System checks the fields '***Dunn.procedure***' and '***Last dunned***' in the customer master record to determine whether the arrears date or the date of the last dunning run lies far enough back in the past.

   ii. Checks whether the account is blocked for dunning according to the ***dunning block*** field in the customer master record

   iii. Program processes all open items, relating to the accounts thus released in (ii) above, that were posted to this account on or before the date entered in the field '***Documents posted up to***'.

   iv. Program checks all the open items, as released in (iii) above, in an account to decide:

      - Is the item blocked?
      - Is overdue according to the date of issue, the base date, the payment conditions, and the number of grace days granted

   v. Program then proceeds to process all open items thus released, in (iv):

      - How many days the item is overdue
      - Which 'dunning level' for a particular open item

   vi. Program determines the highest 'dunning level' for the account based on (v) above. The highest 'dunning level' determined is stored in the master record of the account when you print the letters. This 'dunning level' determines the 'dunning text' and a 'special dunning form', if defined.

   vii. Program then proceeds to check each account:

      - Does the customer / vendor have a debit balance with regard to all open overdue items selected?
      - Are the total amount to be dunned and the percentage of all open items more than the minimum amount and percentage defined in the 'dunning procedure'?
      - Is the 'dunning level' for the account or the overdue items higher than it was for the last 'dunning run'? If not, are there new open items to be dunned (with a previous dunning level of 0)? If not, does the 'dunning procedure' for this level specify that dunning be repeated?

b. Program creates the **dunning proposal list**

c. Edit dunning proposal list

   You can edit the *Dunning Proposal* so as to:

   - Raise or lower the 'dunning level' of an item

- Block an item from being dunned
- Block an account for the current 'dunning run' or remove the block
- Block an account in the master record for dunning or remove the block
- Block a document for dunning or remove the block

d. You can view the sample print out, to ascertain how the printed notice would look like. (Maximum 10 notices can be seen on the screen).

e. You may also display 'logs' to see the changes made in the editing earlier, as a confirmation of what you wanted to change in the system generated proposal earlier. If necessary, you can go back and change the proposal.

3. Print dunning notices

You can use a 'single form' or 'multiple forms', which will have different text, based on the 'dunning levels'. There may also be a requirement to use a completely different form for '**legal dunning**'. Once the print option is activated, the program prints the notices, and the dunning related information like the 'dunning level', 'last dunned' etc are updated in the customer / vendor masters. SAP provides the option to optically 'archive' the notices as the system prints the dunning notices. There is also a provision to re-start the printing if the same is interrupted before complete printing.

27. Can you 'dun' customers across 'Clients' in a single 'Dunning Run'?

No. All the data processing is carried out *per Client*.

28. What differentiates one 'Dunning Level' from another?

This **dunning level** determines the 'dunning text' and (if required) a 'special dunning form'. The 'dunning program' determines what 'dunning level' should be used in the 'dunning run'. The dunning level so determined is stored in the master record of the account when the 'dunning letter' is printed. The dunning level may also determine whether there will be some 'dunning charges' (Figure 3.11).

29. How many 'Dunning Levels' can be defined?

You may define up to nine dunning levels. If there is only one dunning level, then it is called as the ***'payment reminder'***.

30. Explain 'Account Payables' sub-module.

Accounts payables, a sub-module under Financial Accounting (FI) takes care of vendor related transactions as the module is tightly integrated with the purchasing transactions arising out of '***procurement cycle***'. The module helps in processing the outgoing payments either manually or automatically through '***automatic payment program***'. Also helps in '***vendor evaluations***'.

Maintain Dunning Procedure: Dunning levels

Charges | Minimum amounts | Dunning texts

Dunn.Procedure 0001

Name Four-level dunning notice, every two weeks

Dunning Level	1	2	3	4
Days in arrears/interest				
Days in arrears	2	16	30	44
Calculate interest?	☑	☑	☑	☑
Print parameters				
Always dun?	☐	☐	☐	☑
Print all items	☑	☑	☑	☑
Payment deadline	2	1	10	7

Legal dunning procedure

☐ Always dun in legal dunning proc.

Figure 3.11: Dunning Level

31. What documents result from 'Procurement Processes'?

In ***Materials Management*** (MM):

- **PR**: Purchase Requisition (manual or automatic using MRP)
- **PO**: Purchase Order

In ***Financial Accounting*** (FI):

- Invoice Verification
- Vendor Payment (manual or automatic)

Both MM and FI areas:

- Goods Receipt

You may also group these documents into (1) Order documents, (2) GR (Goods Receipt) documents and (3) IR (Invoice Receipt) documents. While GR/IR documents can be displayed both in MM and FI views, the order documents can only be viewed in MM.

32. Describe 'Purchase Cycle'.

The **purchase cycle or procurement cycle** encompasses all the activities starting from purchase requisition, purchase order, goods movement, goods receipt, invoicing, invoice verification, payment to vendors and ending with updating of vendor account balances.

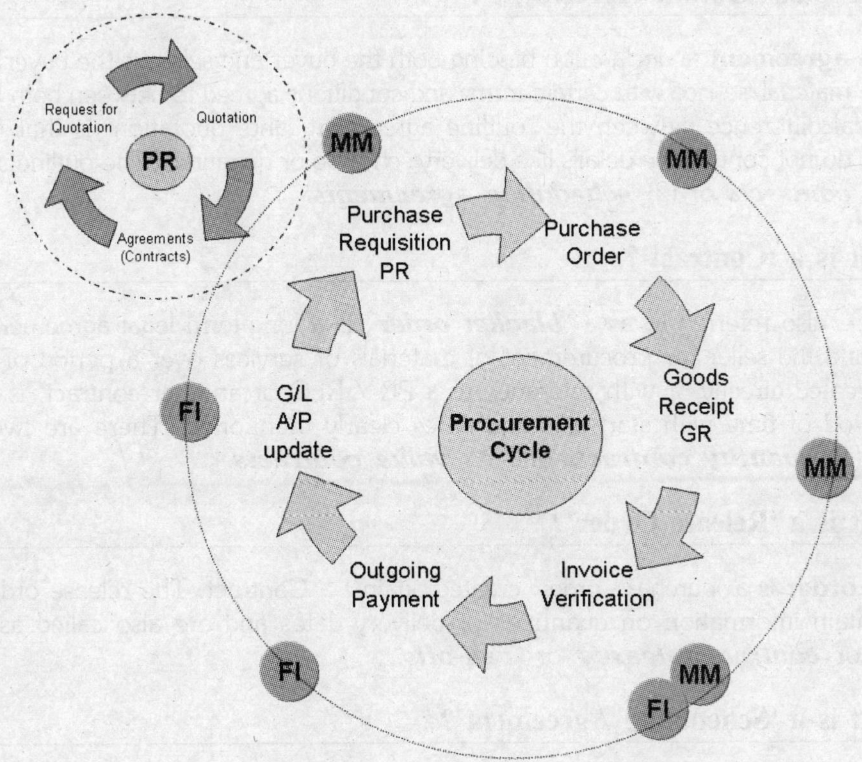

Figure 3.12: Procurement Cycle

33. What is 'Purchase Requisition'?

A **Purchase requisition**, **PR**, is the document which outlines a company's purchasing needs of a material/service from vendor(s). A PR, typically an *internal document* that can be created automatically or manually, identifies the demand for a product and authorizes the purchasing department to procure the same. In automatic creation of PR, this is done as a result of **MRP** (***Material Requirements Planning***). The PR, after identifying the vendor, is processed further to result in a **RFQ (*Request for Quotation*)** or directly to a ***Purchase Order*** (**PO**).

34. What is 'Request for Quotation (RFQ)'?

A **RFQ (Request for Quotation)**, which can be created directly or with reference to another

RFQ or a PR or an Outline Agreement, is actually an invitation to vendor (s) to submit a 'quotation' for supplying a material or service. The RFQ will contain the terms and condition for supply. You may send the RFQ to a single or multiple vendors, and you can monitor the same by sending reminders to those who have not responded to the RFQ.

35. What is an 'Outline Agreement'?

An **outline agreement**, a declaration binding both the buyer and seller, is the buyer's intention to purchase material/service with certain terms and conditions agreed to between both the parties. The essential difference between the 'outline agreement' and 'quotation' is that the outline agreements do not contain the details like delivery schedule or quantities. The outline agreements can be (1) ***contracts*** or (2) ***scheduling agreements***.

36. What is a 'Contract'?

A **Contract**, also referred to as a '***blanket order***', is a long-term legal agreement between the buyer and the seller for procurement of materials or services over a period of time. The contract, created directly or with reference to a PR / RFQ or another contract, is valid for a certain period of time with start and end dates clearly mentioned. There are two types of contracts: (1) ***quantity contracts*** and (2) ***value contracts***.

37. What is a 'Release Order'?

A **release order** is a 'purchase order' created against a Contract. The release orders usually do not contain information on quantities or delivery dates and are also called as '***blanket releases***' or ***contract releases***' or '***call-offs***'.

38. What is a 'Scheduling Agreement'?

A **scheduling agreement** is also a long-term agreement with the buyer and seller for procurement of certain materials or services subject to certain terms and conditions. These agreements can be created directly or with reference to other documents like another scheduling agreement, or RFQ or PR. These agreements help in promoting ***Just-In-Time (JIT)*** deliveries, less paper work, reduce supply lead times and ensures low inventory for the buyer.

39. What is a 'Quotation'?

A **quotation** contains information relating to the price and other conditions for supply of a material or a service by a vendor, and is termed as the vendor's willingness to supply the same based on those conditions. You will be able to compare the data from quotations using a ***price comparison list*** and will help in identifying the most reasonable vendor for supply of that item(s). After you receive the quotations, you will typically enter the quotation data (pricing/ delivery) in RFQ. The SAP system can easily be configured to automatically print '***rejections***' for vendors whose quotation are not selected.

40. What is a 'Purchase Order'?

A **purchase order (PO),** is a legal contract between a vendor and a buyer, mentioning the material/service to be purchased / procured on certain terms and conditions. The order mentions, among other things, the quantity to be purchased, price per unit, delivery related conditions, payment/pricing information etc.

A PO can be created:

- Directly or
- With reference to a PR / RFQ / contract or another PO. Remember, all items on a PO should relate to the same Company Code.

41. What is a 'PO History'?

The **purchase order history** (PO History) lists all the transactions for all the items in a PO like the GR/IR document numbers.

42. Will FI document be created during Purchase Order (PO)?

No. There will not be any document created on the FI side during creation of a PO. However, there can be a document for posting 'commitment' to a Cost Center in CO. (The offsetting entry is posted at the time of GR).

43. Explain FI-MM Integration.

The **FI-MM integration** is based on the following:

- Movement Types
- Valuation Class
- Transaction Keys
- Material Type

MvT	Movement Type Text
101	GR goods receipt
102	GR for PO reversal
103	GR into blocked stck
104	GR to blocked rev.
105	GR from blocked stck
106	GR from blocked rev.

Figure 3.13: Movement Types

Movement type is the 'classification key' indicating the type of material movement (for example, goods receipt, goods issue, physical stock transfer). The movement type enables the system to find pre-defined posting rules determining how the accounts in FI (stock and consumption accounts) are to be posted and how the stock fields in the material master record are to be updated.

Valuation class refers to the assignment of a material to a group of G/L accounts. Along with other factors, the valuation class determines the G/L accounts that are updated as a result of a valuation-relevant transaction or event, such as a goods movement. The valuation class makes it possible to:

- Post the stock values of materials of the same material type to different G/L accounts
- Post the stock values of materials of different material types to the same G/L account

Transaction key (also known as the '**event key** or **process key**') allows the users to differentiate between the various transactions and events (such as physical inventory transactions and goods movements) that occur within the area of inventory management. The transaction / event type controls the filing/storage of documents and the assignment of document numbers.

Material type groups together materials with the same basic attributes, for example, raw materials, semi-finished products, or finished products. When creating a material master record, you must assign the material to a material type. The material type determines:

- Whether the material is intended for a specific purpose, for example, as a Configurable Material or Process Material
- Whether the material number can be assigned internally or externally
- The Number Range from which the material number is drawn
- Which screens appear and in what sequence
- Which user department data you may enter
- What Procurement Type the material has; that is, whether it is manufactured in-house or procured externally, or both

Together with the plant, the material type determines the material's inventory management requirement that is:

- Whether changes in quantity are updated in the material master record
- Whether changes in value are also updated in the stock accounts in financial accounting.

44. What happens when you post a 'Goods Receipt'?

When you post a **goods receipt** (**GR**), the stock account is debited (stock quantity increases) and the credit goes to ***GR/IR clearing account*** which is the intermediate processing account before you actually process the vendor invoice or payments to the vendor:

- Debit: Inventory Account
- Credit: GR/IR Clearing Account

During this (1) a material document is created, (2) an accounting document to update the relevant G/L account is created, (3) PO order history is updated and finally (4) system enables you to print the GR slip.

45. Explain 'Invoice Verification (IV)' in SAP.

Invoice verification involves:

a. Validating the accuracy of the invoices (quantity, value etc)
b. Checking for 'blocked' invoices (which varied to a greater extent from that of the PO)
c. Matching of invoices received from vendors with that of the Purchase Order/Goods Receipt. At this point of time PO History is updated for the corresponding PO Line Item(s) of the matched invoice.
d. Passing of matched invoices to FI module. The system posts the following entries:
    - Debit: GR/IR Clearing Account
    - Credit: Vendor A/c (Accounts Payable open line item)
    - Credit: G/L Reconciliation Account

The different scenarios in invoice verification include:

- *GR based Invoice Verification indicator is **not** set in the PO detail screen:* Although this setting enables you to post the invoice referenced to a PO prior to making a GR, the system will block the invoice for payment (as this kind of posting results in a ***quantity variance*** as there has not been a GR).
- *GR based Invoice Verification indicator is set in the PO detail screen:* When the PO number is referenced the system brings up all the unmatched items of GR in the selection screen. You will not be able to post the invoice for its full value, unless the PO has been fully received.

46. How do you deal with the 'Tax' when you post an invoice?

When you enter an invoice, based on the configuration settings, the system checks the **tax code**, and calculates the applicable tax or validates the Tax Amount entered by you:

- ***Manual entry***: Input the ***tax code*** and the ***tax amount.*** The system will validate and issue a message in case it does not find the tax code or if the amount is different.
- ***Automatic entry***: Leave the tax code and tax amount fields blank. Tick the 'Calculate Tax' indicator. The system picks up the corresponding tax code and calculates the tax amount automatically.

47. What 'Variances' you will come across in Invoice Verification?

The system needs to be configured properly with '*tolerances*' so that you are not hampered with variances when you try *invoice verification*. You need to define the lower and upper limits for each combination of the Company Code and the tolerance key defined for the various variances. The system, then, checks these tolerance limits and issues warnings or prevents you from proceeding further, when you process an invoice.

The **variances** arise because of mismatch or discrepancies between the invoice and the PO against which the invoice has been issued. Normally you will encounter:

- ***Price variance:*** If there is a discrepancy in invoice price and PO item prices

- ***Schedule variance:*** if the planned delivery date is later than the invoice postings
- ***Quantity variance:*** If the delivered quantity (or delivered quantity less previously invoiced quantity) is not the same as that of the invoiced quantity. When the invoiced quantity is more than the GR, the system requires more GRs to square off the situation.

48. Outline the 'Payment Program' in SAP system.

The **payment program,** in SAP, enables you to process international payment transactions – outgoing as well as incoming - both with customers and vendors. It comes with a lot of flexibility that you can define several payment features that vary from country to country such as payment method, payment form, or data carrier specifications. As always, the standard SAP system contains the common payment methods (check, transfer, bill of exchange etc) and the corresponding forms that have been defined separately for each country; it also comes with the country-specific payment methods (like, POR procedure for Switzerland).

The payment program also supports (a) clearing open items between customers and vendors, (b) inter-company payments with one company code paying centrally for others, (c) paying or clearing any type of open item (say, down payments), (d) restricting access to the payment program through authorizations etc

The payment program is used by Accounts Receivable (FI-AR), Accounts Payable (FI-AP), Treasury (TR), and Bank Accounting (FI-BL).

49. Explain the settings required for controlling the 'Payment Program' in SAP.

Besides making the specifications like from which company code the payments are made, how many days of tolerance is provided in processing the payments, you also need to maintain the following control settings that are required for processing a payment by the payment program:

- **What is to be paid?** To do this, you specify rules according to which the open items to be paid are selected and grouped for payment.
- **When payment is to be carried out?** The due date of the open items determines when payment is carried out. However, you can specify the payment deadline in more detail via configuration.
- **To whom the payment is made?** You specify the payee (the vendor or the alternate payee as the case may be).
- **How the payment is made?** You determine rules that are used to select a payment method.
- **From where the payment is made?** You determine rules that are used to select a bank and a bank account for the payment.

50. Where you maintain the specifications for controlling the Payment Program?

The specifications for controlling the payment program are made when:

- Configuring the payment program

- Entering data in your business partner master records
- Entering data in the open items
- Entering data for the payment run

51. Explain the pre-requisites before you run the 'Payment Program'.

Before you are ready to run the **automatic payment program**, the following should have been defined / configured in the system:

- **House bank** and the corresponding bank accounts
- **Payment methods** to be used for the Company Code. SAP comes with pre-defined payment methods, both for AR and AP. The following payment methods are available for you to select from depending upon the requirements:
    - o Accounts Payable

      Cheque / Transfer / Postal Giro transfer / Bill of exchange
    - o Accounts Receivable

      Bank collection / Bank direct debit / Refund by check / Refund by bank transfer / Bill of exchange payment request
- **Bank chain**, if necessary. Bank chains are used to make payment via more than one bank, for example via the correspondence banks of the house bank, the recipient bank, or the intermediary banks. You can define up to three banks.
- **Payment forms**. SAP delivers standard forms, which can be modified, or new forms can be created for use.

52. How do you configure 'Payment Program'?

You may do most of the configuration settings by accessing the various configuration tasks on 'Customizing: Maintain Payment Program' screen (Figure 3.14).

Transaction Code
FBZP

53. What is a 'Sending Company Code'?

The '**sending company code**' is the one which is normally known to your business partners: when you make cross-company code payments, you can specify the sending company code as well as the paying company code for each company code. If the sending company code is different from the paying company code, the system notes the sending company code in the payment transfer medium or payment advice, as information for the business partner. The sending company code affects how the system groups items from different company codes into one payment (Table 3-2).

Table 3.2: Sending Company Code: Illustration

Company Code	Paying Company Code	Sending Company Code	Remark
Company Code 1000 pays for itself, and also on behalf of Company Codes 2000 & 3000			
1000 2000 3000	1000 1000 1000	1000 1000 1000	All items are grouped into a single payment
Company Code 1000 pays for itself, and also on behalf of Company Codes 2000 & 3000			
1000 2000 3000	1000 1000 1000	1000 2000 3000	A separate payment is created for each of the Company Codes

Items are only grouped into one payment for company codes with the same paying company code and the same sending company code. If the sending company code is not specified, the system automatically regards the paying company code as the sending company code. You only need to specify the sending company code if you want to pay using a cross-company code transaction but do not want to pay the items of all participating company codes together.

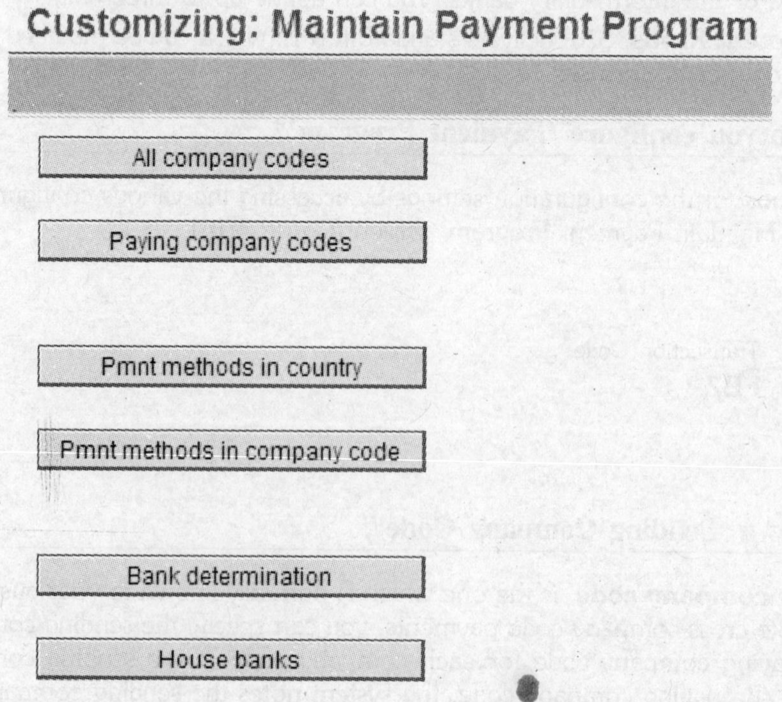

Figure 3.14: 'Customizing: Maintain Payment Program' Screen

54. Explain configuring 'Sending' and 'Paying' Company Codes for Payment Program.

Use the following Transaction Code and configure the sending company code, tolerance days and paying company code specifications.

Transaction Code
OBVU

a. *Sending company code* – if Company Code 'A' is making payments on behalf of Company Code 'B', then 'B' is the *Sending Company Code.* If you do not specify the Sending Company Code, then it is construed that the paying company code is the sending company code.
b. Tolerance days
c. Paying company code specifications – In the case of centralized payments, you will make all the payments through a particular company code known as the 'paying company code'. However, even if there is no centralized payment, you need to have one of your company codes as the paying company code.

Change View "Company Codes": Details

New Entries

Company Code 0001 SAP A.G. — Paying company code

Control data
Sending company code
Paying company code 0001 SAP A.G.
☐ Separate payment per business area
☐ Pyt meth suppl.

Cash discount and tolerances
Tolerance days for payable
Outgoing pmnt with cash disc.from %
☐ Max.cash discount

Figure 3.15: (Sending) Company Code Specifications

The paying company code and the company code to which payment is made must be in the same country and have the same local currency and parallel currencies. Both company codes must also have the same settings for enhanced withholding tax functions (active or not active).

Change View "Paying Company Codes": Det

New Entries

Paying co. code 0001 SAP A.G.

Control Data

Minimum amount for incoming payment	1.00	EUR
Minimum amount for outgoing payment	5.00	EUR

- [ ] No exchange rate differences
- [ ] No Exch.Rate Diffs. (Part Payments)
- [ ] Separate payment for each ref.
- [x] Bill/exch pymt

Figure 3.16: Paying Company Code Specifications

You will make the following specifications:

- Minimum amounts for incoming and outgoing payments.
- Forms for payment advice and EDI
- Bill of exchange parameters

55. What is a Payment Method?

The '**payment method**', in SAP, specifies the procedure, such as check, transfer or bill of exchange, by which payments are made. The payment methods are defined in two steps:

a. Maintain all the specifications that are required for each *payment method in each country*. This is necessary for all the payment methods used by your organization in each country.

b. Maintain the *payment methods you use for each company code*. Here, you also specify the conditions of their use.

56. What payment methods are normally available in SAP?

In a standard SAP system, you will see the following **payment methods** already defined and ready to use:

Accounts Receivable

- Bank collection
- Bank direct debit
- Refund by cheque / bank transfer
- Bank bills
- Bill of exchange request

Accounts Payable

- Cheque
- Transfer
- Postal giro transfer
- Bill of exchange

57. Explain configuring 'Payment Methods in Country' for Payment Program.

You will use the following Transaction Code to define all the payment methods that will be permitted for a country and the specifications for each of these permitted payment methods.

Transaction Code
OBVCU

Here, you may define all the payment methods permitted per country.

Payment Method/Country			
Country	Name	Pmt method	Name
AU	Australia	T	Transfer
BE	Belgium	D	Customer collection - Domicil.
		F	Foreign banktransfers
		K	TFB Kredietbank Foreign Transf
		T	Domestic banktransfers
		X	Customer repayments

Figure 3.17: Payment Methods/Country

The following are to be configured under this category, for each of the payment method for that country:

- Payment method for outgoing/incoming payment?
- Payment method classification
- Master data requirements
- Posting details – document types
- Payment medium details - Print programs
- Permitted currencies (leave blank to allow all currencies)

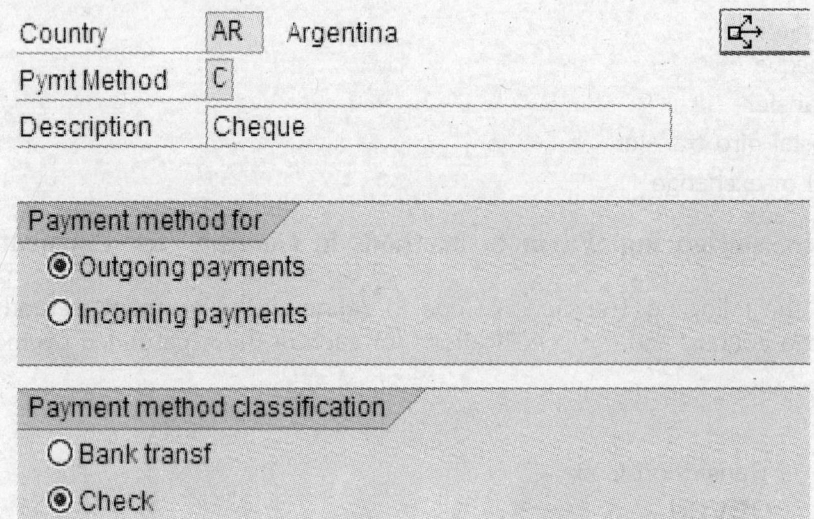

Figure 3.18: Specifications for Payment Method/Country

58. Explain configuring 'Payment Methods in Company Code'.

You will use the following Transaction Code to define all the payment methods that will be permitted for a company code and the specifications for each of these permitted payment methods.

Transaction Code
OBVU

Here, you may define all the payment methods permitted per company code.

Maintenance of Company Code Data for a Payment Method				
CoCd	Name	City	Pmt met	Name
AU01	Country Template AU	Australia	C	Cheque
			T	Transfer
BE01	Country Template BE	Belgium	D	Customer collection - Domicil.
			F	Foreign banktransfers
			K	TFB Kredietbank Foreign Transf
			T	Domestic banktransfers
			X	Customer repayments

Figure 3.19: Payment Methods/Company Code

The following are to be configured under this category, for each of the payment methods permitted for that company code:

- **Amount limits (minimum / maximum payment amounts)**

  This provides the value range within which the payment method can be selected by the payment program. It is important that you specify a maximum amount, without which payment method cannot be used at all. Note that the value range maintained here does not apply if you have specified the payment method in the open item.

- **Whether payment abroad or in foreign currency is allowed (foreign payments / foreign currency payments)**

  This specification as to 'foreign payments' is necessary (a) when you have your customer or vendor abroad and or (b) when the payment is made through a bank abroad. In the case of 'foreign currency payments', specify whether it is possible to use the payment method in question to pay in foreign currency in which case any currency can be used. It is also possible to specify particular currencies per payment method and country: in this case if that particular payment method is selected, then the payments are processed only in one of the currencies specified.

- **Payment item grouping**

  You have two options of grouping the payment items: 'single payment for marked item' and 'payment per due date'

- **Bank optimization (bank selection control)**

  SAP provides you with three options in bank selection: (a) optimize by bank group, (b) optimize by postal code and (c) no optimization.

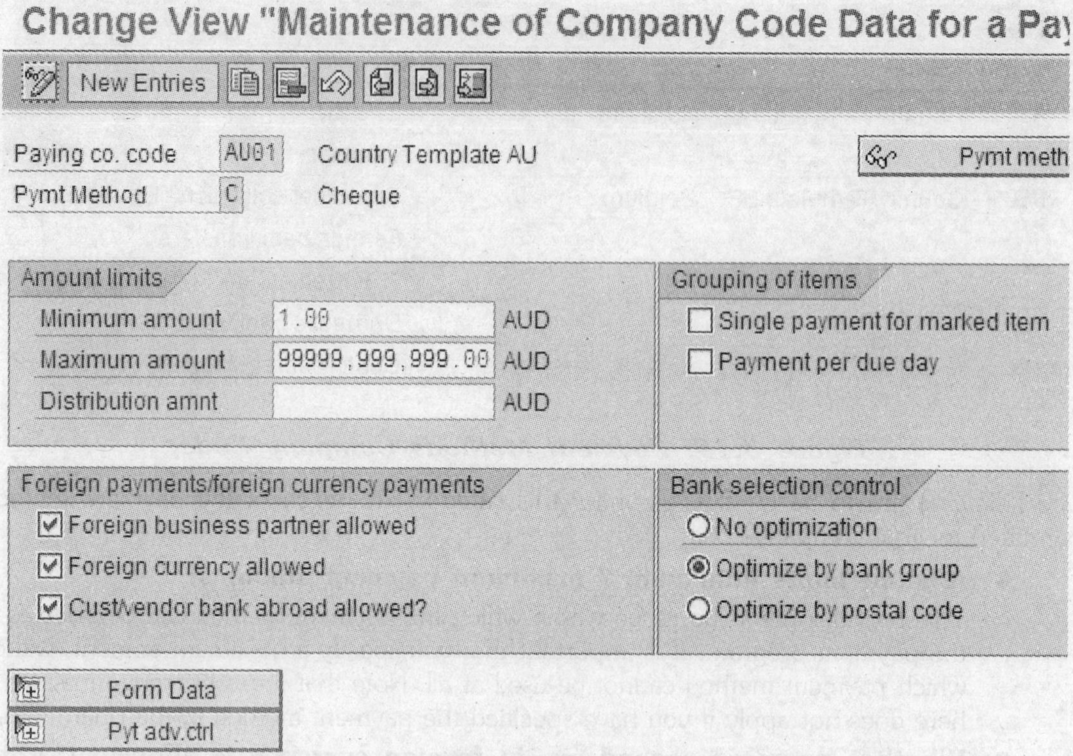

Figure 3.20: 'Payment Method / Company Code' Specifications

59. Explain 'Payment Method' selection by the payment program.

You must specify which payment methods are to be used in the payment run, at the start of every payment run. However, the selection of the payment method for a particular payment run is subject to the payment methods permitted for that payment run, payment methods maintained in the master record and the payment method in the open item. Even the order in which the payment methods are maintained makes the difference (Table 3-3).

For a payment method to be used by the payment program:

- The payment method must be specified in the customer/vendor master record or open items. Note that the method in the open item takes the precedence, when payment methods are mentioned both in the master record and open items.
- The specifications needed for the payment method are mentioned in the master record.
- A bank permissible for the payment method under consideration is determined, for payment.
- The permissible minimum and maximum amounts must be adhered to for the payment amount.

- In the case of payments abroad, the payment method in question should allow for payments to customers / vendors or their banks abroad. For foreign currency payments, the payment method must allow such a payment.

When the program determines a payment method meeting the above conditions, then that payment method is used: else, the program carries out all these checks for the next payment method in the list, till it comes across a payment method meeting the conditions.

Table 3.3: Payment Method selection by Payment Program: Illustration

Payment Method				**Remarks**
In the Open Item	**Maintained in Master Record**	**Permitted for the specific Payment Run**	**That will be considered by the Payment Program**	
C	T	CT	C	Payment method in the open items takes precedence over any payment method defined in the master record
	TC	CT	T	If several payment methods are specified in the master record and none in the open item, then the payment program selects a payment method, in the order in which the payment methods have been maintained

60. Explain 'Optimization by Bank Group'.

If you specify *optimization according to bank groups* for a payment method, then the payment program selects two banks that belong to the same bank group (To make use of bank selection by bank group, you need to assign a freely definable bank group to all banks in your master records). If several house banks come into consideration, the bank with the highest priority (ranking order) is selected. If an optimization is not possible, the optimization function does not apply.

In the Table 3-4, Part-A depicts the house banks with their priority and the bank group. Part-B shows the banks as in the customer/vendor master data.

Table 3.4: Settings for Bank Optimization by Bank Group: Optimization Possible

Part-A: House Banks			**Part-B: Vendor / Customer Master**		**Remarks**
Bank	**Priority**	**Bank group**	**Bank group**	**Bank**	
American Express Bank	1	AB	BA	Bank of America	Bank optimization by 'bank group' is possible. The payment program selects Standard Chartered Bank as it has the highest priority (2)
Standard Chartered Bank	**2**	**SB**	**SB**	**Standard Chartered Bank**	
CitiBank	3	CB	CB	CitiBank	

Now, look at the Table 3-5:

Table 3.5: Settings for Bank Optimization by Bank Group: Optimization not Possible

Part-A: House Banks			**Part-B: Vendor / Customer Master**		**Remarks**
Bank	**Priority**	**Bank group**	**Bank group**	**Bank**	
American Express Bank	1	AB	CB	Chase Manhattan Bank	Bank optimization by 'bank group' is NOT possible. The payment program selects American Express Bank as it is the house bank with highest priority (2)
Standard Chartered Bank	2	SB	FB	Federal Bank	
CitiBank	3	CB	IB	Indian Bank	
Bank of America	4	BA			

This kind of bank optimization by bank group ensures that money is transferred from your house bank to your customer/vendor's bank at the earliest.

61. Explain 'Bank Optimization by Postal Code'.

The bank optimization by postal code ensures that the payment program selects the appropriate house bank according to the location (postal code) of the customer / vendor. It is recommended that, you assign your house banks to a range of postal codes so that this optimization works well (Table 3-6).

Table 3.6: Settings for Bank Optimization by Postal Code

Country	Postal code		House Bank
	From	To	
IN	600001	600099	Indian Bank
IN	600100	600900	Canara bank

If no house bank is defined for the postal code area of the customer/vendor, or if the selected house bank cannot be used, the payment program selects the house bank with the highest priority from the priority list. In this case, optimization does not take place.

62. When you will use 'Payment per due date' grouping option?

If you select 'payment per due date' indicator in 'grouping of items' while configuring the payment methods per country, then it is an instruction to the payment program that a payment needs to be created for each due date. All the items that are to be paid are then grouped according to due date, and several payments are generated grouped by due dates instead of a single payment.

63. Explain configuring 'Bank Determination' for the Payment Program.

You will use the following Transaction Code to define all the necessary specifications for configuring the 'bank determination' for the payment program.

Transaction Code
OBVCU

You will be defining:

- Ranking order
- Bank accounts
- Available amounts
- Value date
- Expenses / charges

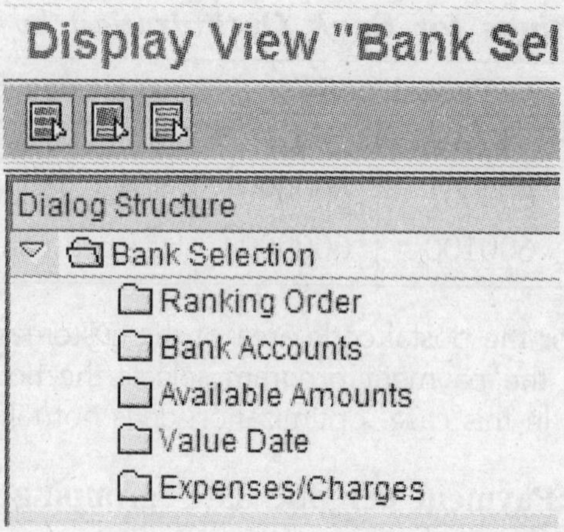

Display View "Bank Sel

Dialog Structure

- Bank Selection
  - Ranking Order
  - Bank Accounts
  - Available Amounts
  - Value Date
  - Expenses/Charges

Figure 3.21: Specifications for 'Bank Determination'

Ranking order

Specify which house banks are allowed for:

- Every payment method or
- Both payment method and currency

Maintain the priority, and sort the list of permissible banks in ranking order according to this priority.

Paying co. code 0001

Ranking Order

P...	Crcy	Rank.order	House Bk	House bk	Acct for bill/exch.
2		1	DB		
2	DEM	1	DB		
2	DEM	2	DRE		
2	USD	1	DB		
A		1	DRE		

Figure 3.22: Ranking Order in Bank Selection

Bank accounts

For every combination of payment method and house bank, specify via which bank account (for example giro) the payment should be made.

Paying company code 0001 SAP A.G.

Bank Accounts

House b...	P...	Curr...	Account ID	Bank subaccount	Clear.acct	Charge ind	Bus
DB	2		GIRO	113102			
DB	2	DEM	GIRO	113102			
DB	2	USD	US$	113150			
DB	A		GIRO	113102			

Figure 3.23: Bank Accounts for 'Payment Method / House Bank' combination

Available amounts

For every account at a house bank, you now need to specify the amounts that are available for the payment run. You may specify the amounts both for incoming and outgoing payments.

Paying company code 0001 SAP A.G.

Available Amounts

House ba...	Account ID	Days	Currency	Available for outgoing payment	Scheduled incoming pa...
DB	GIRO	3	EUR	750,000.00	100,000.00
DB	GIRO	3	USD	750,000.00	100,000.00
DB	GIRO	10	EUR	1,000,000.00	
DB	GIRO	100	EUR	40,000.00	

Figure 3.24: Available Amounts per Account per House Bank

Value date

Value dates are the number of days that elapse between the posting date of the payment run and the value date at the bank. This is required to take into account the delay between the payment and its reflection in the books of the bank. Maintain the value dates for all the combination of payment method / house bank and the amount limit.

Paying company code 0001 SAP A.G.

Value Date					
Pmt met	House b	Acco	Amount Limit	Curr	Days
U	DB	GIRO	300.00	EUR	1

Figure 3.25: Value Date settings in Paying Company Code

Expenses / Charges

Maintain the required charges, for each of the amount limits, using a 'charge indicator' for the paying company code.

Paying company code 0001 SAP A.G.

Expenses/Charges				
Charge ind	Amount Limit	Currency	Charges 1	Charges 2
G1	10,000	EUR	30	
G2	19,999	EUR	47	

Figure 3.26: Maintain Expenses/Charges

64. Explain 'Value Dates' in detail.

As mentioned elsewhere, the **value dates** are the number of days that elapse between the posting date of the payment run and the value date at the bank. The value dates can e either be defined by you based on your experience of previous payments made with that payment method, bank account, payment amount and currency, or you can allow the system to automatically determine the value date. In the case of automatic determination of value dates, the system will use a bank calendar and individual agreements with the bank as decision criteria to arrive at these days.

The payment program makes use of the valued dates in two ways:

- By adding the number of days needed for the payment to be debited from your account to the posting date of the payment run and thereby establishing the value date of the payment. This date is noted in the payment document. Such information is particularly important for the Cash Management and Forecast application. If no value dates are determined by this way, then the system takes the posting date of the payment run as the value date.
- To check the available amounts at each of the accounts / house banks. In this case the value dates are used to plan the available amounts on a graduated time scale. You

generally only need this facility if you post payments by bill of exchange before the due date. In all other cases, you just need to maintain this as '999'.

Since all the payments (regardless of the amount) that are made by transfer are debited from your bank account on the next day, you should enter 1 in the field '*Days to value date*'. However, the period within which a check is cashed can be dependent on the amount: say, for amounts of up to 10,000 USD, the time between the posting date and the value date may be four days, and for all other amount limits this may two days (Table 3-7).

Table 3.7: 'Value Date' settings for Payment Program

Payment Method	House Bank	Account ID	Amount Limit	Currency	Days to value date
T	DB	GIRO	9999,999,999	USD	1
C	DB	GIRO	10,000	USD	4
C	DB	GIRO	9999,999,999	USD	2
T	DB	US$	9999,999,999	USD	1

65. How you will configure 'Available Amounts'?

The configuration of **available amounts** is to enable the payment program to check whether the selected bank accounts have sufficient funds for payment. You may specify available amounts separately for incoming payments / outgoing payments, for the different accounts maintained at the house banks. Define the size of the amount that can be paid for all the outgoing payments and you specify the amount up to which such payments can be made into a bank account for the incoming payments. When this limit is exceeded, the payment program selects another account of the bank. The program does not carry out amount splitting, should it comes across a bank account wherein the available amount is not sufficient for making a payment. Also, if it finds no bank account from which it can post the entire amount for a payment, it does not carry out the payment at all.

You can also specify the amounts based on currency and probable value date (days) at the bank. The value date helps in determining the available amounts as there is a time lag between payment run date and value dating at the bank. You generally need to include this value date facility only if you post payments by bill of exchange before the due date. In all other cases, you can enter 999 (Table 3-8).

Table 3.8: 'Available Amounts' settings for Payment Program

House Bank	Account ID	Days to value date	Currency	Available Amount	
				Incoming Payment	Outgoing Payment
DB	GIRO	999	USD	200,000	100,000
DB	GIRO	999	EURO	100,000	100,000
DB	US$	999	USD	200,000	80,000

66. Outline the steps in executing the 'Payment Program'?

The following are the steps involved in executing the payment program:

1. **Maintain Payment Parameters**

   To start with, you need to maintain the parameters for the payment run like date of execution of 'payment run', 'payment run identifier' etc. Once this is done, you need to specify:

   - What should be the 'posting date' for the payments
   - The 'document date' up to which the program should consider the items for payment
   - The paying company code,
   - Payment methods to be considered
   - What will be the 'next posting date'
   - Are there certain accounts which need to be excluded from the run etc

   The payment run, then needs to be scheduled either immediately or at a specified time/date

2. **Payment Proposal**

   The system creates a 'payment proposal', based on the payment parameters maintained in (1) above. The system selects the eligible ***open items*** based on the following sequence:

   a. ***Due date*** is determined via the ***base line date*** and the ***terms of payment*** for each of the line items

   b. Program calculates the ***cash discount period*** and due date for the ***net payment***

   c. ***Grace periods*** (company code-specific grace periods for payables, maintained in the field 'Grace period in days for payable' under 'cash discount & tolerances') are then added to this due date

   d. Which '***Special G/L*** accounts are to be included (by entering the special G/L code of the transaction in question when you make the company code specifications), based on what you have already maintained as the parameters in (1) above

   e. The system will determine whether to include an item during the current payment run or for the future one based on the specifications you made in (1)

   f. The program also determines whether to ***block*** an item

   The ***payment proposal*** thus created can be displayed for further processing; the 'log' can be checked to see the system messages, and the exception list generated for further evaluation.

3. **Edit Payment Proposal**

   With the payment proposal available, you can now edit the proposal to:

   a. Change house bank, from what was maintained earlier or suggested by the payment program

b. Change payment method, if necessary
c. Change payment due date so as to relax or restrict certain open items
d. Block / unblock line items

4. **Payment run**

After the payment proposal has been edited, you can run the payment program that creates the payment documents and prepares the data for printing the forms or creating the tape / disk / DME. Before printing the forms, check the logs to determine that the payment program run was successful.

5. **Print run**

Payment medium programs use the data prepared by the payment program to create forms (payment advice, EDI accompanying sheet) or files for the data media. The data created by payment program are stored in the following Tables:

- REGUH Payee or Payment Method data
- REGUP Individual Open Items data
- REGUD Bank Data and Payment Amounts data

You need to define ***variants*** for print program:

- Per *Payment Method* per country -> assign a *Print Program*
- To run the *Print Program* ->at least one *Variant* per *Print Program* per *Payment Method*

Transaction Code
F110

67. How the Payment Program determines the House Bank for payment?

During the payment run, the payment program attempts to determine a house bank and a bank account that has a sufficient amount available for payment. The sequence of events is as under:

a. The payment program searches a house bank (bank ID) for the given combination of payment method and currency. If there is no matching entry, then the program checks to find out whether a bank exists for 'payment method without currency specification'.
b. Then it goes on to determine the account ID on the basis of the 'bank ID', the payment method and the currency.
c. At last, it finds out whether sufficient amounts are available for both 'bank ID' and account ID.

During this processing, the following may happen:

- The *program finds no house bank* fulfilling all the conditions: this means that the payment cannot then be made with that particular payment method with which the check was carried out. Now, the system proceeds to carry out the same sequence of checks for the next possible bank: if no bank is determined, then this payment method also can not be used. The program goes further to check whether another method is available, and so on. All these are noted in the log for the payment run.

- The *program determines only one house bank*: the payment is made through that house bank.
- There is more than one bank determined: the payment is made from the house bank with the highest priority according to the defined ranking order of the banks (note that this is not valid in case you have specified payment optimization).

68. Can the Payment Program consider 'check cashing time' for value dating?

You can instruct the payment program to add the number of days it will take for cashing a cheque, so that the value date is correctly arrived at from that of the posting date. For this, you need to enter the number of days in 'check cashing time' in the customer / vendor master record. If this field is blank, then the program determines the value date based on the entries maintained while configuring the 'value dates'.

Consider that the payment posting date was 10-June-2009, for a payment of USD 10,000 to one of your vendors. The payment method was 'cheque' (Table 3-9).

Table 3.9: Check Cashing Time: the possibilities for Value Date

Entry in 'check cashing time' in vendor master record	Entry in 'Days to value date' while configuring 'Value Dates'	Value date arrived by the system
2	4	12-June-2009
Blank	4	14-June-2009
Blank	Blank	10-June-2009

69. What do you mean by 'Local Payment'?

When you deal with an organization having branch offices, the payment program normally pays to the head office, unless otherwise specified. This is because of the reason that the program takes the required information from the master record of the head office. However, it is possible to make payments to the branch offices and such a payment is called as '**local payment**'. For such a payment, the required details like bank, address etc are taken from the master record(s) of the branch office(s). The pre-requisites for a local payment include:

- If you want separate payment methods for different branch offices, then you need to set up these methods in the master records of the branch offices. If the branches require the same payment methods as that of the head office, then it is sufficient to maintain these at the head office's master record. If the payment methods are defined in the master records of branch and head office, then any of these payment methods can be used.

- The field 'Local processing' in 'Correspondence' in the 'Company code data' of the vendor/customer master record needs to be selected.

70. Explain the factors influencing when an open item is paid by the payment program?

There are several factors which influence when an open item is considered for payment:

- Payable or receivable?

  In the case of payables, the items will be selected based on the following:

  - o With the grace period taken into account, the item will be selected for the current run if it:
    - Achieves a higher cash discount if paid in the current payment run than if paid in the following run.
    - Would become overdue in the following payment run
  - o The item is always due together with the invoice it is linked to, for all invoice-related credit memos
  - o All other open items will be paid in the next payment run

  In the case of receivables, the payment program always aims to pay soon enough to take advantage of the highest possible cash discount: the payment is made with the first payment run that is carried out on or after the due date of the first cash discount term.
- Cash discount / net payments strategy
- Bill of exchange payment strategy: pay before the due date?

71. How to arrive at an appropriate 'Cash Discount Strategy' for payments?

The cash discount strategy can be one of the following three options:

a.. Pay as early as possible to get maximum possible discount

To achieve this, select the check-box '*Always max. Cash Discount*' in the company code specifications while configuring the payment program: the program applies cash discount term 1 to these open items.

b. Delay payments as much as possible, even foregoing cash discount

This is achieved by entering the discount percentage in the '*Outgoing payment with cash discount from*' field in the company code specifications of payment program configuration. Once this is done, then the payment program settles items only if the discount percentage rate entered can be reached in the current payment run. Else, payment is made when the amount is due net. If you wish to make payment as late as possible, enter 99 percent as the minimum percentage rate (during payment program configuration): now the payments are always made 'net', and you will be foregoing all the discounts.

c. A middle strategy between (a) and (b)

72. Can you pay a vendor in a currency other than the invoice currency?

With the release 4.5A, it has been made possible that you can pay to a vendor in a currency which is different from that of the transaction / invoice currency. This is achieved by entering the required currency code directly in the open item. Prior to this release, to pay in a different currency, you have to manually process the payment.

73. What is a 'Payment Block'?

A **payment block** prevents you from paying an open item of a vendor. The payment block is entered in the '*payment block*' field in (1) a vendor master record or directly in the (2) open line item.

Use the payment ***'block indicators'*** to define the '***payment block reasons***'. You may use the SAP delivered payment block indicators (**A, B, I, R** etc) or create your own. An indicator like "*" is used when you want to skip the particular account, and a blank indicator indicates that the account / item is free for payment. However, for each of these 'block indicators', you need to configure whether changes would be allowed during processing the payment proposal. Then, it is also possible that you block a payment or release a blocked one while processing the '*payment proposal*'.

You may also propose a 'payment block indicator' while defining a Terms of Payment.

74. How do you release 'Blocked invoices for payments'?

The system will ***block an invoice*** if it comes across with an item with a '***blocking reason***'. The blocking reason may be due to (1) variances, or (2) inspection related issues. When the system blocks an invoice for payment, 'payment block' field is checked by the system.

You will be using an '***invoice release transaction***' to select the blocked invoices for processing further. The 'release' of blocked invoices for payments can be handled either manually or automatically.

75. Explain Payment Medium Workbench (PMW).

The **Payment Medium Workbench (PMW)** tool helps to configure and create payment media sent by organizations to their house banks. This generic tool is to phase out the classic payment medium programs (RFFO*) as it has the following advantages:

- Better sort functions with payment advice notes
- Easier to maintain / extend, and clearer to work with than the multiple payment medium programs
- Superior control, verification of payment procedure and improved performance with mass payments (> 50,000)

The PMW is embedded in a development environment, and you can access all Workbench objects, (program objects, dictionary objects, and mapping tool objects) with just a double click.

It covers:

a. Payment media customization
   - Defining payment medium formats

     The payment medium format controls how payment orders and debit memo orders to the bank are created. The specifications of the formats serve as the basis for definition of payment medium formats. The payment medium format can be country-dependent or country-independent and is assigned to one or more payment methods.
   - Adjusting payment medium formats
   - Adjusting the 'Note to Payee'
   - Assigning payment medium format and note to payee
   - Creating, Assigning, and Transporting Selection Variants

b. *Payment media creation*
   - Creating payment media without documents in file form
     - o Output of the created data media into DME administration
   - Creation of payment advice notes
     - o Output of the created payment advice notes as letter, fax, or IDoc
   - Creation of an output log (an error log too, if necessary) for each program run

The PMW can be used by several components like FI-AP/AR, FI-TV, HR-PY, TR-CM, and TR-TM.

76. What is 'Account Assignment Category'?

The **automatic account assignment** logic takes care of posting to the correct G/L accounts for a '***stock material***' with the '***material type***' permitting inventory management, and the material master contains this information as to which G/L account needs to be updated. But, there are material line items ('***non-stock***' materials) created manually in Purchase Requisition / Purchase Order / Outline Agreement for which some one needs to decide the account assignment data, and manually enter the same in the Purchase Requisition. It is here, the ***account assignment category*** determines where to allocate the costs relating to such materials. The account assignment category helps you to define (1) the type of account assignment (Sales Order-C, Project-P, Cost Centre-K etc) and (2) which accounts are to be posted to when GR/IR is posted to.

77. What is a 'Credit Memo'?

The **credit memo** is issued by the vendor who has earlier supplied you some services or materials. The occasion is necessitated when the delivered goods are damaged or you have returned some of the goods back to the vendor. The system treats both the invoices and the credit memo in the same way, except that the postings are done with the opposite sign.

If the credit memo is for the entire invoiced quantity, the system generates the credit memo automatically. On the contrary, if credit memo relates to a portion of the invoiced quantity, you need to process the same manually in the system.

78. What are 'Special G/L Transactions'?

Special G/L transactions are not directly posted to the G/L (*reconciliation accounts*) though these are related to sub-ledger accounts like AR/AP. The transactions to these accounts are shown separately in the balance sheet. There are specific posting keys/indicators defined in the system to regulate the postings to these items. You need to specify a ***special G/L indicator*** (like, **F**-*Down Payment Request*, **A**-Down Payment) for processing such a transaction. And, the system will make use of the specially defined posting keys (09-customer debit, 19-customer credit, 29-vendor debit and 39-vendor credit) for posting these special G/L transactions.

There are three types of Special G/L transactions:

- Free Offsetting Entries (Down Payment)
- Statistical Postings (Guarantee)
- Noted Items (Down Payment Request)

A	Down payment on current assets
B	Financial assets down payment
D	Discount
E	Unchecked invoice
F	Down payment request
G	Guarantee received
H	Security deposit
I	Intangible asset down payment
M	Tangible asset down payment
O	Amortization down payment
P	Payment request
S	Check/bill of exchange
V	Stocks down payment
W	Bill of exch. (rediscountable)

Figure 3.27: Special G/L Indicators

79. Differentiate 'Free Offsetting Entry' from a 'Statistical Posting'.

Free offsetting entries postings are part of the regular postings but with a freely definable offsetting entry, and relate to the ***on-balance sheet items***. On the other hand, in a **statistical posting**, you will always be posting to the same offsetting entry, and these are all the ***off-balance sheet items***.

80. What is a 'Noted Item'?

The **noted items** are never displayed on the *Financial Statements* as they serve only as reminders of a financial obligation like outstanding payments to be made or due to us, like the '***down payment request***'. This kind of posting does not update any G/L account in the system but helps to keep track of such obligations for easy follow-up. This is also sometimes referred to as a '***memo entry***'.

It will be interesting to note that while the *Special G/L Indicator* for *Down Payment Request* is '***F***', you need to enter the indicator '***A***' as the target Special G/L indicator, while you are in the ***Down Payment Request Entry Screen***. When you post this entry, the system creates a one-sided memo entry for the customer or vendor but does not update the G/L.

81. Explain 'A/R Pledging'.

The **A/R pledging refers** to the transfer of a receivable from the previous creditor (assignor) to a new creditor (assignee). As part of financing, you can set an *accounts receivable pledging indicator* for receivables from goods and services. The pledging indicator you define in customizing is saved in the customer master record and automatically transferred to the customer line item on posting, and is displayed in the customer line item display and in the customer lists for subsequent evaluation. Please note that setting up of this pledging indicator does not trigger any process with a third party (for example, bank or credit provider).

82. Explain 'Assigning Documents to Customers'.

It is possible to assign documents that have been scanned into the system, such as business reports, newspaper articles, or graphics to each customer. However, to use the document management system, you need to have *SAP ArchiveLink* installed / activated in the system.

83. Explain vendor / customer evaluations in financial information system.

The following evaluations /analyses (Table 3-10) are possible through financial information system:

Table 3.10: Customer / Vendor Evaluations

Customer	Vendor
Currency risk	Due date break-down
DSO (Days Sales Outstanding) analysis	Overdue items
Due date break-down	Payment history
Overdue items	
Payment history	
Terms offered / taken	

The system creates drilldown lists for each evaluation, which are sorted and summarised according to freely-definable grouping criteria (such as country, company code, or group key).

The freely-definable grouping criteria in the standard system include:

- Business area
- Company code
- Country
- Credit control area (customers only)
- Credit representative group (customers only)
- Credit risk category (customers only)

However, you can use the following grouping criteria for 'due date analysis':

- Accounting clerk (customers only)
- Cash management groups
- Dunning level (customers only)
- Industries (customers only)
- Reconciliation account

Besides the above two sets of grouping criteria, you can also break-down the evaluation data according to other relevant fields like the postal code, document type etc from the secondary index and master record. However, it is not possible to use the fields from the document header or document segment for such break-down or sorting or summarization.

84. When you will use 'due date break-down' analysis for customers / vendors?

You can use the 'due **date breakdown**' evaluations to display the following for your customers / vendors:

- Sum total of the open customer or vendor items
- Total of due items
- Total of the items not yet due

It is possible that you can have the system to display the 'totals of the due items' and the 'totals of the items due in the future' according to periods as specified by you.

85. What is 'DSO' analysis?

The '**DSO (Days Sales Outstanding)**' analysis is nothing but an analysis of customer payment history, which is always made within a specific period: it is possible to select monthly values for this analysis. This analysis provides general information about the number of days (DSO days) a customer takes to pay an invoice. Using the drill-down feature of the analysis you can display:

- *Balance* (the average debts outstanding - open customer items - at the end of the selected period)
- *Average sales* per period
- *DSO days* (calculated by using the formula: balance/sales per period x 30)

86. What you can do before posting a document in A/R & A/P?

When you have completed entering the line items in a document, and before posting tat document, you can:

- ***Add additional information***: you can enter additional details in automatically generated line items (such as project or cost center) if supplementary account assignment is defined for the G/L account, or if it is required by the field status definition.
- ***Additional account assignment***. If you have called up the 'Post' function and requested individual, automatically generated items using the field status of the G/L account to which they belong, or using the master record of an additional account assignment, the system automatically branches to the document overview. You will notice that the lines that are to be changed are highlighted.
- ***Change fields in vendor / customer (or G/L) line items***. However, note that you will not be able to change the entries in the fields 'Pstky' and 'Account'.
- ***Display the document*** overview showing the document header and all items you have just entered. It is possible to add a *reference text* to the header. From the overview, you can also enter more line items, call up the line items already entered in order to process them, and delete line items.

87. What are all the options for calculating interest on customer / vendor accounts?

The **interest calculation**, in SAP, is controlled by settings made in the *interest indicator* (assign an interest indicator to the master records of the customer / vendor accounts for which you want to calculate interest, and also make other settings for each interest calculation). The interest is calculated using the *debit interest rate* defined for the interest indicator in the system. The *credit interest rates* are used when interest is being calculated on items paid prior to their due date.

SAP provides you with the several options for calculating interest on customer / vendor accounts (Table 3-11).

Table 3.11: Interest Calculation Options for Customer / Vendor Accounts

To calculate	Follow the Menu path	And, select	Remarks
Interest for cleared items and post the interest	*A/P or A/R > Periodic Processing > Interest Calculation > Arrears Interest >*	*'Without Open Items'*	The system calculates interest as of the due date for net payment.
Interest for open and cleared items and post the interest		*'With Open Items'*	The system calculates interest as of the upper limit date of the last interest run
Interest for open and/or cleared items but do not want to post the interest		*'Without Postings'*	The system calculates interest as of the due date for net payment

		'Custom Selections'	If you want to make a selection that differs from the options mentioned above

88. Explain fields relevant for arrear interest calculation, in customer / vendor master.

The following are the two fields (in the company code data area) of customer / vendor master records that are relevant for the calculation of interest on arrears:

- ***'Interest indicator'***: the interest program that calculates interest on arrears using the interest indicator specified in the customer master record (the most important specifications – like rules determining which items are selected for interest calculation and how the interest is calculated - for the interest calculation run are stored under the interest indicator). The interest indicator must be assigned to the interest calculation type 'Item interest calculation'. If an account is to be included in the interest calculation run, an interest indicator for interest on arrears must be specified in the master record.
- ***Last key date***: after each interest calculation run, the program enters the upper limit of the calculation period into this field by batch input. This is the date you have specified for the calculation run.

4

Bank Accounting (FI-BL)

1. Explain the features of 'Bank Accounting' in SAP.

Bank accounting, a sub-module under Financial Accounting (FI), helps to handle accounting transactions that you process with your bank. It includes:

- Management of bank master data (Bank Directory)
- Cash balance management (Check / Bill of Exchange management)
- Creation and processing of incoming and outgoing payments

Using bank accounting, it is possible to freely define all country-specific characteristics, such as the specifications for manual and electronic payment procedures, payment forms, or data media.

2. What is a 'Bank Directory'?

SAP stores the master data (details like bank key, bank name, bank country, bank accounts, bank address etc) relating to the banks in **bank directory** (Table: BNKA). The bank directory must contain the master data for all the banks that you require for payment transactions with your business partners. This includes your banks and the banks of your business partners.

3. How to create a 'Bank Directory'?

There are two ways with which you can create a bank directory:

- **Automatically**

  Obtain the national bank directory on a data medium (ASCII file) from a banking organization in your country, and import the bank directory into the SAP system using the program RFBVALL_0. This is currently possible for countries like Austria, Germany, Spain, Italy, Canada, Great Britain, South Africa, Switzerland and Denmark. However, you can use the same program to import other file formats for other countries. When you resort to create the bank directory through this method, note that you should update the bank directory regularly.

  You may use the IMG Menu Path: *SAP Customizing Implementation Guide >*

Cross-Application Components > Bank Directory > Bank Directory Data Transfer > Transfer Bank Directory Data - Country-Specific

Transaction Code
BAUP

Country-specific transfer of bank data

Country Selection

Bank Country: US
Format: 1

File Path

◉ Presentation Server
○ Application Server
File Name and Path: C:\Documents and Sett
Code Page:

General Selections

Maximum Number of Records: 99999
☐ Update Run
☑ Set Deletion Flag
☑ Detail List
☑ Display Changed Banks Only
Layout: 1SAP

Figure 4.1: Automatic Creation of Bank Directory (Country-Specific)

For *international bank data*, you will import a bank directory file that you might have created using the 'BIC Database Plus' into the SAP system, using the program RFBVBIC_0. This file can contain data from the banks of one country or of several countries. The following details are imported into SAP:

- Bank key (complete) in field BNKA-BANKL
- Bank name (first 60 bytes) in field BNKA-BANKA
- Bank number (complete) in field BNKA-BNKLZ and BNKA-BANKL, if the bank number is selected as the bank key.
- Branch (first 40 bytes) in field BNKA-BRNCH, if contained in the input file.
- City (first 27 bytes) + postal code (8 bytes) in field BNKA-ORT01, if the postal code has no more than 8 characters; in all other cases, only the city (first 35 bytes) is transferred.
- S.W.I.F.T. (complete) in field BNKA-SWIFT and BNKA-BANKL, if the S.W.I.F.T. code is selected as the bank key.
- Street (first 35 bytes) in field BNKA-STRAS

Transaction Code
BIC

- **Manually**

  You may use the following Menu Path to create the bank master data: *SAP Easy Access: SAP menu > Financial Accounting > Banks > Bank Master Record > Create*.

Transaction Code
FI01

As regards the master data for the business partners' banks are concerned, you can enter these when you are entering or editing the master data for the business partners: when you are entering customer or vendor master data, or entering a document in a one-time customer account, the system automatically branches to bank directory editing if you enter bank details that do not exist in the directory.

4. What is a 'House Bank'?

House bank is the bank (or financial institution) in which the Company Code in question keeps its money and does the transactions from there on. A house bank in SAP is identified by a 5-character alphanumeric code. You can have any number of house banks for your Company Code, and the details of all these house banks are available in the '**bank directory**'. The picture below depicts how the houses banks are modelled within a bank directory in SAP:

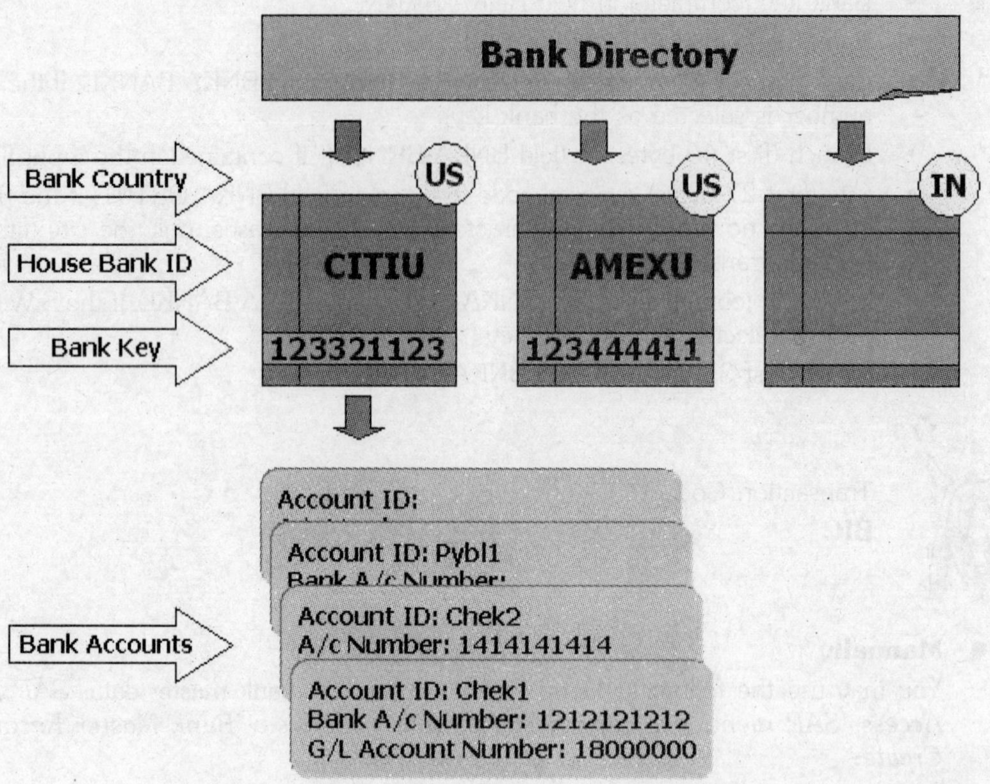

Figure 4.2: House Banks in Bank Directory

- Each 'house bank', in the system, is associated with a ***country key*** (US, IN etc) representing the country where the bank is located, and a unique country specific code called '*bank key*'. The system makes use of both the '*country key*' and the '*bank key*' to identify a '*house bank*'.

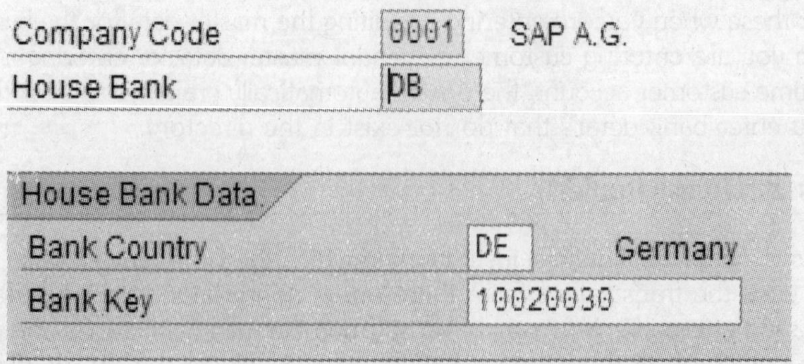

Figure 4.3: House Bank ID (DB), Country and Bank Key

- For each of the '*house banks*', you can maintain more than one bank account; each such account is identified by an ***account ID*** viz., Chek1, Chek2, Pybl1 etc. Here 'Chek1' may denote Checking account 1, 'Pybl1' may denote Payables account 1 and so on. You may name the accounts in such a way that it is comprehensible easily. The 'Account ID' is referenced in the *customer / vendor master record* and the same is used in the *payment program* by the system.

Company Code 0001

Bank Accounts

House Bank	Account ID	Bank acct	Text
DB	GIRO	552096	Current account (Bank 1)
DB	US$	108972	Foreign exchange account for USD (Bank 1)
DB	WERTP	036393060	Account for securities (Bank 1)

Figure 4.4: Bank Accounts of a House Bank (DB)

- For each of this '*account ID*' you will also specify the ***bank account number*** (maximum length of this identifier is 18 characters). You may name this in such a way that it is also comprehensible easily.
- For each 'bank account number' so defined in the 'house bank', you need to create a G/L account master record, and while doing so you will incorporate the 'house bank id' and the 'account id' in that G/L master record.

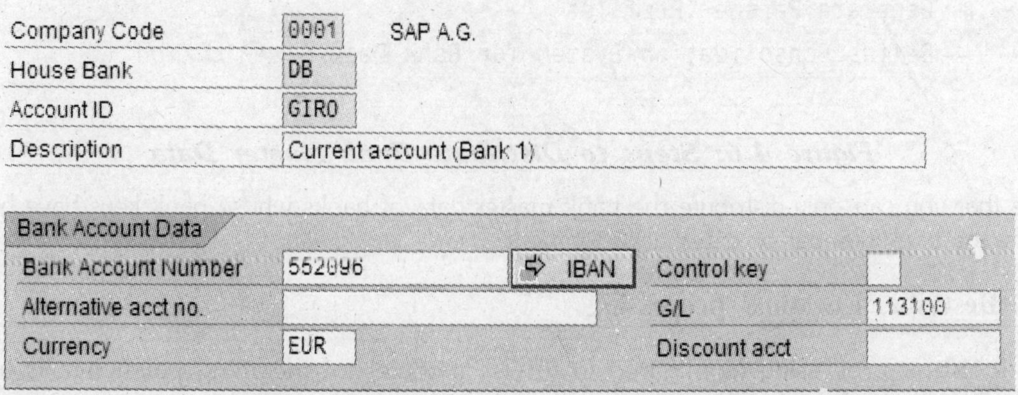
Company Code 0001 SAP A.G.
House Bank DB
Account ID GIRO
Description Current account (Bank 1)

Bank Account Data
Bank Account Number 552096 IBAN
Control key
Alternative acct no.
G/L 113100
Currency EUR
Discount acct

Figure 4.5: Bank A/c Number and G/L Account Number of a House Bank (DB)

Transaction Code
FI12

5. How to distribute the Bank Master Data?

If you wish to process bank master data and the related company addresses in any of the systems of an SAP system group, then the ALE business process allows for all changes to bank master data to be made via a consolidation system. The local systems send all the changes to the consolidation system, and the consolidation system sends the changes back to all the local systems. The banks can also be processed in the consolidation system. The address from the central address management is distributed together with the bank. The address data from central address management must be processed before the banks in the target system.

You need to determine a system, within the system group, as the *consolidation system* wherein you will make all the cross-system settings. Then you need to (a) define all the systems involved in the distribution (logical system settings), (b) maintain the distribution model via 'Add BAPI' and (c) generate the partner profiles to determine the point at which the data should be exchanged between the systems.

Name of Activity
Make Settings for Logical Systems
Maintain Distribution Model
Generate Partner Profiles
Define Consolidation System for Bank Data Distribution

Figure 4.6: Steps to Distribute Bank Master Data

Note that you can only distribute the bank master data of banks whose bank keys have been set by the bank number or external assignment.

6. Describe 'Lockbox' processing.

The **lockbox** processing (configured in FR-TR module), of incoming payments, is used predominantly in the US. Here, the bank receives the checks from customers as incoming payment, creates payment advice for each of these customer check payments and informs the payee about the payment, in BAI file format. This lockbox file is sent to the payee who imports the details into the system using this electronic file. The system updates the payments into the G/L by way of '*batch input*' processing.

7. What are the important 'Control Parameters' for Lockbox processing?

At present, only the procedure 'LOCKBOX' is supported by SAP, as the control data for lockbox processing. The payment information provided in the bank data file will create a payment advice per check. This payment advice will be used by the lockbox procedure to clear sub-ledger open items. This data is needed for importing lockbox files (only BAI and BAI2 file formats are supported by SAP) sent by banks:

- **BAI Record Format**

  Specify the length of the document numbers (10 in the standard SAP System) and the number of document numbers in record types 6 and 4 of the BAI file. Your bank must agree on this format information.

Processing procedure for check payment	LOCKBOX
Record format	BAI

Record format (not for BAI2 format)

Document number length	10
Num. of doc. numbers in type 6	3
Num. of doc. numbers in type 4	6

Postings

☑	G/L account postings	G/L account posting type	1
☑	Incoming customer payments	Partial Payments	☐
☐	Insert bank details		

Figure 4.7: BAI Record Format

- **BAI2 Record Format**

  It is not necessary to specify the length of the document or the number of document numbers in record types 6 and 4. This is because BAI2 file is designed that each document number is on a different record type 4 with its corresponding payment and deduction amounts. Your bank must agree on this format information.

Processing procedure for check payment	LOCKBOX
Record format	BAI2

Record format (not for BAI2 format)

Document number length	
Num. of doc. numbers in type 6	
Num. of doc. numbers in type 4	

Postings

☑ G/L account postings	G/L account posting type	1
☑ Incoming customer payments	Partial Payments	☐
☑ Insert bank details	ADDBNKDETAIL	

Figure 4.8: BAI2 Record Format

Transaction Code
OBAY

- **Posting Functions (Batch Input Sessions)**
  Specify which postings the system creates (G/L cash postings and/or customer cash application). It is recommended that both choices are selected if you are using the G/L and A/R modules. For the G/L, you can decide whether to post one aggregate amount to the incoming cash account or one line per check. This depends on your reconciliation with the bank. In addition, you can choose to create and name a batch input session to insert any missing or new customer bank details into the customer master records (this can only be done if the system identifies a valid document number).

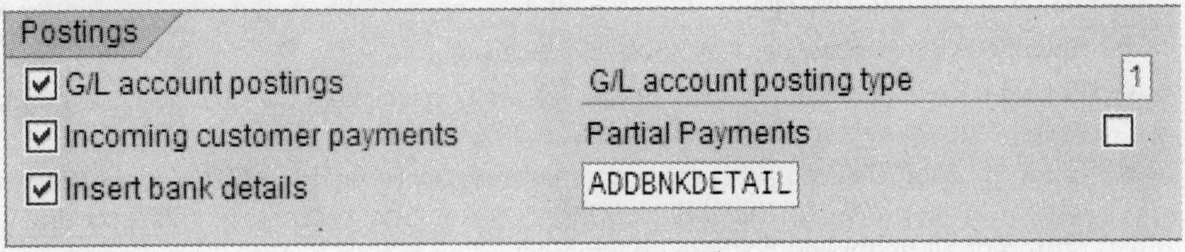

Postings

☑ G/L account postings — G/L account posting type: 1

☑ Incoming customer payments — Partial Payments: ☐

☑ Insert bank details — ADDBNKDETAIL

Figure 4.9: Posting Functions

8. What if the file formats are not exactly the same as that of BAI & BAI2?

While the BAI and BAI2 formats are supposedly standard, experience has shown that they can vary by bank and many SAP clients have contracted for a customized format. What is required is that the format received will need to be mapped to reconcile with the SAP delivered data dictionary layout (Tables FLB01, FLB05, FLB06, etc.) to ensure proper processing.

If the format does not reconcile and the user does not want to have the bank change the format, SAP recommends that a user-written ABAP be used to reformat the file or alternatively the SAP data dictionary can be modified (this is a repair that will need to be re-applied in future releases).

9. How the Lockbox program identifies the customer?

The **lockbox** program first attempts to identify the customer with unique bank information in the customer master record matching to MICR information on the check, so maintenance of unique customer MICR information is important to ensure success. If there is more than one customer with the same MICR bank and account, then the program cannot apply the check to an account. This situation usually means that either the same customer has been set up twice, or maybe what should have been only Ship-to or Sold-to customers for the same Payer have actually been set up as separate Payers. Alternatively, it may be necessary to set up a relationship where one customer is identified as the main Payer and has MICR info, and the related customers do not have MICR info but instead have the main Payers customer number in the Alternate Payer field of the customer master record.

10. How you will define the 'Posting Data' for a Lockbox?

You need to store information needed to process particular lockbox data and generate postings. The '*Destination*' and '*Origin*' are routing information and defined by your bank. For every unique destination/origin, posting information is needed to create the following postings:

- **G/L posting**

  Debit bank account (incoming checks) and credit payment clearing account

- **A/R posting**

  Debit payment clearing account and credit customer account

You need to complete the following:

- Specify a company code that holds the lockbox
- Enter in 'Bank account number' - Bank (clearing) acct - field the G/L account number which corresponds to the lockbox (clearing) bank account
- Enter in 'Bank clearing acct' - Payment clearing acct - field the G/L account number which corresponds to the AR clearing account (the balance in this account will represent all unapplied (lockbox) payments)
- Specify the document types and posting keys for these postings

Destination	DEST1
Origin	ORIG1

Lockbox bank data

Company Code	0001
House Bank	DEBA
Account ID	GIRO
Bank (G/L) acct	113100
Bank clear.acct(A/R)	113109

Posting parameters

Bank pstng doc. type	SA
Cust pstng doc. type	DZ
Pstng key: debit G/L	40
Pstng key:credit G/L	50
Post key:credit cust	15

Figure 4.10: Posting Data for Lockbox

Transaction Code
OBAX

11. How to define a 'Lockbox' for your House Bank?

By defining **lockbox** accounts at the house banks, you can optimize the payment transactions: on the outgoing invoice you can inform your customer of the lockbox to which payment is to be made. You may define the lockbox accounts using the following Menu Path: '*SAP Customizing Implementation Guide > Financial Accounting (New) > Bank Accounting > Bank Accounts > Define Lockboxes for House Banks*'.

- Specify your lockbox links (company code; key of the lockbox to which the customer is to pay; house bank ID; lockbox number at your house bank)
- For customer master data, you can determine to which lockbox number the customer is to pay in the application menu ("Payment Transactions / Company code data").
- Include two new fields in table VBDKRZ, for example, ZZBANK for the house bank ID at which you have the lockbox, and ZZLOCK for the lockbox number. Note that the names of these fields must begin with "ZZ" since SAP has left these name ranges free for new, user-defined fields.
- The user interface for the outgoing invoice needs to be expanded. To do this, you have to enhance program V05NZZEN as follows:

```
TABLES: KNB1, T049L.
SELECT SINGLE * FROM KNB1 WHERE KUNNR = VBDKR-KUNRG
   AND BUKRS = VBRK-BUKRS.
SELECT SINGLE * FROM T049L WHERE BUKRS = VBRK-BUKRS AND
LOCKB = KNB1-LOCKB.
VBDKR-ZZLOCK = T049L-LCKNR.
VBDKR-ZZBANK = T049L-HBKID.
```

- Include the new fields VBDKR-ZZBANK (key of the house bank at which you have the lockbox) and VBDKR-ZZLOCK (lockbox number) in the form for the customer invoices (SD application).

Transaction Code
OB10

12. What is 'IBAN'?

IBAN (International Bank Account Number) is a standardized, uniform representation of complete bank details in accordance with the European Committee for Banking Standards (ECBS). A constant IBAN length has been stipulated for each country. An IBAN is a series of a maximum of 34 alphanumeric characters, and is made up of a combination of the following elements:

- The bank country key (ISO-Code)
- Two check digits
- Country-specific account number (comprises, for example the bank number and account number in Germany, or the bank number, account number and control key in France)

Bank Account Data

Bank Account Number	552096	⇨ IBAN	Control key	
Alternative acct no.			G/L	113100
Currency	EUR		Discount acct	

Figure 4.11: IBAN in Bank Master Data

13. How to configure the 'Checks for Bank Master Data'?

You can specify check rules for country-specific definitions. The rules apply to the ***bank number*** ('1' in Figure 4.12), or the ***bank key and bank account number*** ('2' in the screen-shot). For each country key, enter the length of the bank number and bank account number. The check rule determines whether:

- The entry is numeric or alphanumeric
- The length specified is only a maximum length, or whether this must be strictly adhered to
- Gaps are permitted in the bank account number or bank number

The system always carries out these formal checks. You can also select ***additional special checks*** ('3' in Figure 4.12) to avoid input errors. These include, for example:

- Postal check account number in Germany and Switzerland
- Bank account number in Belgium and the Netherlands
- Bank number and bank account number in France

You may configure the country-specific checks using the following Menu Path: '*SAP Customizing Implementation Guide > SAP NetWeaver > General Settings > Set Countries > Set Country-Specific Checks*'.

Transaction Code
OY17

Country Key US USA

Key for the bank directory

Bank Key 1 Bank number **1**

Formal checks

	Length	Checking rule	
Postal code length	10	1	Maximum value length, without gaps
Bank account number	17	6	Maximum value length, numerical
Bank number length	9	6	Maximum value length, numerical
Post bank acct no.	10	6	Maximum value length, numerical
Tax Number 1	11	5	Maximum value length
Tax Number 2	10	5	Maximum value length
VAT registration no.			
Length of Bank Key			

2

Further checks

☑ Bank data	☑ Postal code req. entry **3**	☐ City file active
☐ Other data	☐ P.O.box code req. entry	☐ Street postcode

Figure 4.12: Country-Specific Checks for Bank Master Data

14. What is a 'Repetitive Code' in Bank Accounting?

Repetitive codes are the payment transfer data that remains unchanged, and are used to simplify frequently recurring payments with the same payment details. The data include the sender bank, sender account, recipient bank, recipient account, payment method, and currency. Maintenance of a repetitive code reduces the administrative work required for frequently recurring payments with the same payment details. The only details that are different for each payment are the amount and the note to payee. In addition, in the USA, a company can agree a repetitive code with its house bank. The bank then only needs the repetitive code, the amount, and (if required) the note to payee in order to process a payment order.

Transaction Code
OT81

Repetitive Code: Rep-001

Processing Bank Data

Paying CoCd	0001	SAP A.G.
House Bank	DEBA	
Account ID	GIRO	Current Account

Business Partner

Bus.Partner	2000017		
Bank details	0001	Bank Country	
Bank Account		Bank Key	
Reference		Control key	
Account holder			

Posting Data

TargetCoCd	0001 SAP A.G.	G/L	172110

Payment Information

Bank chain ID		Bnk Chain	
Pymt Method	T	Currency	EUR

Figure 4.13: Repetitive Code in Bank Accounting

15. What is an 'Intermediate Bank'?

Intermediate banks are used, in SAP, in addition to the 'house banks' and 'partners' banks', for making or receiving payments from business partners abroad. The payment processing, involving an intermediate bank, makes use of the ***'bank chain'*** which may consists of a house bank, a partner bank and an intermediate bank.

16. What is a 'Bank Chain'?

Before SAP brought in 'bank chain' functionality, when making a payment to a business partner abroad, you had to specify your house bank and the business partner's bank when processing payments. These two banks represented the start and end of the payment cycle and it was down to the house bank to determine via which bank(s) the payment should be made. Using the **bank chain** function (for example via the correspondence banks of the house bank, the recipient bank, or the intermediary banks), you can now specify this bank chain yourself, leading to faster payment transaction processing and considerable cost savings through reduced bank charges. SAP allows you to define up to three banks, in a bank chain. To use the bank chain function, you must also implement the function Automatic Payments in either the Financial Accounting (FI) or the Treasury (TR) application component.

17. How the 'Bank Chain' is made use of during a 'Payment Run'?

For each payment, the payment program can determine a combination of intermediary banks that you previously defined. The order of the banks in the bank chain can depend on the following factors:

- Currency
- Customer's bank details
- House bank
- Payment method supplement
- Treasury business partner's bank details
- Vendor's bank details

These factors are represented in the SAP system by means of ***scenarios for bank chain*** determination that you define in Customizing for Bank Accounting.

- Copy one of the scenarios that are delivered in the standard system or define a new scenario

Scenario	Scenario description	Gen.Search	Rec.Search
0001	NO BANK CHAIN DETERMINATION	☐	☐
0002	SENDER BANK ORIENTED	☐	☑
0003	RECEIVER BANK ORIENTED	☑	☑
0004	RECEIVER ORIENTED	☐	☑

Figure 4.14: Scenario for Bank Chain

- Activate the scenario
- If you want payments to be made via a bank chain and independently of a business partner's bank details, define a general bank chain

Transaction Code
FIBC

If you carry out a payment run (whether for open items or for payment requests from Treasury or Cash Management) the system determines the bank chain according to your Customizing settings and those you made in the master data. If, during payment proposal editing, you have changed an entry (house bank or partner bank for example) that is relevant to bank chain determination, the system re-determines the bank chain, which is then displayed on screen. The system is only able to determine the bank chain if a payment method is used for which a bank chain is needed (no bank chain is determined for payments by check for example). When processing payments, you can use program RFZALI20 to create a payment list and an exception list. The payment list contains a summary of all payments and line items. The exceptions list contains blocked line items and open items that the payment program did not propose for payment. In the standard system, the bank chain in not included on either list. The bank chains are transferred each time a payment medium is created.

18. How you will handle 'Cashed Checks'?

If you receive data on **cashed checks** electronically from your bank you can use program RFEBCK00 to import the data into the SAP System, after having converted it to SAP format. This program imports the information on cashed checks delivered by the bank and generates the clearing entries (debit outgoing checks account, credit bank account). It also marks as "paid" the checks in the check register that could be posted. The clearing entries can be placed in a batch input session (batch input mode) or be posted immediately (call transaction mode). Since there is no standard for data on cashed checks in the USA and most other countries, a pre-processing program is needed to convert the bank format to the entry format of this program.

19. What is 'Electronic Check Deposit'?

Electronic check deposit enables you to process data supplied by an external entry system (check reader). However, the data must be delivered in a format defined by SAP, to process the data. The data is transferred from a file to the bank data buffer. Some of the fields have to be entered manually during this process. If the external entry system does not supply the entries for these fields, you must enter them as parameters when you run the program (optional entries for the check deposit list). To avoid importing the same file several times, you can have the external entry system uniquely indicate the file, and then have the SAP System check this indicator.

If data is complete, the electronic check deposit can also create the batch input session directly. If the transfer is incomplete, you can access manual check deposit for post-processing the check deposit list you entered. You may use this as an entry function, and then complete and post individual data with the ***manual check deposit***.

Two batch input sessions are created to post the check deposits:

- One session for bank account postings
- One session for sub-ledger postings

Using the appropriate parameter, you can specify whether the system should create both sessions or only the session for bank postings first. If you want to use the manual transaction for post-processing the data, you cannot create any sessions. Further processing is then carried out by using the manual transaction. You either name the sessions when importing the data or have the program name the sessions with the house bank ID and account ID.

20. What is 'Manual Check Deposit'?

This function '**manual check deposit**' is used to enter checks you receive. After the input is complete, you can access the additional functions to further process the entered checks. On the entry screen, the system will display different fields for each account assignment variant you choose. Depending on the number of account assignment fields in a variant, up to three lines are available for entering a memo record. You can change the account assignment variant at any time during processing. If you have used more account assignment fields than are available in the current variant, the system will display this information in an additional field. You can, for example, enter several document numbers and different invoice amounts for one memo record. This is useful if a customer pays several invoices with one check. The system highlights the account assignment field when you have entered several values in it.

Transaction Code
FF68

22. What is the main function of an 'Electronic Bank Statement (EBS)'?

The **electronic account statement** (EBS) is used to automatically assign payments (by check, bank transfer etc) received by/made from house bank accounts to the appropriate open items (which items have already been posted in the system).

22. What information is made available in an 'Electronic Bank Statement (EBS)'?

The electronic bank statement contains the following information:

- Header data; general information on the house bank (bank number and account number, account currency, statement number, and statement date)
- Line item data: list of individual business transactions that were posted to the account (line items)

23. What are the formats of 'Electronic Bank Statement (EBS)'?

There are three formats available at present:

- **MultiCash format**

  This format is created from the account statement data received from the banks (usually SWIFT MT940) using the BCS (Banking Communication Standard) software.

Standard for all banks, it can be easily run using a spreadsheet program or a word processing program. It consists of two files in format AUSZUG.TXT and UMSATZ.TXT. The AUSZUG.TXT contains the header information for the account statements, UMSATZ.TXT the item information. This format allows you to import data from several account statements at the same time, including those from different banks.

- **Swift MT940**

  SWIFT MT940 should only be used in cases where it is not possible to use the MultiCash format. This format is available in two variants: with or without structured field 86.

- **DTAUS format**

  SAP does not recommend this format unless there are some valid and compelling reasons from the business side to go in for this.

  The DTAUS format originated in the mainframe era and has certain disadvantages:

  - Individual data records are not separated by the special character denoting a "new line" (Carriage-Return Line-Feed <CR><LF>) and this renders the search for errors extremely difficult in cases where the bank has transmitted defective files.
  - Even if a single byte is missing from the file, the whole file is rendered unreadable, since every subsequent data record is displaced by one byte

  This format only contains a single business transaction (for example, cash receipt) per file and therefore only represents a fraction of the items processed in an account. Using the DTAUS format usually entails importing more than one file into the system. In addition, certain business transactions (that are not supported by this format) may need to be posted manually. Moreover, the header record of DTAUS files does not contain any reference to the statement from which the items originated (such as statement date or number). This means that the import program cannot carry out the usual checks, such as those which prevent the same items being imported more than once, or which check that imported data is complete.

24. What are the obstacles in using EBS? How you can overcome these?

There are two main obstacles in customizing the electronic account statement:

- Creating the files UMSATZ.TXT (header data) and AUSZUG.TXT (line items) is a complex process. Experience has shown that many implementation errors arise from incorrect creation (format errors) of these files. Using actual files from the bank is also difficult as the files are usually very big.
- The open items to be found and cleared using the electronic account statement must usually be entered into the (test) system manually and with correct clearing information. This information must also exist in the correct fields in the individual line items in the UMSATZ.TXT file (for example in the note to payee fields).

You may however overcome these obstacles by using the program RFEBKATX to create open items in a company code and the related (MULTICASH) account statement files for a house bank account. You can, then, import this directly using program RFEBKA00, and test both your customizing settings and the general functions provided by program RFEBKA00.

25. What is an 'External Transaction' in EBS?

An **external transaction** (or *business transaction code*) is a bank-specific code for a business transaction. Issued by the bank in the electronic bank statement, each of the external transaction codes involves a different type of payment, and SAP system requires this code in order to identify the business transaction: it converts these bank-defined codes into its own system-internal transaction codes (known as posting rules), which in turn trigger certain specific posting transactions in the system

Some examples of the external transaction code (ETC) are (Table 4-1):

Table 4.1: External Transaction Codes in Bank Accounting

ETC	Business Transaction	ETC	Business Transaction
020	Transfer Order	52	Recurring Entry Credit Memo
051	Transfer Credit memo	206	Foreign Bank Transfer

26. What is a 'Posting Rule' EBS?

To configure the electronic account statement, all the external transactions need to be assigned to a **posting rule** to enable the system to determine which bank or sub-ledger accounts these transactions are to be posted to. The posting rules are represented in the system by a non-bank-specific code (for example, 0001 for debit memos). The posting rules are required to rationalize postings so that you do not duplicate the postings on the SAP side. In the illustration below, there are two external transactions both of which requiring the same posting in your accounts. Accordingly, you just need to assign them to a single posting rule (say, 001 – debit memo).

ETC	Business Transaction	ETC	Business Transaction
004	Direct Debit by Debit Memo	005	Collection Authorization by Debit Memo

27. What is the significance of '+/-' signs in posting rules in EBS?

'+/-' signs are entered in customizing when assigning external transactions to posting rules. The '+' sign represents incoming payments and the '–' sign represents outgoing payments. A different posting rule can apply to the same external transaction depending on the '+/-' sign.

28. What is a 'Transaction Type' in EBS?

The **transaction types** are used to group together banks providing the same external transaction codes in the electronic bank statement. By doing this it is not necessary that you assign the external transaction codes of the banks to internal SAP posting rules for every individual bank but make this assignment just once per transaction type. Once a transaction type is defined, you need to assign each of your house banks to a transaction type.

29. What is a 'Posting Area' in EBS configuration?

There are two posting areas (area 1 & area 2) which you need take note when you configure the electronic bank statement. Depending on the external transaction code and your customizing settings, a single line item from an electronic account statement can automatically trigger up to two posting transactions:

- Area 1 postings are made to bank or G/L·accounts
- Area 2 posting are made to sub-ledger accounts (these are additional postings)

30. How do you configure the 'Global Settings' for EBS?

The following are the recommended sequence of configuring the global settings you need to make in customizing, for electronic bank statement:

a. Define transaction types

Group together all banks that use the same external transaction code for certain business transactions under the same transaction type.

Trans. type	Name
BAI	BAI format for USA Banks
BANCOESP	Banco Español
BE	Belgium : CODA
BRADESCO	Brazil: Banco Bradesco

Figure 4.15: Create Transaction Types

b. Assign bank (accounts) to transaction types

Assign each of your bank accounts to a transaction type. You can specify a worklist of G/L accounts. This enables you to search several bank sub-accounts for open items that the system could not clear during posting of the account statement when you post-process the account statement. If you select the field "No Automatic Clearing", an open item remains, even if the amount of the open item agrees with that in the account statement.

Assign Bank Accounts to Transaction Types											
Bank Key	Bank Account	Tran	Cur	P	Su	Co	C	Wor	N	D	D
075000022	068173602	BAI		ZB	☐	1200			☐		
075000022	086646035	BAI		ZB	☐	1310			☐		
075000022	171379044	BAI		ZB	☐	1100			☐		
075000022	209909271	BAI		ZB	☐	1100			☐		

Figure 4.16: Assign Bank Accounts to Transaction Types

c. Create keys for posting rules

Assign posting rules to possible transactions in account statement file. A list of assignments where one external transaction code is assigned to one posting rule is called a transaction type.

Posting rule	Text
0001	Cash inflow via interim account
0002	Check credit memo through bank
0003	Check deposit via interim account
0004	Direct check deposit

Figure 4.17: Create Keys for Posting Rules

Define Posting Rules											
Posti	Pos	Pos	S	Acct (Debit)	Compr	Posting	Sp	Acct (Credit)	Compr	Doc	Po
0001	1	40		BANK	☐	50		GELDEINGANG	☐	SA	1
0001	2	40		GELDEINGANG	☐				☐	DZ	8
0002	1	40		BANK	☐	50		SCHECKEINGA	☐	SA	1
0003	1	40		SCHECKEINGANG	☐	50		SCHECKVERRE	☐	SA	1
0003	2	40		SCHECKVERRECHNG	☐				☐	DZ	8
0004	2	40		SCHECKEINGANG	☐				☐	DZ	8
0005	1			SCHECKAUSGANG	☐	50		BANK	☐	SA	4

Figure 4.18: Define Posting Rules

d. Assign external transaction types to posting rules

You assign (external) business transaction codes to an (internal) posting rule. This means that the same posting specifications can be used for different business transaction codes.

Trans. type	BE
Name	Belgium : CODA

Assign External Transaction Types to Posting Rules

External transaction	+/- sign	Posting rule	Interpretation Algorithm
0101000	-	BE02	001: Standard algorithm
0103000	-	BE02	000: No interpretation
0105000	-	BE09	001: Standard algorithm

Figure 4.19: Assign External Transaction Types to Posting Rules

e. Define posting rules

You need to complete the following activities, here:

i. *Create the account symbols for the required posting transactions*

Specify G/L accounts (such as bank, cash receipt, outgoing checks) to which postings are to be made from account statement. You assign account symbols to the G/L account numbers. These are required for the posting rules in step 'assign accounts to account symbols'.

Create Account Symbols

Account	Text
<ASSE	Cash on hand
<REDITORENÜBERW	Vendor transfer
<UNDENUEBERWEI.	Customer transfer
<UNDENÜBERWEISU	Customer transfer

Figure 4.20: Create Account Symbols

ii. Define account determination rules for each of the account symbols.

Define postings to be triggered by possible transactions in the account statement (such as bank transfer, debit memo). In the '*posting specifications debit -> credit*' that you define here, use the account symbols from the previous step, not the G/L account numbers. This prevents similar posting rules being defined several times, the only difference between them being the accounts to which postings are made.

Chart of Accts INT Sample chart of accounts

Assign Accounts to Account Symbol

Act Symbol	Acct Mod.	Currency	G/L acct	Acct Symb. Desc.
BANK	+	+	++++++++++	Bank account number
GEBÜHREN	+	+	479000	Charges
GELDAUSGANG	+	+	+++++++++2	Cash disbursement
GELDEINGANG	+	+	+++++++++9	Cash Receipt Account

Figure 4.21: Assign Accounts to Account Symbols

You create posting specifications for postings to G/L or bank accounts (posting area 1) and sub-ledger postings (posting area 2) for those of the posting transactions you choose.

31. Describe the 'Posting / Clearing' flow in EBS.

Consider that you have already imported the EBS into your SAP System. Imagine that one of your customers have paid an open invoice by bank transfer (to your house bank account):

a. The transaction triggers 2-level posting in your system
   i. Bank posting (cash receipt is posted to a clearing account such as a cash receipt account)
   ii. Sub-ledger posting (system locates the customer and clears the item from this account)
b. However, to complete this, the system will look for the following information from the statement:
   i. The business transaction (for example, transfer by credit memo) must be identified. The system must then apply a rule to determine how that business transaction is posted in the system (account determination).
   ii. Clearing information must be found (document numbers for example) so that the customer open items can be cleared.
c. The system will look for the above information in the following sequence:
   i. It finds the transaction type in the customizing table using the bank key (say, 075000022) and the bank account (say, 068173602)
   ii. It determines the posting rule key in the customizing table from the transaction type and the external transaction code/bank's business transaction code
   iii. From the posting rule key, it determines the posting specifications and the account determination rules that you defined in the configuration of the electronic account statement

d. Now the system proceeds to clear the customer open item, and this is accomplished as detailed below:

   The system finds the necessary information for this in the note to payee lines in the statement. Using the document number or the reference document number, the system finds and clears the document. The document number or the reference document number is found for the note to payee information using "interpretation algorithms".

If the entire flow, as detailed above, is successful then the system posts the data in the system. Though the entire process should normally be error-free, there can be situations where post-processing (Transaction Code **FEBAN**) manual intervention would be required to correct errors, if any.

32. What is a 'Currency Class'?

If you import bank statements containing currency keys that are different from the ISO currency keys which SAP delivers with its standard system, then you will require the **currency classes**. It is possible that you can combine alternative currency keys in a single currency class. Then, the alternative currency keys within a currency class are assigned to the SAP currency key. This assignment is required so that the electronic bank statement program can process the currency keys transmitted by your house bank and customers.

Transaction Code
OT74

33. Why Planning Types are to be assigned to certain transactions?

You need to assign **planning types** to certain transactions made in the bank account, so as to determine the bank accounts for which cash management payment advices are generated by certain information from the bank (If a planning type is not assigned for certain cases, an advice note is not created). This type of account statement can currently be processed only when you use the American BAI format or IDoc interfaces (logical message FINSTA - document type ACP). Note that this activity is necessary only when you use account statements from the present day that update cash management and forecast, but do not update accounting. When assigned, the system can generate a cash management payment advice for the following information:

a. Adjustment amounts relating to check presentation amounts from the previous day
b. Current account balance
c. Total of first debit of checks presented on that day (checks within the state)
d. Total of second debit of checks presented on that day (checks outside the state)

34. What is a 'Payment Request'?

A document for generating payment media, **payment requests** can be generated automatically when payments that are due are posted. They are subsequently settled individually or collectively using the Treasury payment program.

5

Asset Accounting (FI-AA)

1. Explain 'Asset Accounting' (FI-AA).

The **Asset Accounting (FI-AA)** sub-module, in SAP, manages a company's fixed assets, right from the acquisition to retirement/scrapping. All the accounting transactions relating to

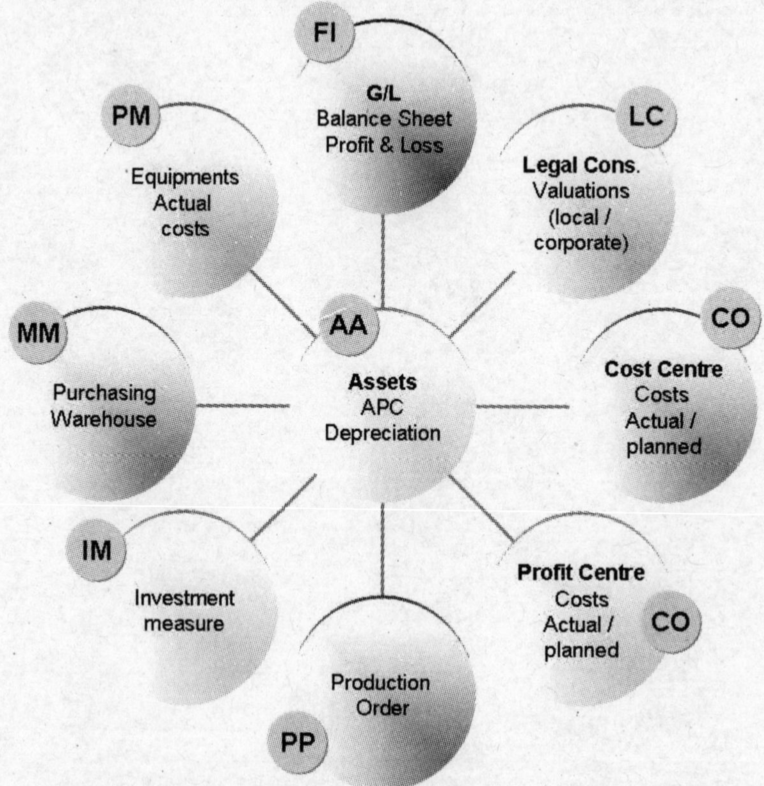

Figure 5.1: FI-AA integration with other modules

depreciation, insurance etc of assets are taken care through this module, and all the accounting information from this module flow to FI-G/L on a real time basis.

You will be able to directly post (the goods receipt (GR), invoice receipt (IR) or any withdrawal from a warehouse to fixed asset) from MM or PP to FI-AA. The integration with FI-AR helps in direct posting of sales to the customer account. Similarly, integration with FI-AP helps in posting an asset directly to FI-AA and the relevant vendor account, in cases where the purchase is not routed through MM module. You may capitalize the maintenance activities to an asset using settlements through PM module. FI-AA and FI-G/L has a real-time integration where in all the transactions like asset acquisition, retirement, transfer etc are recorded simultaneously in both the modules. However, batch processing is required to transfer the depreciation values, interest etc to the FI module.

The FI-AA and CO integration helps in:

- Assigning an asset to any of the ***controlling objects*** like cost centre, internal order / maintenance order, or an activity type. ***Internal orders*** act as a two way link to the FI-AA: (i) they help to collect and pass on the capital expenditure to assets, and (ii) collect the depreciation / interest from FI-AA to controlling objects. (Note that when there is a situation where the asset master record contains an internal order and a cost centre, then the depreciation is always posted to the internal order and not to the cost centre.)
- The depreciation and the interest are passed on to the cost / profit centres

2. What is a 'Lean Implementation' in FI-AA?

The **lean implementation** is the scaled-down version of the regular FI-AA configuration in IMG, with minimal configuration required to enable asset accounting. This is suitable in cases of small companies using the standard functionalities of asset accounting, and also in situations where the '*Asset Catalogue*' is not that large.

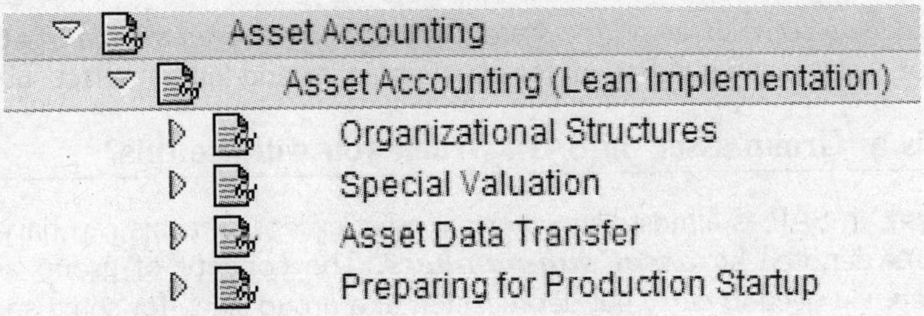

Asset Accounting
Asset Accounting (Lean Implementation)
Organizational Structures
Special Valuation
Asset Data Transfer
Preparing for Production Startup

Figure 5.2: Lean implementation in FI-AA

You should not opt for lean implementation if:

- You need more than to *Depreciation Areas*
- You need to *Depreciate In Foreign Currencies* as well
- You have *Group Assets*

- You need to define your own *Depreciation Keys / Transaction Types / Reports*
- You need a *Group Consolidation*

Transaction Code
OASI

3. What are all the kinds of 'Assets' in SAP?

An asset can be a ***simple asset*** or ***complex asset***. Depending upon the requirement, assets are maintained with ***asset main number*** and ***asset sub-numbers***. A complex asset consists of many ***sub-assets***; each of them identified using an asset sub-number. You may also use the concept of ***group asset***, in SAP.

4. Explain 'Complex Asset' and 'Asset Sub-Numbers'.

A **complex asset**, in SAP, is made up of many master records each of which is denoted by an **asset sub-number**. It is prudent to use asset sub-numbers, if:

- You need to manage the 'subsequent acquisitions' separately from the initial one (for example: your initial acquisition was a PC, and you are adding a printer later)
- You want to manage the various parts of an asset separately even at the time of 'initial acquisition' (for example: initial purchase of PC where in you create separate asset master records for the monitor, CPU etc)
- You need to divide the assets based on certain technical qualities (keyboard, mouse etc)

When you manage a complex asset, the system enables you to evaluate the asset in all possible ways like (i) for a single sub-number, (ii) for all sub-number and (iii) for select sub-numbers.

5. What is a 'Group asset' in SAP? When you will use this?

A **group asset**, in SAP, is almost like a normal asset except that this can have (any number of) ***sub-assets*** denoted by ***asset sub-numbers.*** The concept of group asset becomes necessary when you need to carry out depreciation at a group level, for some special purposes like tax reporting. Remember that SAP's way of depreciation is always at the individual asset level. Hence, to manage at the group level, you need the group asset. Once you decide to have group assets, you also need to have 'special depreciation areas' meant for group assets; you will not be able depreciate a group asset using a normal depreciation area.

Unlike ***complex assets***, you can delete a group asset only when all the associated sub-numbers have been marked for deletion.

6. What is 'Asset Super Number' in SAP?

The concept of **asset super number**, in FI-AA, is used only for reporting purposes. Here, you will assign a number of individual assets to a single asset number. By using this methodology, you will be able to see all the associated assets with the asset super number as a single asset (for example: brake assembly line) or as individual assets (for example: machinery, equipments in the brake assembly line).

7. What is 'Chart of Depreciation'? How it differs from 'Chart of Accounts'?

The **chart of depreciation** contains list of country-specific depreciation areas. It provides the rules for the evaluation of assets that are valid in a given country or economic area. SAP comes supplied with default charts of depreciation that are based on the requirements of each country. These default charts of depreciation also serve as the 'reference charts' from which you can create a new chart of depreciation by copying one of the relevant charts of depreciation. After copying, you may delete the depreciation areas you do not need. However, note that the deletion must be done before any assets are created.

Chart of depreciaton for asset valuation

ChDep	Name
1AT	Sample chart of depreciation: Austria
1BE	Sample chart of depreciation: Belgium
1CH	Sample chart of depreciation: Switzerland
1DE	Sample chart of depreciation: Germany
1ES	Sample chart of depreciation: Spain
1FR	Sample chart of depreciation: France
1GB	Sample chart of depreciation: Great Britain

Figure 5.3: Sample Charts of Depreciation

You are required to assign a chart of depreciation to your Company Code. Remember that one Company Code can have only one chart of depreciation assigned to, even though multiple Company Codes can use the same chart of depreciation.

The chart of accounts can be global, country specific and industry specific based on the needs of the business. The chart of depreciation is only *country specific*. Both the charts are independent of each other (Table 5-1).

Table 5.1: Chart of Depreciation & Chart of Accounts: Differences

Chart of Depreciation	Chart of Accounts
Established in FI-AA.	Established in FI.
A chart of depreciation is a collection of country specific depreciation areas.	The chart of accounts is a list of G/L accounts used in a Company Code. The chart of accounts contain (1) chart of accounts area and (2) Company Code area.
The chart of depreciation is country specific. Usually you may not require more than one chart of depreciation. SAP comes delivered with many country specific charts of depreciation as 'reference charts' which can be copied to have your own chart of depreciation.	Depending upon the requirement you may have an 'operating chart of accounts', 'country specific chart of accounts', 'global chart of accounts' etc
One Company Code uses only one chart of depreciation.	One Company Code uses only one chart of accounts (operating).
Many Company Codes, in the same country, can use the same chart of depreciation.	Several Company Codes within the same country can use the same chart of accounts.

8. How do you create an 'Asset Accounting Company Code'?

- Define the Company Code in FI configuration, and assign a chart of accounts to this Company Code
- Assign a chart of depreciation to this Company Code in FI-AA configuration
- Add necessary data for the Company Code for use in FI-AA, and your 'asset accounting Company Code' is now ready for use.

9. What is 'Depreciation'? Explain the various types of depreciation.

Depreciation is the reduction in the ***book value*** of an asset due to its usage over time ('decline in economic usefulness') or due to legal framework for taxation reporting. The depreciation is usually calculated taking in to account the ***economic life*** of the asset, ***expected value*** of the asset at the end of its economic life (***junk / scrap value***), ***method of depreciation calculation*** (straight line method, declining balance, sum of year digits, double declining etc) and the defined percentage decline in the value of the asset every year (20%, or 15% and so on).

10. What is 'Planned Depreciation'? How it is different from 'Unplanned'?

The depreciation can either be (1) planned or (2) un-planned:

- ***Planned depreciation*** is one which brings down the value of the asset after every planned period; say every month, till the asset value is fully depreciated over its life period. By this you will know what will be the value of the asset at any point of time in its active life.

- On the contrary, ***unplanned depreciation*** is a sudden happening of an event or occurrence not foreseen (there could be a sudden break out of a fire damaging an asset, and forcing you to depreciate fully as it is no longer useful economically) resulting in a permanent reduction of the value of the asset.

11. What are the three types of depreciation in SAP?

In SAP, you will come across three types of depreciation:

- ***Ordinary depreciation*** which is nothing but the 'planned depreciation'
- ***Special depreciation*** which is over and above the 'ordinary depreciation', used normally for taxation purposes
- ***Unplanned depreciation*** which is the result of reducing the asset value due to the sudden occurrence of certain events

12. Define 'Depreciation Area'.

The fixed assets are valued differently for different purpose (business, legal etc). SAP manages these different valuations by means of **depreciation areas**. There are various depreciation areas like book depreciation, tax depreciation, depreciation for cost-accounting purposes etc).

Chart of dep. 0IN Sample chart of depreciation: India

Define Depreciation Areas

Ar.	Name of depreciation area	Real	G/L	Trgt Group
1	Book depreciation	☑	1	
15	Depreciation as per Income Tax Act 1961	☑	0	
20	Cost-accounting depreciation	☑	3	
30	Consolidated balance sheet in local currency	☑	0	
31	Consolidated balance sheet in group currency	☑	0	
32	Book depreciation in group currency	☑	0	
41	Investment support deducted from asset	☑	0	
51	Investment support posted to liabilities	☑	1	

Figure 5.4: Depreciation Area

A depreciation area decides how and for what purpose an asset is evaluated. The depreciation area can be 'real' or a 'derived one'. You may need to use several depreciation areas for a single asset depending upon the valuation and reporting requirements.

The indicator under the column 'G/L' determines how that particular depreciation area updates the values to a G/L Account:

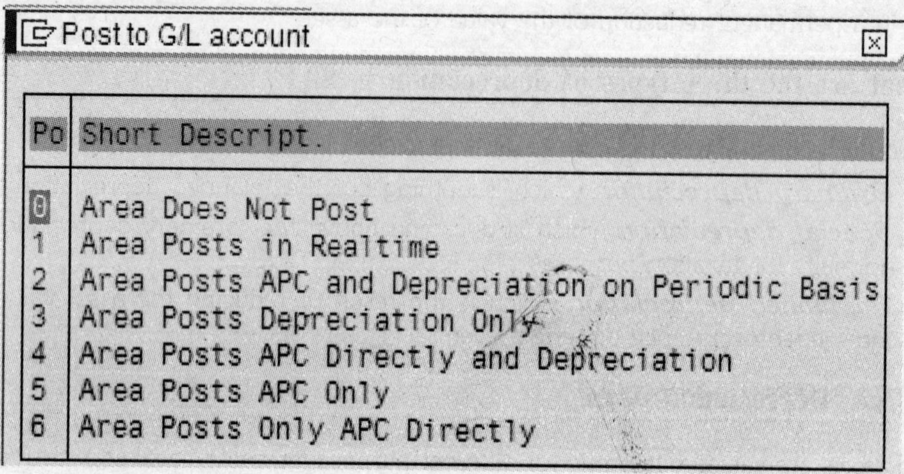

Figure 5.5: How a Depreciation Area posts to G/L

The depreciation area is denoted by a 2-character code in the system. The depreciation areas contain the depreciation terms which are required to be entered into the ***asset master*** records or ***asset classes***. SAP comes delivered with many depreciation areas; however, the depreciation area ***01 – Book depreciation*** is the major one.

The other depreciation areas include:

- Book depreciation in group currency
- Consolidated versions in local/group currency
- Tax balance sheet depreciation
- Special tax depreciation
- Country-specific valuation (e.g., net-worth tax or state calculation)
- Values/depreciations that differ from depreciation area 01 (example: cost-accounting reasons)
- Derived depreciation area (difference between book depreciation and country-specific tax depreciation)

13. What is 'Depreciation Area Type'?

The fixed assets are valued differently for different purpose (business, legal etc). SAP uses an additional attribute, called depreciation area type, for use in the Annex 16 legal report to classify depreciation areas for fixed assets (Annex-16, is a legal report that Japanese companies must submit with their tax returns, containing data about a company's fixed assets and the amount of depreciation relevant for the fixed assets). Annex-16 uses the depreciation area type to determine how each depreciation area is used. The type is assigned according to the primary purpose of the depreciation area. Note that all the depreciation areas in the standard charts of depreciation have a depreciation type assigned already (for example, depreciation area 01 is of the type "balance sheet valuation"), and when you create a chart of depreciation, the system takes over this type from the standard reference chart of depreciation.

Transaction Code
OADC

14. What is a Derived Depreciation Area?

The **derived depreciation** is a separate depreciation area which is 'derived' from two or more 'real depreciation' areas using a pre-determined rule. You can use derived depreciation areas, for example, to calculate *special reserves* as the difference between tax and book depreciation. The book value rule in a derived depreciation area is checked each time a posting is made or depreciation is changed in the corresponding real area. Since the values are derived, the system does not store any values in the database, but updates the derived values whenever there are changes in the real depreciation area or its depreciation terms. You may also use the derived depreciation only for reporting purposes.

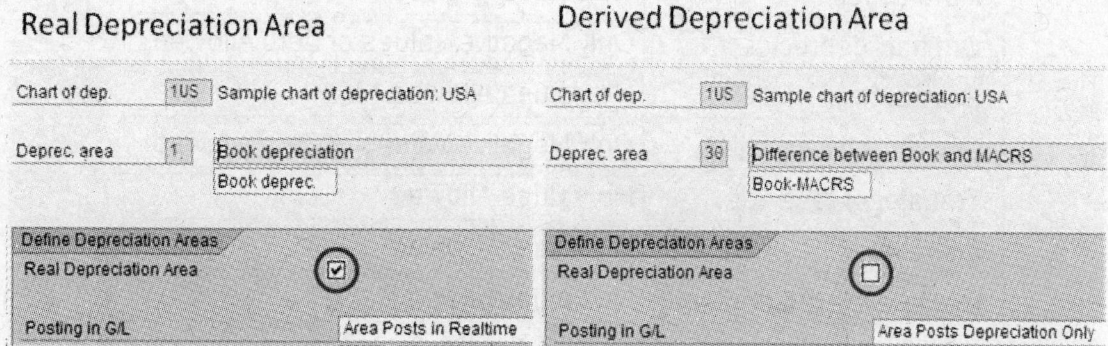

Figure 5.6: Real & Derived Depreciation Areas

15. Describe the function of Depreciation Areas

Depreciation area 01, which can be set up as the Book Depreciation, can make automatic postings to the G/L.

Deprec. area 1 Book depreciation

Book deprec.

Define Depreciation Areas

Real Depreciation Area	☑
Posting in G/L	Area Posts in Realtime
Target Ledger Group	
Different Depreciation Area	
Cross-syst.dep.area	

Value Maintenance

Acquisition value	Only Positive Values or Zero Allowed
Net book value	Only Positive Values or Zero Allowed
Investment grants	Only Negative Values or Zero Allowed
Revaluation	No Values Allowed
Ordinary depreciat.	Only Negative Values or Zero Allowed
Special Depr.	No Values Allowed
Unplanned Depreciat.	Only Negative Values or Zero Allowed
Transfer of reserves	No Values Allowed
Interest	No Values Allowed
Revaluation ord.dep.	No Values Allowed

Figure 5.7: Book Depreciation (01): Typical Settings

Other depreciation areas may get their values from depreciation area 01 but calculate and post different depreciation values to the general ledger. Other depreciation areas can be set up to show: country specific valuation (i.e., tax depreciation); values/depreciations that differ from depreciation area 01 (i.e., cost-accounting reasons); consolidated versions in local/group currency, book depreciation in group currency; and the difference between book, 01, and country-specific tax depreciation ('derived depreciation area').

16. How you will setup 'depreciation areas postings' from FI-AA to FI?

You need to define how the various depreciation areas need to post to FI-G/L. It can be any one of the following scenario:

- Post depreciation through 'periodic processing'
- Post both the APC (Acquisition and Production Costs) and depreciation through periodic processing
- Post the APC in 'real time' but depreciation through periodic processing
- No values are posted

However, you need to ensure that at least one depreciation area is configured to post values automatically to the FI-G/L. Normally, this depreciation area will be 01 (book depreciation). For rest of the depreciation areas, it may be configured that they derive their values from this area and the difference thus calculated is automatically posted to FI-G/L. There may also be situations wherein you may define depreciation areas just for reporting purposes, and these areas need not post to the G/L.

17. What is an 'Asset Class?

Asset class, in SAP, is the basis for classifying an asset based on business and legal requirements. It is essentially a grouping of assets having certain common characteristics. Each asset in the system needs to be associated with an asset class.

Asset class is the most important configuration element which decides the type of asset (like land, buildings, furniture & fixtures, equipment, assets under construction, leased assets, low-value assets etc), the document number range, data entry screen lay out for asset master creation, G/L account assignments, depreciation areas, depreciation terms etc. An asset class is defined at the Client level and is available to all the Company Codes of that Client. It is possible to assign any number of charts of depreciation to each asset class: so, you can have country-specific depreciation terms (the default values in the given chart of depreciation) for each combination of asset class and chart of depreciation.

Class	Short Text	Asset class description
1100	Buildings	Buildings
2000	Machines decl. depr.	Machines declining depr.
2100	Machines str.-line	Machines straight-line-depr.
2200	Group assets	Group assets (USA/Canada only)
3000	Fixture and fitting	Fixture and fittings

Figure 5.8: Asset Class

Transaction Code
OAOA

The asset class consists of:

- A <u>header</u> section - control parameters for master data maintenance and account determination
- A <u>master data</u> section - default values for administrative data in the asset master record
- A <u>valuation</u> section - control parameters for valuation and depreciation terms

The control parameters and the master data section of the asset class are always valid for all company codes within a client. However, it is also possible to specify that certain general master data is dependent on the chart of depreciation, and to use it to provide default data.

The asset class can be:

- Buildings
- Technical assets
- Financial assets
- Leased assets
- AuC (Assets under Construction)
- Low Value Assets (LVA)

18. Why do you need 'Asset Classes'?

An **asset class** is the *link* between the asset master records and the relevant accounts in the G/L. The ***account determination*** in the asset class enables you to post to the relevant G/L accounts. Several asset classes can use the same account determination, provided all these asset classes use the same chart of accounts and post to the same G/L accounts.

19. What is an 'Asset Class Catalog'?

An **asset class catalog** contains all the asset classes in an enterprise and hence valid across the Client. Since an asset class is valid across the Client, most of the characteristics of the asset class are defined at the Client level; however there are certain characteristics (like the depreciation key, for example), which can be defined at the chart of depreciation level.

20. Is it possible to create 'Asset Classes' automatically?

One of the benefits of lean implementation configuration is the ability to create asset classes automatically from the asset balance sheet G/L accounts (system generates these asset classes automatically, in a one-to-one relationship to the accounts). This tool selects the only necessary system settings so that the asset classes are created automatically in a very short time. During the process of creation, the system allows you to delete all the existing objects viz., asset classes, number ranges, account allocations, field selections etc. before creating the new ones.

The pre-requisites for automatic asset class creation include:

- Company Code is assigned to a chart of depreciation
- Depreciation areas have been defined
- G/L account number is not more than 8 digits (else you need to assign the classes manually)

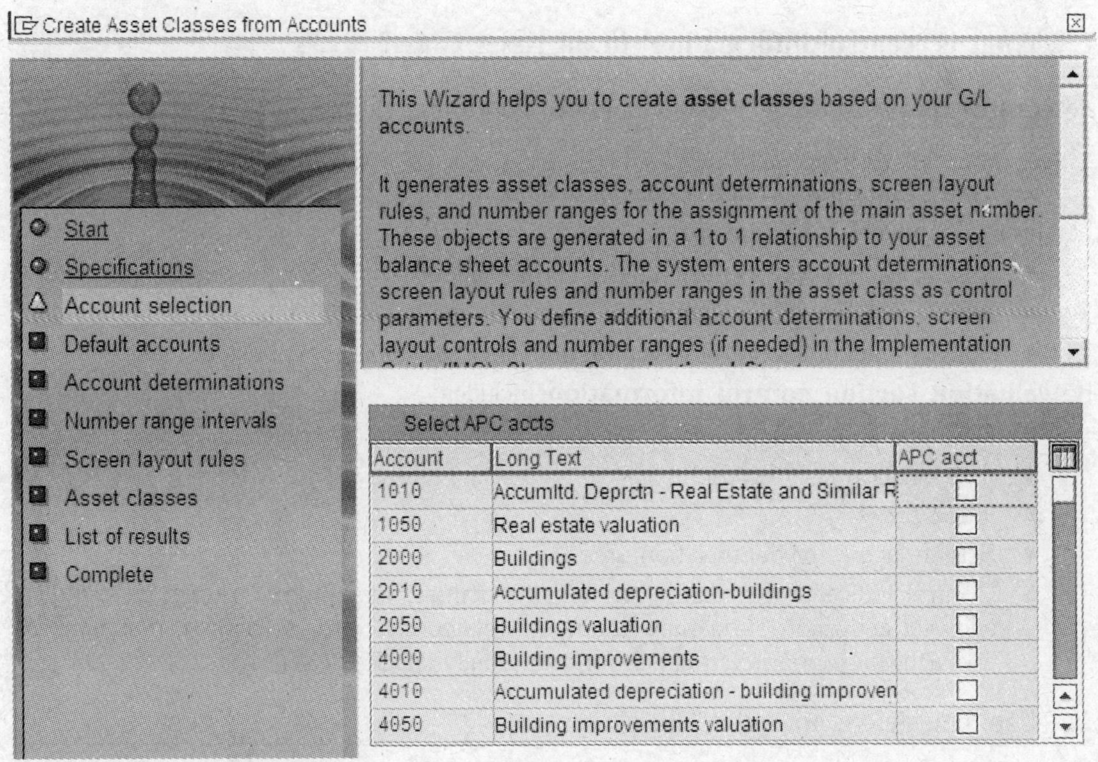

Figure 5.9: Generate Asset Class from G/L Accounts (1 to 1)

This processing view has seven navigation levels. The first navigation level is the overview screen containing the generating function. The next six navigation levels are detail screens for this overview screen. Work through all of the detail screens before you can start the generation of the asset classes in the first navigation level. The first detail screen (account selection) has to be processed first. There is no hierarchy for the remaining detail screens (no detail screens for the prior navigation level). They are not dependent on each other: you can work through each of these screens independently from the other.

It is to be noted that you may need to maintain the G/L account for 'accumulated depreciation' manually. The system maintains the necessary account assignment only with regard to the depreciation area 01 (book depreciation): if you need more areas other than 01, you may need to do that manually in the IMG.

Transaction Code
ANKL

21. What is 'control information' in an Asset Class?

The **control information** in an asset class can be grouped into 2 sections:

a. General control information
b. Control information in the valuation section

The **general control information** includes:

- Asset type (account determination, screen layout control for the master data etc)
- Number /sub-number assignment
- Special functions (control indicators for AuC, lock status, real estate etc)

The **valuation section control information** includes:

- Deactivation of a depreciation area
- Depreciation key and useful life
- Index series
- Screen layout for depreciation area
- Control indicator (for managing negative values, maximum / minimum useful life allowed, activation of quantity & amount related check for collectively managed LVA and activation of amount check for individually checked LVA)

22. Can you delete an Asset Class?

Yes, you can **delete an asset class** as long as the company code is in the 'implementation' status. Because, when the company code is in implementation status and:

- *No assets have been created* in an existing asset class; that class is deleted and generated again
- *There are assets in an existing asset class* (but no transactions)
  - o You can delete all asset classes and their assets and generate them again or
  - o You can only add new asset classes.
- *Transactions exist for the assets*: you can only add new asset classes

If the company code is in *production status*: the system creates only asset classes that were not yet created. Existing classes remain unchanged.

23. What is an 'Index Series'?

The **index series** is used for calculating replacement values. To make use of the index series functionality, you must have provided for using revaluation when the depreciation area involved was defined. You also need to use a depreciation key that allows you to depreciate from replacement values.

Index series	00060	Iron, Steel Goods

Control entries		
Index class	1	FI-AA: Dependant on year, no historical indexing
Sim.annual rate	101.900	

Figure 5.10: Index Series

You need 'index figures' if you want to calculate replacement values: maintain the index figures beginning with the point in time that the oldest asset with an index series was acquired, up to the time of the takeover of old assets data. The system needs these past index figures in order to correctly calculate the replacement values and insurable values for assets transferred during the old assets data takeover. It is absolutely necessary that you maintain your index series with the correct index figures before old assets data is taken over. Index figures of years prior to the data takeover (after the old assets data takeover has taken place) can only be changed with considerable effort.

Transaction Code
OAV5

24. How to calculate replacement value without index series?

It is possible to calculate replacement values for all assets in later fiscal years even after the productive start of the system, even if there is no 'index series' at the time of the old assets data takeover. However, for previous acquisitions, you can then only use index series that provide for "historical calculation" in their index class. You can calculate the current replacement value with such an index series using the following formula:

Value (current year) = APC * index (current year) / index (acquisition year)

After calculating the replacement value in this way, you can change to a different index series in the following year, which calculates on the basis of the replacement value from the previous year.

25. What is an 'Asset Value Date'?

The **asset value date** will be the start date of depreciation for the asset. The 'planned depreciation' is calculated by the system based on this depreciation start date and the selected 'depreciation term' for that asset. Be careful with the posting date and asset value date: both these dates need to be in the same fiscal year.

26. What is an 'Asset Master'?

An **asset master** can be created by copying an existing asset in the same Company Code or another Company Code; it can also be created from the scratch when it is done for the first time. Again, while creating the master, SAP allows to create multiple assets in one go, provided, all such assets are similar (having the same asset class and all belonging to the same Company Code).

From Release 4.5, the transaction codes for creating asset master has been changed to AS series instead of the earlier AT series (for example create asset is by **AS01** (***AT01*** earlier), change asset is **AS02** (***AT02*** earlier) and so on. If you are still comfortable with creation of assets using the conventional screen than with the 'tab' feature available now in AS transaction series, the news is that you are welcome to do so, but you can not find these transactions under **'ASMN'**!

Each asset master contains the necessary information to calculate the depreciation:

- Capitalization date / acquisition period
- Depreciation areas relevant for the asset
- Depreciation key
- Useful life / Expired useful life
- Change over year, if any
- Scrap value, if any
- Start date of (ordinary depreciation)

27. What kind of data is maintained in an Asset Master?

The master data an asset master relate to the following:

- General data (description, capitalization date, inventory date)
- Time-dependent assignments (for example, cost center)
- Allocations (evaluation groups, investment support measures)
- Information on the origin of the asset
- Specifications for net worth tax
- Insurance data

- Leasing information (especially the relevant data for the opening entry and, if necessary, determination of present value)

28. What is known as 'Maintenance Level'?

Maintenance level, in FI-AA, defines the level (asset class, main asset number, sub-number) at which a field in an asset master record is to be maintained. Maintenance level definition is part of the screen layout rule. If, for example, you define the maintenance level as the 'main asset number' for a field, then the field will be filled with a default value from the asset class. However, you will be able to change the field when maintaining master data at the asset main number level.

The three maintenance levels are:

- Asset class
- Asset main number
- Asset sub-number

29. When you would use Asset Sub-Numbers?

A **complex fixed asset** can be represented in the system using several master records, that is, sub-numbers. Assets may be divided using sub-numbers if:

- Managing the values for subsequent acquisitions in following years (i.e., buildings) separately
- Managing the values for individual parts of assets separately
- Dividing the asset according to various technical aspects

30. How to create an Asset Master?

The creation of an asset master depends on whether you are (a) creating an entirely new asset or (b) adding to an existing asset in the system.

In case you are creating an entirely new asset, you can create the asset by:

- Entering the appropriate asset class in the initial screen of asset master creation transaction
- Referencing to an existing asset already in the system

In case you are adding to an existing asset, you need to locate the asset main number and add the new one as a sub-number; the system will use the same asset class of the main asset to the newly created sub-asset.

31. Can you create multiple assets in a single transaction?

SAP enables you to create multiple (but *similar*) assets in one transaction. You can use the standard transaction for creating an asset: but, enter the number of assets you need to create in '*Number of similar assets*' field. Ensure that all these assets belong to the <u>same</u> asset class and <u>same</u> Company Code.

After creating the assets, you will be able to change the individual descriptions / inventory numbers when you are about to save the master records. When you save the master records, the system assigns a range of asset numbers. The only drawback of using this method of creating assets in bulk is that you will not be able to create *long text* for any of these assets.

Transaction Code
AS01

Create Asset: Initial screen

Master data | Depreciation areas

Asset Class	3100
Company Code	9000
Number of similar assets	12

Reference

Asset	
Sub-number	
Company code	

☐ Post-capitalization

Figure 5.11: Create Asset: Initial Screen

32. What are all the 'Time Dependent Data' in asset master?

All the cost accounting assignment related data like cost centre, internal orders or investment projects etc need to be maintained as **time dependent data** in asset masters. Additionally, the information relating to ***asset shut-down*** and ***shift operation*** also needs to be maintained as time dependent. SAP maintains all the time-dependent data for the entire life span of the assets.

Interval from 01/01/1900 to 12/31/9999	
Cost Center	1010044
Resp. cost center	

Figure 5.12: Time-dependent Cost Centre Data

33. How to make changes to an Asset Master?

SAP handles the changes to an asset master in several ways, based on what kind of information is changed:

- *General Master Data / Time-dependent allocations that are* <u>*not*</u> *relevant to balance sheet:* the normal or general information relating to an asset master can be changed simply by changing the information in the relevant fields. This is true with regard to the time-dependent allocations that are not relevant to balance sheet (say, 'plant')
- *Time-dependent allocations that are relevant to balance sheet:* there are two ways of doing this:
    - o Changing the assignment using the master data transaction However, you can only use this method if the business area and cost center master data fields are not managed as time-dependent (set the business area and cost center to time-independent in Customizing). When you use this method, the system displays the new business area or cost center/profit center in all subsequent reports (even if the report is for a time period prior to the change) as it is not able to create a history for the earlier assignment to a cost center/profit center.
    - o Change the assignment of business area or cost center/profit center by posting an asset transfer to a new master record, rather than making the change in the asset master data. Use this method if the business area and cost center master data fields are managed as time-dependent. When you use this method, the system displays the business area or cost center that is valid for the given time period in all reports.
- *Change in asset class:* this is possible only by posting a transfer to a new asset master record. Copy the asset master record that you want to change; by creating a new master record using the 'reference' method and making the necessary changes in the new master record. Either create the new master record with a new asset class, or enter a new business area in the time-dependent data for the new asset.

34. Why it is necessary to 'Block' an asset master record?

In case you decide that you do not want to post any more acquisitions to an existing asset, then it is necessary that you set the **block indicator** (also known as '*acquisition lock*') in the asset master record: the default is '*none*', and you can select the radio-button '*locked to acquis*' to block further acquisitions. This is usually the case with AuC, where after the capitalization you no longer want any further additions to the asset. The block indicator prevents only further postings but not transfers or retirements or depreciation; even after blocking, the asset can continue to be depreciated the same way as in the case of other assets.

Acquisition year 0 Plnd. retirement on

Acquisition lock

None

Locked to acquis.

Figure 5.13: Block Indicator (Acquisition Lock) in Asset Master

Transaction Code
AS05
AS23 (Group Asset)

35. What is 'Deactivation' of an asset?

The system automatically assigns a **deactivation date** to an asset (as a result of the retirement posting) when you scrap or sell it. Such deactivated assets can be removed from the database and transferred to an archive file. However, since the asset history sheet includes transactions from the previous year, the deactivated assets from the previous year cannot be reorganized or archived (minimum residence time = 1 year).

If you reverse the retirement posting, the system removes the deactivation date. You can also cancel the deactivation date manually in the master record, if, at a later point of time, you want to post subsequent acquisitions to the asset.

36. How do you delete an asset?

It is possible to can **delete** an asset (master record) to which no postings have been made, directly online, without archiving. It is also possible to manually delete old assets (legacy assets from your previous system) during the asset data transfer process.

- Delete all the transferred values for the old asset using the old asset change transaction.
- Set the deactivation date for the old asset using the old asset change transaction (in the first master data screen)

- Delete the old asset using the delete transaction

Transaction Code
AS06
AS26 (Group Asset)

37. What is a '(Asset) Transaction Type' in FI-AA?

Transaction types in FI-AA identify the nature of asset transaction (acquisition or transfer or retirement) so as to specify what is that updated, among (a) Depreciation area, (b) Value field and (c) Asset accounts (in B/S).

TType	Transaction type name
020	Acquisition:Cost-accounting area only
030	Acquisition in group area only
100	External asset acquisition
101	Acquisition for a negative asset
105	Credit memo in invoice year
106	Credit memo in invoice year to affiliated company
110	In-house acquisition
115	Settlement from CO to assets
116	Acquisition - internal settlement to AuC
120	Goods receipt
121	Goods receipt for production order
122	Goods receipt from affiliated company (net)
130	Withdrawal from stock
131	Goods issue (in-house production)
140	Incidental costs without capitalization

Figure 5.14: Transaction Types

The following are some of the common transaction types used:

- 100 Asset Acquisition – Purchase
- 110 Asset Acquisition – In-house Production

- 200 Asset Retirement – without revenue
- 210 Asset Retirement – with revenue

The transaction type is extensively used in most of the asset reports, including the ***asset history sheet***, to display the various asset transactions differentiated by the transaction types. SAP comes with a numerous transaction types which will take care of almost all your requirement. However, should there be a specific case; you may also create your own transaction type.

Every transaction type is grouped into a ***transaction type group*** (for example: 40 -> Post-capitalization) which characterizes the various transaction types (for example transaction types 400 & 490) within that group. The system makes it possible to limit the transaction type groups be associated with certain asset classes.

Trans. Type 400 Post-capitalization
Transaction type grp 40 Post-capitalization

Account assignment
(•) Debit transaction
( ) Credit transaction
[✓] Capitalize fixed asset
Document type AA Asset posting

Other features
[ ] Cannot be used manually [ ] Set changeover year
Consolidation transaction type 275 Write-ups
Asst hist sheet grp 40 Post-capitalization
[ ] Call up individual check

Figure 5.15: Transaction Type Group

38. Explain 'Asset Acquisition'.

Asset acquisition can be through any one of the following three routes:

1. **External acquisition through purchase**

   External acquisition of assets will be primarily from vendors, who are either your business partners or third parties. It can also be from your affiliated companies (use *Transaction Code: **ABZP***). The external asset acquisition can be through different ways:

i. The asset can be posted in MM module

ii. The asset can be created in FI-AA with automatic clearing of the offsetting entry (Transaction Code: **ABZON**). This can be achieved either of the following ways:

- The posting is made initially in FI-AP and the clearing account cleared when the posting is made to the asset (FI-AA)
- Post the asset with the automatic offsetting entry(FI-AA), then clear the clearing account through a credit posting by an incoming invoice (FI-AP)

When not integrated with FI-AP, you may acquire the asset in FI-AA with an automatic offsetting entry without referencing to a Purchase Requisition (PR). This kind of acquisition is necessary when:

- You have not yet received the invoice or
- When the invoice has already been posted in FI-AP

When integrated with FI-AP, acquire the asset in FI-AA using an incoming invoice but without a reference to a Purchase Order PO)

2. In-house Production / Acquisition

In-house asset acquisition is primarily the capitalization of goods/services produced by your company. The costs associated with the complete or partial production of the goods/services from within the company needs to be capitalized into separate asset(s). Usually, the capitalization is done as under:

- Create an order/project (in Investment Management) to capture the production costs associated with the goods/services produced in-house
- Settle the order/project to an AuC (Asst under Construction)
- Distribute/Settle the AuC so created in to new asset(s)

You will be using the transaction type 110 for asset acquisition from in-house production.

3. Subsequent Acquisition

When the asset /vendor accounts are posted, the system updates the corresponding G/L accounts (FI-AP & FI-AA) through relevant account determinations. SAP uses various kinds of 'transaction types' to distinguish the different transactions. During acquisition the system makes the following entries in the asset master data:

- Date of initial acquisition / period & year of acquisition
- Capitalization date of the asset
- Start date for ordinary depreciation (start date is determined from the asset value date/period/year of acquisition)
- Vendor is automatically entered in the 'origin'

39. What data are automatically set-in the asset masters during 'Initial Acquisition'?

The following information is automatically set-in the asset masters during initial acquisition:

- Acquisition period
- Date of capitalization
- Depreciation start date (per depreciation area)
- Posting date of original acquisition

40. Can you post Asset Acquisition in two steps (or two departments)?

Yes, it is possible to post asset in two steps or in two departments.

When the asset acquisition is posted in two steps or two different departments, you normally post to a clearing account. Use a general ledger account with open item management so that this account can be cleared. Either the FI department includes this clearing account in their periodic run (of automatic clearing program) or the clearing account has to be cleared in an additional step.

41. Explain implications of valued /non-valued transactions in FI-AA

For non-valued, the goods receipt (GR) takes place before the invoice receipt (IR) and the values are not yet posted to FI-AA. The line items are created and the values are updated, instead, at the time of the invoice receipt. However, the system uses the date of the goods receipt as the capitalization date. At time of invoice receipt the asset is capitalized, line items are created, and the value fields are updated.

On the other hand, for the valued transaction, the GR takes place before the invoice receipt and the values are posted directly to Asset Accounting. The asset is capitalized, line items are created, and the value fields in the asset are updated. When the invoice is received later, there may be differences between the invoice amount and the amount posted at the time of goods receipt. In this case, the corresponding adjustment postings are made to the asset.

42. Explain 'Assets under Construction (AuC)' in SAP.

The goods and/or services produced, in-house, can be capitalized into asset(s). But, there are two distinct phases during this process:

- Construction phase (AuC)
- Utilization phase (useful or economic life phase)

It, then becomes necessary, to show the assets under these two phases in two different balance sheet items:

The 'construction phase' is one in which you start producing or assembling the asset and is not yet ready for putting into economic utilization. SAP categorizes these kinds of assets into a special asset class called '**Assets under Construction**' (**AuC**). The AuC is to be managed through a separate asset class with a separate asset G/L account. SAP allows posting 'down payments' to AuC. It is also possible to enter credit memos for AuC even after its complete capitalization, provided you are managing this asset class allowing *negative* ***APC (Acquisition and Production Costs)***. The ***IM*** (***Investment Managemen***t) module helps to manage internal orders / projects for AuC. It is necessary that you use the **depreciation key** '0000' to ensure that you are not calculating any depreciation for AuC. But, you can continue to have s***pecial tax depreciation*** and ***investment support*** even on these assets.

43. How to capitalize AuC in SAP?

An **AuC** can be managed in two ways, as regard the asset master is concerned:

- As a 'normal' asset
- As an asset with 'line item management'

Later on, the AuC is capitalized and transferred to regular asset(s), by 'distribution' / 'settlement'. While doing so, the system with the help of different *transaction types* segregates the transactions relating to the current year with that of the previous years. The capitalization can be:

- Lump sum capitalization
- With line item settlement (when capitalized using line item settlement, it is not necessary that you need to settle (a) all the line items and (b) 100 % in a particular line item)

In case of integration with SAP-IM (Investment Management), capital investments can be managed as AuC by:

- Collecting the production costs associated to an order/project
- Settling the collected costs to an AuC
- Capitalizing the AuC into new assets by distribution/settlement

Transaction Code
AIAB (Capitalize AuC by Distribution)
AIBU (Capitalize AuC by Settlement)

44. What do you mean my 'Low Value Assets (LVA)'?

SAP uses the tem **Low Value Assets (LVA)** to denote assets which will be depreciated in the year of purchase or in the period of acquisition. This categorization usually follows the statutory requirements of the country of the Company Code, wherein you define a monetary limit and consider all those assets falling below the value, say $1,000, as LVA. You have the flexibility of managing these assets either on an individual (***individual check***) basis or collective basis (***quantity check***).

SAP uses a special ***depreciation key*** called *LVA*, and the expected useful life of such an asset is considered to be one period (month).

45. Explain 'Asset Transfer', in SAP.

Asset Transfer is of two types, namely:

1. Inter-company asset transfer
2. Intra-company asset transfer

Inter-company asset transfer is between the Company Codes, resulting in creation of the new asset in the target Company Code (the receiving one). The transaction posts the values as per the 'posting method' selected during the transfer. In doing so, the system:

- Retires the asset in the source/sending Company Code by an 'asset retirement'
- Posts acquisition in the new/target Company Code by an 'asset acquisition', and creates the new asset in the target Company Code
- Posts inter-company profit/loss arising out of the transfer
- Updates FI-G/L automatically

An inter-company asset transfer is usually necessitated when (a) there is a need for physically changing the location from one Company to the other or (b) there is an organization restructuring resulting that the new asset to be attached with a new Company Code. You may use the standard ***transfer variants*** supplied by SAP. The selection of a suitable transfer variant will be based on (1) the legal relationship among the Company Codes and (2) the methods chosen for transferring the asset values.

Inter-company asset transfer can be handled:

- Individually using the normal transaction for a single asset
- For a number of assets using the 'mass transfer'

If you need to transfer assets cross-system, you need to use ALE functionality.

Transaction Code
ABT1N

Intra-company Asset Transfer is the transfer of an asset within the same Company Code. This would have been necessitated by:

- Change in the asset class or business area etc.
- Settlement of an AuC to a new asset
- Transfer of stock materials into an asset (by posting a GI to an order through MM or settlement of a production order to an asset)
- Splitting an existing asset into one or more new assets.

Transaction Code
ABUMN

46. What is a 'Transfer Variant'?

A **transfer variant** is dependent upon the whether the Company Codes involved are legally dependent or independent.

Variant	Name
1	Gross method
2	Net method
3	Revaluation method
4	Transfer within a company code
5	Investment measure settlement
6	Line item settlement from independent AuC
7	Gross variant (affiliated company)
8	Gross variant (non-affiliated company)

Figure 5.16: Transfer Variant

Transfer variants specify (1) the *transfer method* (one of the four methods) for the capitalization of the transferred assets in the target Company Code and (2) the *type of transaction* (acquisition or transfer) used for the transaction. You can specify in each transfer variant which master data fields should be copied from the transferred asset to the target asset, if a new asset has to be created in the target company code.

Transfer var. 2 Net method

Rel. type	Crs-sys.ar	Rel.cr-syst area	Trans.meth	Retmt tr.type	Acq.trans.typ
1	*	Generic entry	2	230	157
2	*	Generic entry	1	300	310

Figure 5.17: Specifications in a Transfer Variant

47. Explain 'Asset Retirement' in FI-AA.

Asset retirement is an integral part of asset management. The asset retirement results in removal of an asset or a part of an asset from an asset portfolio. The retirement can be through (a) sale or (b) scrapping.

During asset sales transactions, the system removes the ***APC*** and also the corresponding ***accumulated depreciation***; then the ***profit or loss*** arising out of the sale is recorded in the system. Even, in case of 'partial retirement' or 'partial sales', the system records the proportionate gain/loss arising out of the transaction. Any tax posting arising out of the transaction is automatically created by the system.
SAP recognizes the following types of asset retirement in the system:

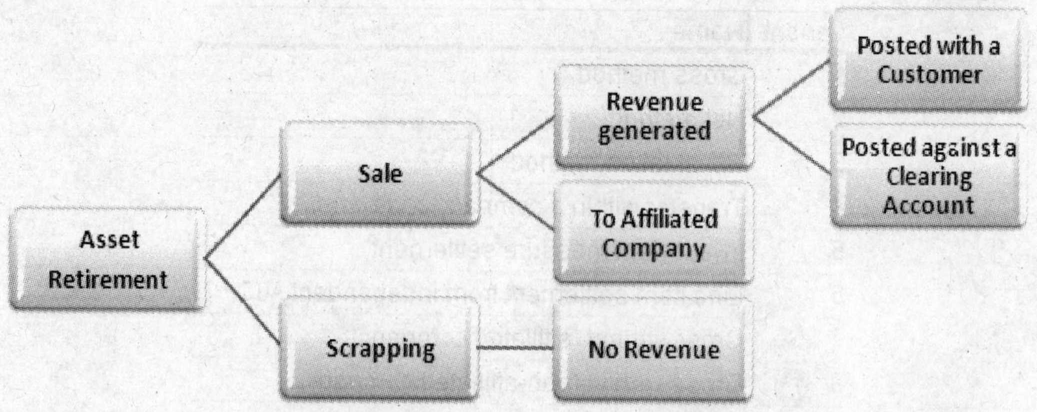

Figure 5.18: Asset Retirement

48. What is known as 'Scrapping' in FI-AA?

The **scrapping** (also known as the **asset retirement without revenue**) is the removal of an asset from the asset portfolio without any revenue. During scrapping, the system does not create revenue and gain/loss postings; but it creates a 'loss' from an asset retirement without revenue posting in the amount of the net book value being retired.

Transaction Code
ABAVN

Enter Asset Transaction: Asset Retirement by Scrapping

Line items | Change company code | Multiple assets

Company Code 1000 Operations

Asset 1000042 0 Land

Transaction data | Additional details | Partial retirement | Note

Document Date

Posting Date 07/18/2009

Asset Value Date

Text

Figure 5.19: Asset Scrapping

49. How SAP handles 'Partial Retirement' of an asset?

The asset retirement can be (a) complete retirement (relating to an entire fixed asset) or (b) partial retirement (relating to a part of a fixed asset). In either case, the system automatically determines (based on the asset retirement date you enter) the amounts to be charged off for each depreciation area.

The **complete retirement** of a fixed asset is only possible if all transactions to the asset were posted with a value date before the asset value date of asset retirement. Note to clear or reverse down payments and investment support measures, which are in the same posting year as the retirement, before you post the complete retirement.

The **partial retirement** of a fixed asset can be initiated by entering any one of the following:

- *APC amount being retired*: when you enter the APC amount that is being retired, the system determines the percentage to be retired from the asset using the first depreciation area in which posting is to take place, and uses the same percentage for other areas.
- A percentage rate
- *A quantity*: you can enter a quantity, if you have not specified the APC amount or percentage rate. The system interprets the quantity as a ratio to the total quantity of the asset and thereby determines the asset retirement percentage rate.

The asset value date of the retirement is recorded in the asset master record. You cannot post any transactions with a value date before the value date of the last retirement. If you nevertheless need to post such a transaction, you must first reverse all retirements that lie after the value date of the belated posting. After posting the belated transaction, you can then re-post the retirements.

50. What is the significance of selecting the right Transaction Type for Retirement?

It is imperative that you select the correct **transaction type** for both partial and complete retirement. For the complete retirement of a fixed asset acquired in previous years, always select a transaction type intended for prior-year acquisitions. A partial retirement can always relate either to prior-year acquisitions or to current-year acquisitions. Prior-year asset acquisitions and current-year acquisitions are shown separately from one another in the document.

51. Explain 'Asset Sale with Customer'.

In the case of asset sale with customer, the system enables you to post the entry to FI-A/R, the revenue posting and the asset retirement in one step: you post the revenue first, and then post the asset retirement. An indicator in the posting transaction specifies that the system posts the asset retirement after the revenue posting. The prerequisite for this is that the sales revenue account in FI, to which the revenue should be posted, has a field status variant in its master data in which the 'Asset retirement' field (category Asset Accounting) is defined as a required or optional entry field.

- Asset sale with revenue
  - o With customer (involving integration with FI-A/R)
    - Debit customer, credit assets

Transaction Code
F-02

52. What is 'Proportional Value Adjustments' in asset retirement?

The system automatically determines the reference period for the retirement, based on the value date and period control: it automatically determines any depreciation (value adjustments) that is applicable to the part of the asset being retired, up to the reference period (retirement). It, then, automatically retires this depreciation at the time of the retirement transaction. This procedure ensures that the percentage of the book value that is retired is identical with the percentage of the APC that is retired.

The system automatically posts the **proportional value adjustments** retired during an asset retirement. The system uses the *transaction type* 290 for proportional values with retirements. For transfers, it uses transaction types 390/395 (transfer retirement / acquisition). These transaction types are entered in the Customizing definition of the retirement or transfer transaction types (Value adjustments function). These special transaction types for the proportional value adjustments are particularly important for group consolidations, so that the individual transaction can be identified as retirement of transfer.

53. Is there a special requirement for Retiring LVA?

There are certain special considerations for the retirement of low value asset (LVA) due to the large number of assets that are being retired, calling for a simplified business transaction. It is not necessary to actually post the retirement of LVA in order for the assets transactions to be displayed correctly in the asset history sheet. It is possible to simulate the retirements of low value assets during a time period you specify. Enter the LVA asset classes and the simulation time period in the initial screen of the asset history sheet.

54. Can you retire several Asset Sub-Numbers simultaneously?

It is possible to post complete retirement of several sub-numbers of a fixed asset in one step (generic entry using an asterisk (*) in the sub-number field). However, instead of using this generic entry with an asterisk, you can use complete retirement of several sub-numbers of an asset:

In the transaction '*SAP Easy Access screen > Accounting > Financial Accounting > Fixed Assets > Posting > Acquisition > External Acquisition > Acquis. w/ Autom. Offsetting Entry*', maintain the asset number, choose [Multiple assets], choose [Subnumbers]. All sub-numbers for the asset are displayed in the 'List of assets'. You can remove sub-numbers from the list, which you do not want to retire.

55. What is 'Mass Retirement' of assets?

When you plan to sell a large portion of your company's asset portfolio (say, a rolling mill), it is necessary to post the retirement of all the individual assets which make up the whole. Since the number of assets involved can be extremely high, the FI-AA component makes it possible to carry out the retirement using mass posting. To carry out a **mass retirement**, you need the "normal" authorization for asset transactions, as well as authorization for the authorization object A_PERI_BUK (authorization for periodic processing) with activity 40. This authorization is contained in the standard profile A_ALL. The selection of the assets involved and the basic procedure for mass retirement is carried out using the same functions as a **mass change** to asset master data. Create / use a work list, make the entries like posting date, transaction type and revenue/type of revenue distribution needed for posting the mass retirement, and then follow the rest of the procedure as in a mass change.

56. Define Work Lists

Work lists are used for mass retirements, mass changes and work on incomplete assets. There are three steps in using work lists:

- Select the objects (assets) to be changed
- Assign the task to be performed on the objects
- Release the work list and process the Workflow

57. What are Depreciation Keys?

Depreciation is calculated using the **depreciation key** and ***internal calculation key***, in the system.

Depreciation keys are defined at the chart of depreciation level, and are uniform across all Company Codes, which are attached to a particular chart of depreciation. The depreciation key contains all the control parameters defined, for the calculation of planned depreciation. The system contains a number of pre-defined depreciation keys (like *LINA, DWG, DG10* etc) with the controls already defined for calculation method and type. A depreciation key can contain multiple internal calculation keys.

Chart of dep. 1US Sample chart of depreciation: USA

DepKy	Name for whole depreciation
DG20	Declining balance 2 x
EP2	E&P S/L - Mid-Month - All Lives
GD10	Buildings decl.bal.10.0/ 5.0 / 2.5 %
GD35	Buildings decl.bal.3.5/ 2.0 / 1.0 %
GD50	Buildings decl.bal. 5.0 / 2.5 / 1.25 %
GD70	Buildings decl.bal. 7.0 / 5.0 / 2.0 / 1.25 %
GL20	Buildings straight-line 2%
GL25	Buildings straight-line 2.5%
LEAS	Leasing
LINA	Str.-line via acq.value below zero
LINK	Str.-line from acq.value to zero without interest
LINR	Str.-line from rem.life to book value zero
LINW	Str.line dep.from rep.val.below zero No curb
LVA	LVA 100 % Complete depreciation
M150	MACRS 15, 20 years property
M200	MACRS 3,5,7,10 years property
MANU	Manual depreciation only

Figure 5.20: Depreciation Keys

58. What in an Internal Calculation Key?

Internal calculation key makes up a part of the depreciation key and it defines a method, base value and rate of percentage for depreciation, changeover rules (for declining depreciation), and treatment of depreciation after useful life and period control for transactions.

Each internal calculation key contains:

- Depreciation type (ordinary or unplanned)
- Depreciation method (straight-line or declining balance),
- Base value
- Rate of percentage for depreciation calculation
- Period control for transactions (acquisition, retirement etc)
- Change-over rules (in case of declining/double declining methods of calculation)
- Treatment of depreciation after useful life period

Chart of dep.	1US	Sample chart of depreciation: USA
Dep. key	LINW	Str.line dep.from rep.val.below zero No curb
DepType	Ord.depreciation	
Phase	From the start of depreciation	
Assignment of Calculation Methods		
Base method	0010	Ordinary: percentage from life (below zero)
Decl.-bal. method	001	0.00x / 0.0000% / 0.0000%
Prd cont	008	01/06/02/02
Multilev.meth.	052	0.0000%
Class	Straight-line depreciation	
Chnge. method		
Changeover%rate		
Multiple shift	Increase in depreciation and expired useful life	
Scrap value	Consideration is controlled by cutoff value key	
Shutdown	No	

Figure 5.21: Internal Calculation Key

59. What is the significance of Depreciation Key '0000'?

Depreciation key '0000' is a SAP delivered key that ensures depreciation and interest is not calculated and posted. This key can be used for the Assets under Construction (AuC).

60. What is a 'Periodic Processing' in FI-AA? Explain.

Periodic processing, in FI-AA, comprises the tasks that must be performed at periodic intervals. Since only the values from one depreciation area can be automatically posted online in Financial Accounting, the changes to asset values (transactions) from other areas with automatic postings have to be posted periodically to the appropriate reconciliation accounts.

The following are the tasks under periodic processing in FI-AA:

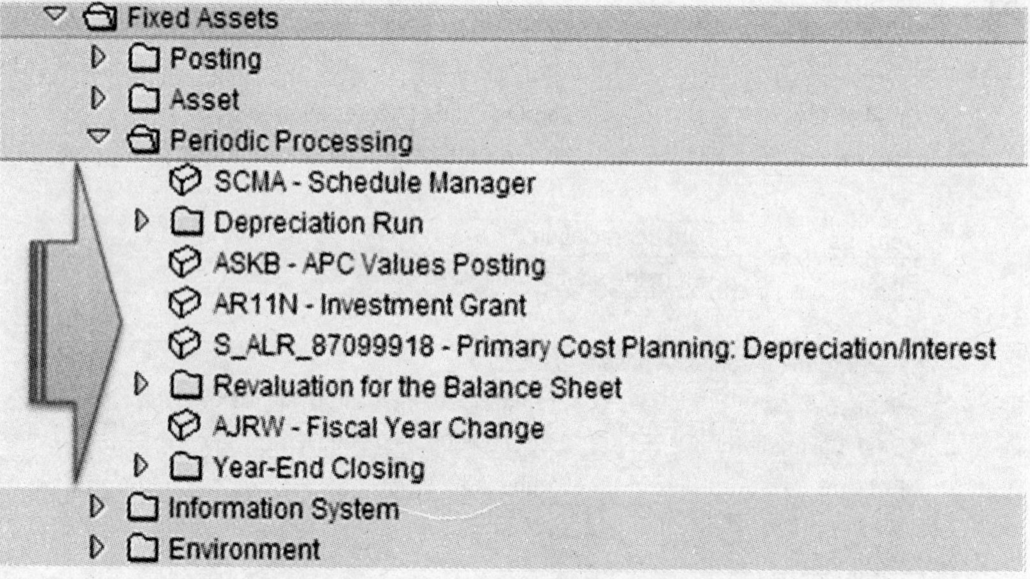

Figure 5.22: Periodic Processing

You may use the *Schedule Manager* (Transaction Code: SCMA) to schedule and monitor the various tasks which need to be processed periodically.

61. How does the system post 'imputed interest' to CO?

In case you calculate **imputed interest** on the capital tied up in assets, then the system posts this interest simultaneously during the periodic depreciation posting run. It posts to the accounts that are entered in the relevant account determination for each depreciation area. Furthermore, an additional account assignment can be made to the cost center or the internal order entered in each asset master record (same for depreciation).

62. What is known as 'Depreciation Run' in SAP?

The **depreciation run**, an important periodic processing, takes care of calculating depreciation for the assets and posting the corresponding transactions in both FI-AA and FI-G/L. The depreciation calculation is usually done in sessions, and the ***posting session*** posts the different depreciation types, interest/ revaluation, and also writing-off / allocating special reserves. The depreciation run is recommended to be started with a 'test run' before making it as the '***production run***' which will update the system. The system provides the facility to re-start a run session should there be problems in the earlier run. The depreciation run needs to be completed per period. During every depreciation run, the system will create summarized posting documents per business area and per account determination; no individual posting documents are created.

63. Explain the various steps in a 'Depreciation Run'.

The following are the sequence of steps in a typical depreciation run:

- Maintain the parameters for the depreciation run on the initial screen of the Transaction **AFAB** (Company Code, fiscal year & posting period).
- Select a 'reason' for the posting run (repeat run, planned posting run, restart run or unplanned run).
- Select the appropriate check boxes in the 'further option' block if you need a list of assets, direct FI posting, test run etc. Please note that it is a good practice to select the 'test run' initially, see and satisfy the outcome of the depreciation run, then remove this 'check box' and go for the 'productive run'.
- Execute the test run (if the assets are less than 10, 000 in numbers, you may then do the processing in the foreground; else execute the run in the background).
- Check the results displayed.
- Once you are convinced that the test run has gone as expected, go back to the previous screen, uncheck the 'test run' check-box, and execute (in the background).
- Complete the 'background print parameters', if prompted by the system. You may also decide to schedule the job immediately or later. The system uses the 'depreciation-posting program' ***RABUCH00***, for updating the asset's values and generating a batch input session for updating FI-G/L. The 'posting session' posts values in various depreciation areas, interest, revaluation besides updating special reserves allocations and writing-off, if any. If there are more than 100, 000 assets for depreciation calculation and posting, you need to use a special program ***RAPOST00***.
- Process the 'batch input session' created by the system in the previous step. You may use the Transaction Code **SM35**. Again, you have the option of processing the session in the foreground or in the background.
- System posts the depreciation in FI-G/L.

64. How the system calculates the 'Depreciation'?

The system calculates the depreciation as in the following process flow:

i. The system takes the 'depreciation terms' from the asset master record, and calculates the annual depreciation for the asset taking into account the 'useful life' and the 'depreciation key'. The start date for depreciation is assumed to be the first date of acquisition of the asset.

ii. The system may also calculate other values like, interest, revaluation etc

iii. The depreciation and / other values as in (ii) are calculated for each of the depreciation areas.

65. How the depreciation start date is determined by the system?

Normally, the system determines the **depreciation start date** from the asset value date of the first acquisition posting.

66. What is known as a 'Repeat Run' in depreciation process?

Repeat run is normally used at the end of the fiscal year to carry out posting adjustments or corrections which may arise due to changes in depreciation terms or manual depreciation calculations. However, you can also use this to repeat but within the same posting period. The 'repeat run' also provides the flexibility to restrict the calculations to specific assets.

67. What is 'Restart a Depreciation Run'?

Restart depreciation run is used only when there has been a problem with the previous run resulting in termination of that run. To make sure that all the steps in a depreciation run is completed without errors; the system logs the status at every stage of the processing and provides 'error logs' so as to find out the problem. This option of 'restart' is not available during the 'test run' mode.

68. What is 'Depreciation Simulation'?

Depreciation simulation refers to 'what if' valuation of assets. This is achieved by changing and experimenting with the 'parameters' required for depreciating the assets. The simulation helps you to 'foresee' what would be the depreciation should there be changes in various 'depreciation terms'. You may simulate to see the valuation for the future fiscal years. ***Sort versions*** and options for ***totals report*** are also available in simulation. The depreciation simulation can be applied to a single asset or your entire asset portfolio.

69. Can you select 'Direct FI Posting' for a 'Depreciation Run'?

If the 'check box' to enable '**direct FI posting'** is ticked then the system will not create the 'batch input session' for depreciation posting; instead the FI-G/L is posted directly. Be careful when checking Direct FI Posting check box, because there will not be an opportunity to correct mistakes, if any, in accounts and account assignments like business area, cost objects etc when you execute the depreciation run. Also, there will be no possibility to check and correct postings. Note that if this option is selected during a depreciation run, and if the run is terminated for any reason and needs to be re-started, this has to be kept checked during that time as well.

The standard system comes with the document type '***AF***' (number range defined as '*external numbering*') configured to be used in '*batch input*'. Hence, with this default configuration, you will get an error when you try depreciation posting run by selecting the option 'direct FI posting'. You can, however, overcome this by not restricting the same in FI-AA customization (Use Transaction Code **OBA7** and remove the tick mark form 'Btch input only' check-box).

70. Does the system post individual documents when you run RABUCH00?

No. The depreciation posting program RABUCH00 updates the assets values and generates a batch-input session for the update of the G/L. The posting session also posts the different depreciation types, interest and revaluation, in addition to the writing-off and allocation of special reserves. *The system does not create individual documents, only summarized posting documents (per business area per account determination).*

71. What Document Number Range you will use for automatic depreciation postings?

For each Company Code, a document type must be defined for posting depreciation. The depreciation program should only use a document type that is limited to being used for batch input. In this way, unintentional use of the document type can be prevented. It is also essential that the document type is assigned a number range with an **external** number assignment. The depreciation program can then assign the document numbers by itself. If the numbers are assigned in this way, the depreciation posting program can keep a check on posting to FI. If errors occur, this numbering also makes it possible to make corrections. The document type 'AF' is supplied by SAP for depreciation posting.

72. Differentiate 'Smoothing' from 'Catch-up'?

SAP uses two methods of distributing the forecasted depreciation to the various posting periods:

- Smoothing
- Catch-up

The **smoothing** method distributes depreciation evenly to the periods from the current depreciation period to the end of the fiscal year (regardless of the value date of the transaction). On the other hand, with the **catch-up** method, the depreciation on the transaction (from the start of capitalization up to the current period) is posted as a lump sum.

Details	Catch-up	Smoothing
Value of the Asset	USD 1,200	
Rate of Depreciation	10%	
Depreciation start in period	1	1
Planned annual depreciation (10%)	120	120
Depreciation posted up to period 8	0	0
Planned Depreciation up to period 8 (=120/12 *8)	80	80
Depreciation to post in period 8	80	0
Depreciation to post per period from period 9	10	30
	(i. e.,40/4)	(i.e., 120/4)

Figure 5.23: Smoothing Vs Catch-up

73. Describe transfer of 'Legacy Asset Data' to SAP.

One of the challenges in the implementation of FI-AA is the transfer of **legacy asset data** from your existing systems to SAP FI-AA. Though SAP provides multiple options and appropriate tools to carry out this task, you need a carefully planned strategy for completing this task. You may resort to transfer the old asset values through any one of the following ways:

- Batch data inputs (large number of old assets)
- Directly updating the SAP Tables (very large number of old assets)
- Manual entry (few old assets)

Normally, you will not be resorting to manual process as it is time consuming and laborious; however, you may do this if you have very limited number of assets. Else, you may use either of the other two options, though batch data input with error handling would be the preferred way of doing the same. You need to reconcile the data transferred, if you resort to any of the two automatic ways of transferring the data. You may also use, ***BAPI***s (***Business Application Programming Interface***) to link and process the asset information in SAP FI-AA, from non-SAP systems.

The transfer can be (i) at the end of the last closed fiscal year, or (ii) during the current fiscal year following the last closed fiscal year. You will be able to transfer both (a) master data as well as (b) accumulated values of the last closed fiscal year. If required, you can also transfer the asset transactions, including depreciation, during the current fiscal year. It is important to note that the G/L account balances of the old assets need to be transferred separately.

74. Outline 'Automatic Transfer of Old Assets'.

SAP provides you with the necessary interfaces for converting your' legacy asset data' into prescribed formats for upload into the SAP system. The ***data transfer workbench*** allows you to control the entire data transfer process.

i. These interface programs convert the data to be compatible with the SAP data dictionary Tables like BALTD for master data, and BALTB for transactions. If you have more than 10 depreciation areas, then you need to change the transfer structures for both BALTD and BALTB.

ii. The converted data are stored in sequential files.

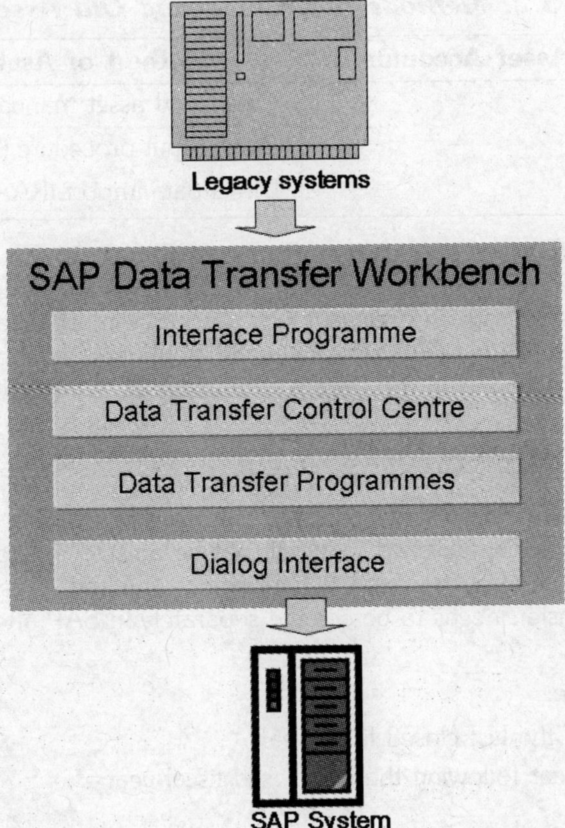

Figure 5.24: Legacy Asset Transfer to SAP FI-AA

iii. Use the data transfer program RAALTD01 (for batch input) or RAALTD11 (direct Table update) for transferring the data to SAP.

- Do a *test run*. This will help to correct errors, if any.
- Do a *production run*, with a few asset records, to update the relevant Tables in FI-AA.
- Reset the values in the asset Company Code.
- Continue with the production run for all the assets

iv. All the asset records without errors will be updated immediately through background processing, in the relevant Tables like ANLH, ANLA, ANLB, ANLC etc.

v. The records with errors will be stored in a separate batch input session which can be processed separately.

75. What are the three methods of old asset data transfer, based on number of assets?

The Table 5-2 outlines the three methods of data transfer in FI-AA.

Table 5.2: Methods of Transferring Old Asset Data

Number of Old Asset Accounts	Method of Asset Transfer
Small	Create old asset manually (dialog transaction)
Large	Batch-input procedure (RAALTD01)
Very Large	Direct data import (RAALTD11)

76. With any of old asset transfer methods, will G/L in FI be updated?

No. Balance reconciliation with the relevant G/L accounts must take place separately. G/L personnel can input these via FI or AA personnel can input them via the transfer balance screen in AA. With up-to-date accounts in the already productive FI there is no need to update them.

77. What is 'Asset Transfer Date'?

The **asset transfer date** refers to the 'cut-off' date for the transfer of old assets data from your existing system. Once established, you will not be able to create any old asset in SAP, before this reference date. Any transaction happening after the transfer date but before the actual date of asset transfer, needs to be created separately in SAP after you complete the old asset transfer.

The two possibilities are:

- At the end of the last closed fiscal year
- In the fiscal year following the last closed fiscal year

78. What data is transferred at the year-end transfer and the sub-annual transfer?

Year-end transfer and transfer during fiscal year:

- Master data
- Cumulative values as of the end of the last closed fiscal year

Sub-annual transfer (if the 'transfer date' is after the closed fiscal year)

- Master data
- Cumulative values as of the end of the last closed fiscal year
- Depreciation and asset transactions posted in the current year (transfer parameters)

79. What are the 2 methods of transferring depreciation posted in current year?

You can use any one of the following two methods:

- *Transferring the depreciation posted in the current fiscal year up to the point of transfer*- it is necessary to specify the last posted depreciation period in the legacy system for each depreciation area for every asset company code.
- *Posting the total depreciation for the current fiscal year up until the transfer date after the old data transfer* – it is done in AA by performing a posting run for unplanned depreciation.

80. What (transfer / postings) is allowed in different SAP environments?

The Table 5-3 outlines what kind of posting is allowed in different environments namely test, transfer or production:

Table 5.3: Different Environments in FI-AA

Environment	Old Data Transfer	Postings
Test	✓	✓
Transfer	✓	⊗
Production	⊗	Only current

81. Describe 'Mass Change'. How to achieve this?

Mass change enables you to make changes (like mass retirements, changes to incomplete assets etc) in FI-AA, to a large number asset master records at one go. The mass change functionality is achieved through ***work lists*** which are FI-AA standard tasks pre-defined in the system. These tasks are assigned with 'work flow objects' which can be changed according to your specific requirements. The work lists are created in several ways from asset master records, asset value display, from asset information system etc.

For effecting a mass change you need to:

i. Create ***substitution rule(s)*** in which you will mention what are all the fields that are required to be changed. This rule will consist of an 'identifying condition' (for example: if the cost centre = 1345), and a 'rule to substitute' new values (for example: replace the 'field' cost centre with the 'value' '1000')

ii. Generate a list of such assets which needs to be changed

iii. Create a 'work list' to carryout the changes

iv. Select the appropriate 'substitution rule' (defined earlier in step-(i) above)

v. Process the 'work list'. You may also release the same to some one else in the organization so that he/she can complete the task

vi. Run a 'report' to verify the changes

82. Explain the 'Year Closing' in FI-AA.

The year-end is closed when you draw the final balance sheet. But, to reach this stage, you need to ensure that the depreciation is posted properly: you can achieve this by checking the 'depreciation list' and also the 'asset history sheets'. After this is done, draw test balance sheet and profit & loss statement and check for the correctness of the depreciation. Correct the discrepancies, if any, by adjustment postings. You need to re-run the depreciation posting program if you change any of the depreciation values.

When you, now, run the **year-end closing program**, the system ensures that the fiscal year had been completed for all the assets, depreciation had been fully posted and there were no errors logged for any of the assets. If there were errors, you need to correct the errors before re-running the year-end program. When you reach a stage where there is no error, the system will update the last closed fiscal year, for each of the depreciation areas for each of the assets. The system will also block any further postings in FI-AA for the closed fiscal year. If you need to re-open the closed fiscal year for any adjustments postings or otherwise, ensure that you re-run the year-end program so that the system blocks further postings.

83. Explain 'Asset History Sheet'.

SAP comes delivered with country specific **asset history sheets** which will meet the legal reporting requirements of a country. The asset history sheet is one of the important reports which can be used either as the ***year-end report*** or intermediate report when ever you need it. Asset history sheets help you to freely define the report layout, headers, and most of the history sheet items.

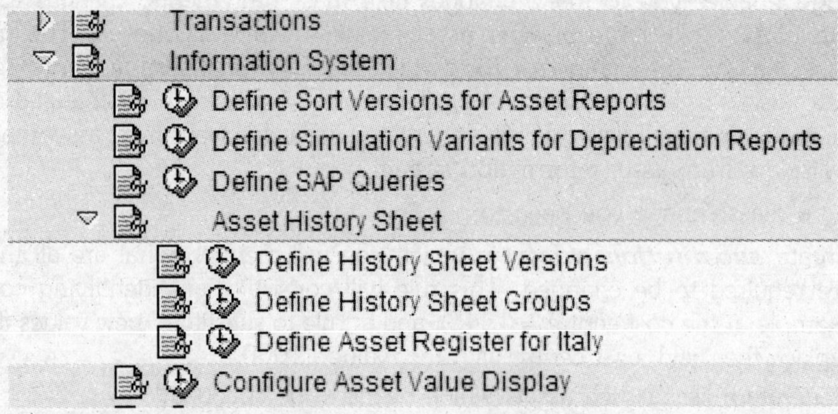

Figure 5.25: Configuring Asset History Sheet

You may create various version of asset history sheet:

Asset hist. sheet versions

Language	Hist.sht.vers.	Asset history sheet name
EN	0003	Depreciation by depreciation type
EN	0004	Acquisition values
EN	0005	Asset Register (Italy)
EN	0006	Cost-accouting w/revaluation (derived from HGB2)
EN	0007	Transferred reserves
EN	0008	History of res.for spec.depr.

Figure 5.26: Asset History Sheet Versions

For each of the versions, you will be able to define various columns according to your requirement:

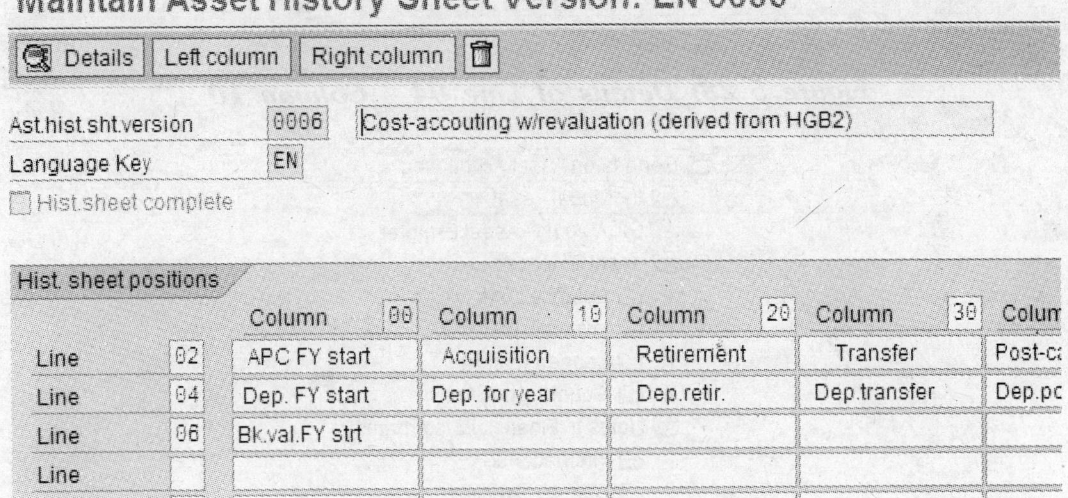

Figure 5.27: Asset History Sheet Version: Field Positions

You can look at the details of a particular column by double-clicking on the same:

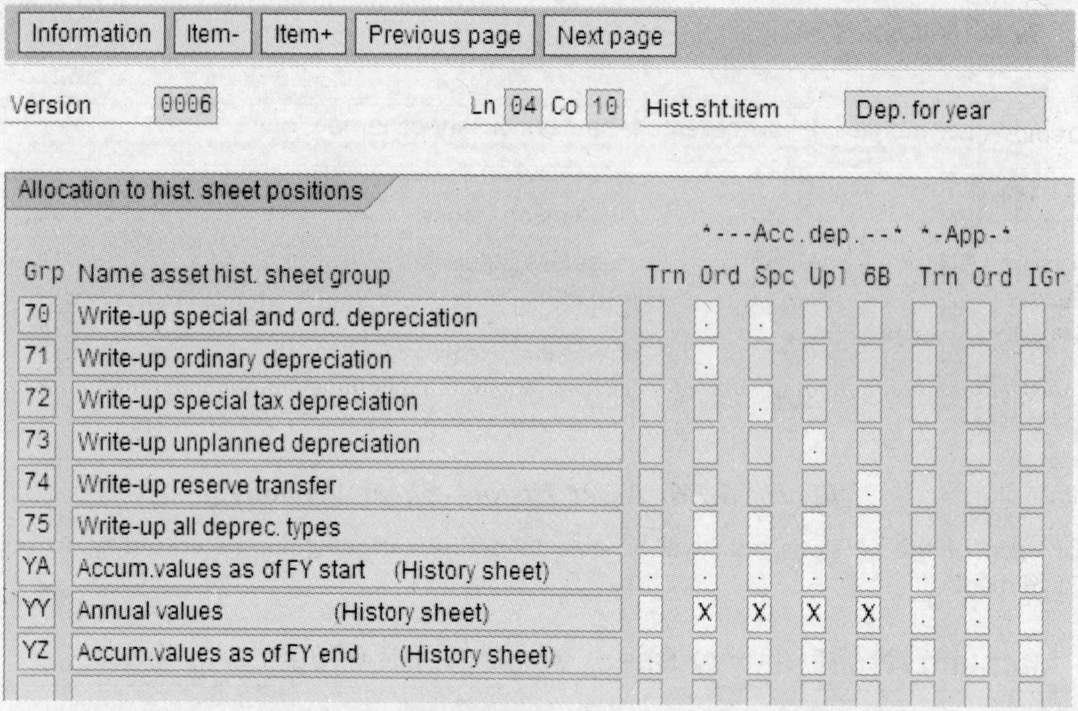

Information	Item-	Item+	Previous page	Next page

Version 0006 Ln 04 Co 10 Hist.sht.item Dep. for year

Allocation to hist. sheet positions

Grp	Name asset hist. sheet group	Trn	Ord	Spc	Upl	6B	Trn	Ord	IGr
			*---Acc.dep.		--*		*-App-*		
70	Write-up special and ord. depreciation		.	.					
71	Write-up ordinary depreciation		.						
72	Write-up special tax depreciation			.					
73	Write-up unplanned depreciation				.				
74	Write-up reserve transfer					.			
75	Write-up all deprec. types								
YA	Accum.values as of FY start (History sheet)	.	.	.	.	.	.	.	
YY	Annual values (History sheet)		X	X	X	X	.	.	
YZ	Accum.values as of FY end (History sheet)	.	.	.	.	.	.	.	

Figure 5.28: Details of Line 04 / Column 10

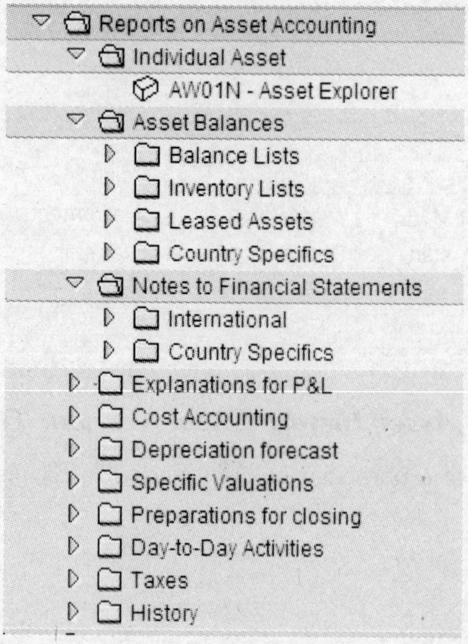

- Reports on Asset Accounting
  - Individual Asset
    - AW01N - Asset Explorer
  - Asset Balances
    - Balance Lists
    - Inventory Lists
    - Leased Assets
    - Country Specifics
  - Notes to Financial Statements
    - International
    - Country Specifics
  - Explanations for P&L
  - Cost Accounting
  - Depreciation forecast
  - Specific Valuations
  - Preparations for closing
  - Day-to-Day Activities
  - Taxes
  - History

Figure 5.29: Asset Report Tree

84. Is it possible to change the reports in a report tree in FI-AA?

Yes. The standard reports provided by SAP can be copied and modified. Branches can be added or removed from a report tree.

85. What is Sort Version?

The **sort version** defines the formation of groups and totals in an asset report. All fields of the asset master record can be used as group and/or sort criteria for defining of a sort version. It consists of a maximum of 5 sort levels determined via fields.

86. What is Asset Explorer?

Asset explorer helps you to display the asset values, depreciation details etc from single screen (Transaction Code: AW01N).

Designed for easy navigation and ease of use, the interface is made up of:

- *Asset values window*

  The top-left area/window is the 'asset values' window which is in a tree-like structure expanding to various depreciation areas like 01, 03, 10 etc. By selecting any one of these depreciation areas, you will be able to view the value of an asset in the 'asset value details window'.

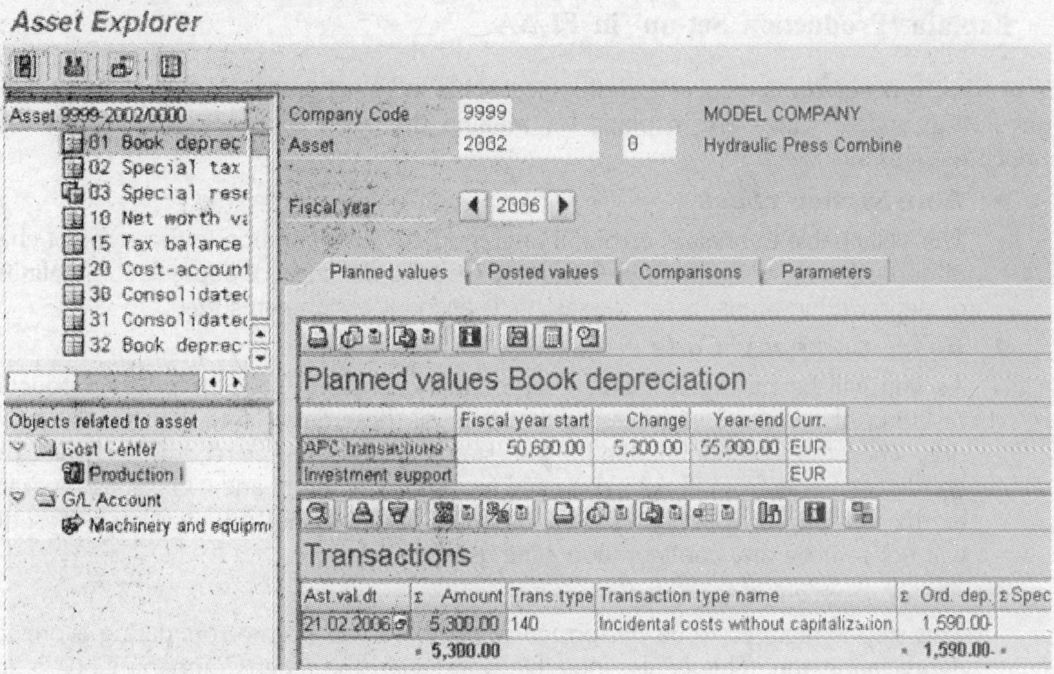

Figure 5.30: Asset Explorer

- *Objects related to asset window*

  This is also on the left hand side of the display page, just below the 'asset values window'. With a drill-down tree-like structure you will be able to navigate between cost centres and GL accounts relating to the asset.

- *Asset value detail window (with tab pages)*

  This is the main window on the right, usually occupying most of the page area. Here, you will see the information like Company Code, asset number selected, fiscal year etc. This window is made of, completely re-sizeable, two components: the top area displaying the asset values and the bottom showing the asset transactions

Using asset explorer you can:

- Move from one asset number to another
- Display asset values (planned / posted) for any number of depreciation areas
- Jump to the asset master or cost centre master or GL account master
- Call up various asset reports
- Look at the various transactions relating to an asset
- Look up all the values for different fiscal years
- Distinguish between real and derived depreciation areas with two differentiating symbols
- Display *depreciation calculation function*, and if necessary, recalculation of depreciation

87. Explain 'Production Set-up' in FI-AA.

The **production set-up** is a collection of logical steps in FI-AA to ensure that all the required configuration and activities are in place for making the asset accounting Company Code 'productive'. This includes:

- ***Consistency check***

  This will enable to analyze errors, if any, in FI-AA configuration in the areas of charts of depreciation, assignment of Company Code to the chart of depreciation, definition of depreciation areas, asset classes, G/L account assignments etc.

- ***Reset Company Code***

  As you will be having test data, before the Company Code becomes productive, resetting of company is necessary to delete all these data. Note that this is possible only when the Company Code in 'test' status. All the master records and values will be removed only from FI-AA. You need to remove all the FI and CO values separately as the resetting of asset account Company Code does not remove these. Resetting will not remove any configuration settings of FI-AA.

- ***Reset posted depreciation***

  This step is required to be performed when there had been errors during a previous depreciation run. This is also possible only when the asset Company Code is in a status of 'test'.

- ***Set / reset reconciliation accounts***

  Define G/L accounts for FI-AA reconciliation, if not done already. You may also reset already defined reconciliation accounts in case of wrong account assignments earlier.

- ***Transfer asset balances***

  Transfer the asset balances to the G/L accounts that have been defined as the asset reconciliation accounts.

- ***Activate asset accounting Company Code***

  This is the last step in the production set-up. All the previous status of the Company Code (test status / transfer status) becomes invalid now. No more transfer of old asset data is allowed when the asset Company Code become productive.

88. Explain how FI-AA is integrated with CO, in SAP

The postings to depreciation can be made through a cost object such as a cost center or internal order. Also, an asset can be assigned to any of the CO objects like cost centre, internal order / maintenance order, or an activity type.

The *internal orders* act as a two way link to the FI-AA:

- They help to collect and pass on the capital expenditure to assets, and
- Collect the depreciation / interest from FI-AA to controlling objects. (Note that when there is a situation where the asset master record contains an internal order and a cost centre, then the depreciation is always posted to the internal order and not to the cost centre.)

6

Lease Accounting (FI-LA)

1. Explain SAP Lease Accounting (FI-LA).

The **lease accounting** in SAP enables you to carry out and display the accounting-relevant aspects of the leasing deal. SAP FI-LA covers all the postings needed in asset accounting, the execution of contract-related accrual postings in G/L accounting, and one-time postings that are made for a lease. Based on the "Lease" contract object, all postings in asset accounting and G/L accounting are made fully automatically.

SAP FI-LA is also known as FI-LAE (Lease Accounting Engine).

Lease accounting is controlled by the ***Lease Accounting Engine***. This is tightly integrated with the CRM system and accounting. In accounting, this includes the Lease Accounting Engine, Accrual Engine, one-time postings, and asset accounting.

2. Explain the key components of Lease Accounting.

The SAP Lease Accounting is made up of the following key components:

- ***CRM Leasing***

  The front end for all lease processing begins with the CRM system. CRM utilizes principally Quotations and Contracts along withIPC and FIMA to price leases.

  - *CRM Billing*- Contracts generate Billing Requirement Items (BRIs) which are selected via the Billing Due List
  - *CRM TTE* - Transaction Tax Engine for calculating sales and lease taxes on transactions. You can also integrate with third party solutions likeVertex O Series.

- ***FI-CA(of FI-AR)***

  Contracts Accounts Payable and Receivable is the standard choice of the leasing application for handling AR and Cash Application

- ***Syndications***

  This is a very new module that was created by an external company, TXS, and handles the process of securing outside financing companies to fund the lease deals

- ***SAP Banking/CML***

  The Commercial Loans Management (CML) module integrates with Syndications to turn the funding stream into Notes Payables for remitting lease payments back to the banks

- ***Lease Accounting Engine(FI-LA or FI-LAE)***

  This is a core module within Financial Accounting and provides all of the posting support for leases.

3. Explain the Lease Accounting Engine (FI-LAE).

The **Lease Accounting Engine** (LAE) is responsible for incoming administration of leases in Accounting.

In Customizing, you need to define how the system processes the values for the lease transferred from SAP-CRM. As soon as a new lease is created in the CRM system (NEWL process) or a change process (for example, BLEX process) is carried out for a lease in the CRM system, SAP-CRM automatically transfers the contract data to the LAE in the SAP system. Using the value identifiers defined in Customizing, the LAE automatically determines the values from the CRM contract that are to be forwarded to Accounting. The LAE then uses these values to classify the lease. In other words, the contract is checked to determine the type of lease involved (capital lease or operating lease).

Leases are classified on the basis of verification rules defined in Customizing. Depending on the result of the classification, the Lease Accounting Engine automatically carries out postings in the Asset Accounting, Accrual Engine, and One-Time Postings applications.

4. Outline the sub-components of Lease Accounting Engine (FI-LAE).

The FI-LAE is the core of the lease accounting in SAP. The sub-components include:

- *Classification*- Using FI Substitutions, you take information from the leased asset and determine its classification, e.g. operating/capital (Direct Finance, Sales Type) asset with or without Bargain Purchase Option (BPO).
- *Fixed Assets*- You can directly integrate with Fixed Assets module to create and capitalize assets. With parallel accounting you can create the book and tax elements of the assets. With subsequent changes to leases, e.g. terminations, extensions, you can handle updates to the assets, calculation of net book values, etc.
- *Accrual Engine*- FI-LAE shares the power of the ACE FI Accrual Engine to post accruals, e.g. Unearned Income, etc.
- *One Time Postings*- For those accounting entries that take place once, there are also ways to let the FI-LAE generate one time postings, e.g. inventory relief, miscellaneous costs etc

5. What is known as 'Value ID' in Lease Accounting?

Value IDs are the actual controlling elements in lease accounting, and they are similar to typical programming variables and act as buckets for key information that are used to feed other critical processing in the Lease Accounting Engine (LAE) like Asset creation/capitalization, Accruals, and One Time Postings. Values can be established within a Value ID either directly from various source transactions or can be derived with different formulas and processing methods.

The value IDs provide information about:

- The origin of a value: a value can come from a contract item, a material master record, customer master record, or condition types, for example.
- Its business function: for example, a financing amount or residual value.

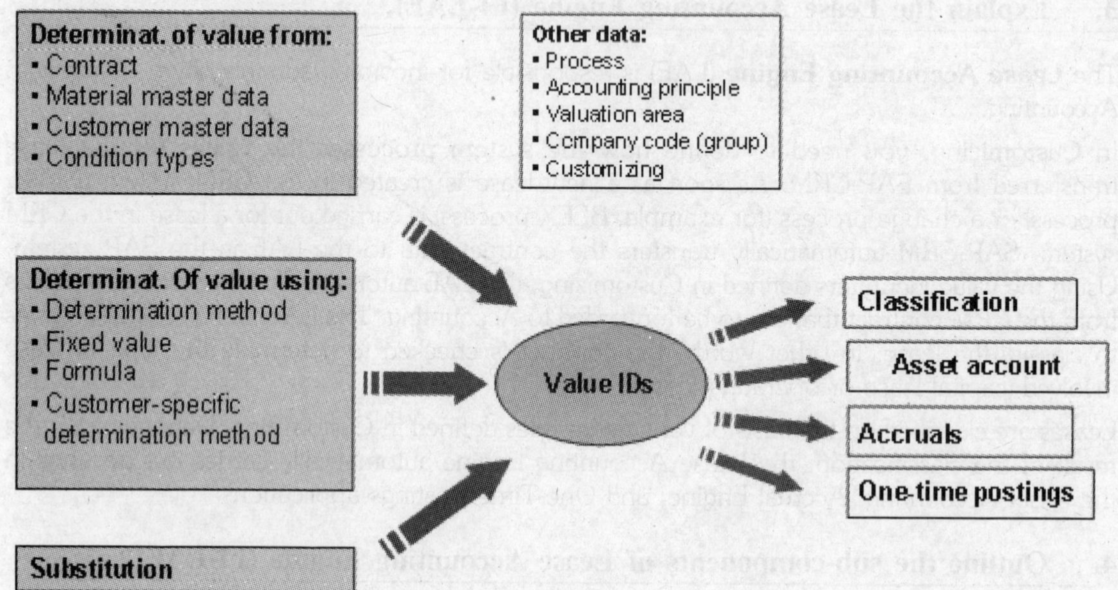

Figure 6.1: Value IDs *(Image © SAP)*

The value IDs are used:

- **As Component of creating, calculating, or deriving other value ids.** -The building block for everything in the LAE, even deriving value ids takes value ids. Simply put, they act like variables throughout.
- **For passing values to Lease Classification routines**-Utilize the same FI Substitution Engine to calculate and determine how leases are classified. Necessary values, e.g. PV of the Rents, are passed for calculations.
- **For creating Fixed Asset Master Records** -The Lease Accounting Engine can automatically create Fixed Assets in Financial Accounting. All the attributes of the fixed asset are established through value ids.
- **Fixed Asset Postings** -Values for capitalizations, retirements, are passed through the Lease Accounting Engine for further processing including determining the Fixed Asset's transaction type to define the posting.
- **For calculating and processing accruals through Accrual Engine** -The Lease

Accounting Engine heavily utilizes FI's Accrual Engine (ACE) to calculate and process accruals. In addition to defined accrual methods (enabled through delivered and customer programmed function modules), you can pass values to the ACE to both define the accrual and its calculations.

- **For one-time Posting** -Value ids not only provide the amounts to be posted, but also the can assist in determining which GL accounts are posted.

6. How you can manage the leased assets in FI-AA??

In the FI-AA system, you can manage the leased assets in two ways:

- As statistical assets (without values)
- Assets capitalized according to the *capital lease* method.

Currently, the capitalization using the capital lease method is possible only if the book depreciation area is included: if you want to capitalize a leased asset only in the cost accounting depreciation area, then you have to do it manually. You have to use special transaction types, which only post to the depreciation areas you want.

7. What is a 'Leasing Type'?

The **leasing type** is an indicator that controls how the leased asset is handled (either as operating lease or capital lease) for book-keeping purposes. Specify the leasing type in the asset class or in the asset master record, and classify the leased assets with the leasing type.

Change View "Leasing Types": Details

New Entries

Leasing type	01	Capital lease
Transact. type	100	External asset acquisition
Doc. type	ZB	Capital Lease Assets
Input tax		
Posting key	31	Invoice
SGL indicator		

Figure 6.2: Leasing Types

The leasing type also contains the essential parameters for posting the acquisition of an asset that is to be capitalized using the capital lease procedure (such as, transaction type). The system determines the accounts to be posted and the amount to be capitalized with the help of (a) active depreciation areas in the respective asset class, and (b) leasing conditions in the asset master record. This way, you can capitalize leased assets according to the capital lease method using the present value of future payments.

SAP provides the 'leasing type 1' as an example.

Transaction Code
OAC1

8. What is a 'Classification'?

The **classification** of financing is a step performed during the processing of leases. A classification in the Lease Accounting Engine (LAE) is performed for all processes apart from terminating processes. The system determines which class the financing belongs to and how a financing transaction is to be mapped in accounting:

- The CRM system uses the CRM interface to transfer the contract data to the system containing the LAE.
  - o The contracts are classified on the basis of various parameters such as the accounting principle, useful life of the asset, and contract term.
- The LAE first determines which validation rule or check sequence is to be used to determine the classification.
  - o Depending on the Customizing settings, it evaluates either individual validation rules or a check sequence of several rules. The system processes the check steps of a check sequence one after the other until it determines a classification. The result is linked with the validation rule or check sequence as per the principle of substitution (access key).
  - o Depending on the result of the classification, the LAE triggers the asset posting and one-time postings in the general ledger and the accrual postings.

9. What are the processes carried out by Lease Accounting Engine in 'Classification'?

The following are the processes carried out by the LAE in the **classification**:

- ***New lease (NEWL)***

  For *operating leases*, the LAE capitalizes the asset in the lessor's asset management system. If the result of the classification process is an operating lease, the system automatically creates an asset master record in FI-AA. This asset master record is assigned to an asset class in Customizing for FI-AA. In turn, the asset class is assigned to one or more accounts in the general ledger.

For *capital leases*, asset acquisition postings are not generated, and only the accrual postings are triggered and posted in the G/L.

- ***Base lease extension (BLEX) or restructuring (REST)***

  The original lease continues with a follow-on contract or follow-on contract item. In SAP CRM, the old contract is ended and a new contract or contract item is created. The new contract or contract item is classified. The old asset is decapitalized.

  For *operating leases*, the old asset is decapitalized in asset management and a new asset is created with the appropriate values. In addition, any accrual postings that have not been released yet are cleared and then posted again.

  For *capital leases*, only the accruals are posted.

- ***Contract termination at end of the contract term (TERM) or earlier (ETER)***

  The classification is not carried out in processes that terminate a contract. The existing assets and accruals are cleared. In addition, depending on the entries in Customizing, one-time postings are made in the general ledger for each accounting principle.

10. Give some examples for 'one-time' postings in FI-LAE.

As explained else where, the 'one-time' postings allow you to allocate and post a variety of charges and adjustments on a one-off basis. This function also offers considerable flexibility when choosing accounts.

Some of the examples include:

- *CHARGE*: Charges levied for termination of contracts (for contracts that are terminated prematurely and those that are terminated normally at the end of the contract term).
- *CORROREV*: Correction of the OREV schedule if the contract is terminated prematurely in the middle of the period.
- *IDC, Initial Direct Cost*: Posted once for incidental acquisition costs relating to operating leases.

7

Travel Management (FI-TV)

SAP Travel Management (FI-TV), is an integrated online solution offering a '360-degree' travel management that supports all the processes involved in handling business trips. With its comprehensive functionality encompassing settlement, taxation, and payment processes, it enables you to:

- Request trips
- Plan trips
- Book trips
- Create travel expense reports
- Transfer expense data to other functional areas

1. What are the implementation considerations for FI-TV?

You need to analyze the travel processes in the company and ascertain:

- What is the approval workflow for business trips?
- Which trip rules have to be considered for which employee groups?
- Will it be necessary to first define trip rules?
- Are there any agreements with external travel service providers that need to be taken into consideration?
- How is the reimbursement process implemented?
- Which organizational units are involved?

Based on the outcome to the above questions, you then need to determine which business tasks you can conduct using SAP Travel Management to increase efficiency, and determine which sub-components (like travel requests, travel planning and travel expenses) you will need to install / activate.

2. How you can combine the sub-components of FI-TV?

Of the three sub-components (viz., travel requests, travel planning and travel expenses), you can use 'travel expense' independent of the other two. Touted as the 'anchor', the travel expense forms the back-bone of SAP travel management, and you can combine this subcomponent with the others as shown in the following combination matrix (Table 7-1):

Table 7.1: SAP Travel Management – Sub-Components

Combination	Travel requests	Travel planning	Travel expenses
A			✖
B	✖	✖	✖
C		✖	✖
D	✖		✖

3. How 'Travel Requests' can support the business processes?

The sub-component **travel requests** streamlines approval processes within SAP Travel Management to reduce process costs to a minimum:

- Sends data such as trip destination, purpose, estimated cost, and preliminary distribution of costs to the approving manager or his portal inbox automatically.
- Pays advances that the traveller requested in this self-service scenario by cash, check, or bank order automatically once the request has been approved.
- Uses workflow conditions for automating approval, e.g., a maximum limit for estimated costs.
- With SAP Duet, this allows users to requests travel within the Outlook Calendar.
    - o Duet workflow routes travel requests, travel plans and expense reports including associated travel budget information to the approving manager's Outlook Inbox.
    - o Approval notifications are returned to the requester's Outlook Inbox. In addition, Duet makes the travel cost information available to the SAP ERP application for expense reporting.

4. Explain 'Travel Planning'.

The **travel planning** in FI-TV enables business travelers through a self-service scenario to book flights, hotels, cars, country-specific rail options, and look up related information.

- Performs online booking by connections to central reservation systems such as Amadeus, Galileo and Sabre.
- With SAP NetWeaver Exchange Infrastructure (SAP NetWeaver XI), it allows direct connections to hotel reservation systems, low cost carrier consolidators and Deutsche Bahn (German rail).
- Supports communication with travel agencies fully and makes it more efficient.
- Cuts agency fees substantially for online bookings and lets the agency concentrate on ticketing and strategic quality assurance.
- A 100% data synchronization of bookings and, if requested, profiles is supported too

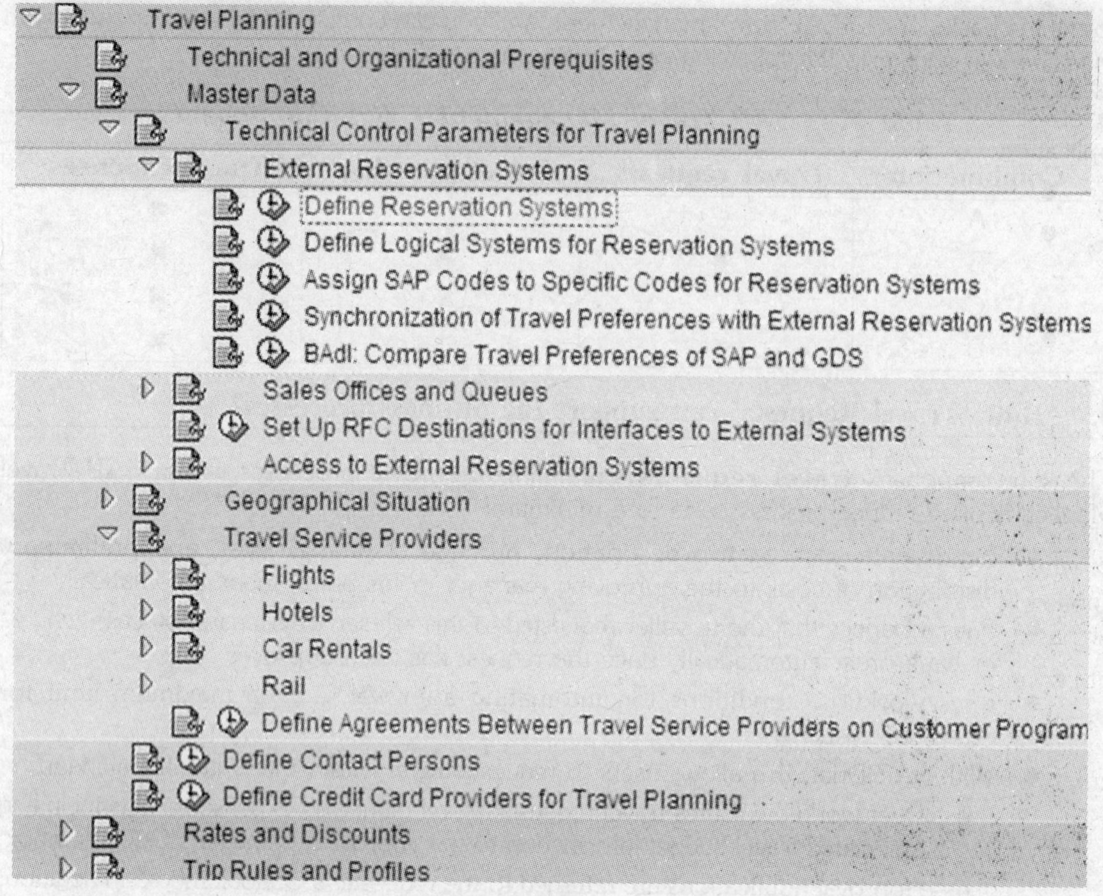

Figure 7.1: Travel Planning in SAP Travel Management

5. How 'Travel Expenses' in FI-TV can help you in travel management?

The sub-component **travel expenses** supports the entire business trip lifecycle - from online buying to expense reimbursement and integration into SAP ERP Financials and SAP ERP HCM:

- Supports receipts and per diems reimbursement, cost assignments, multiple payment modes, etc., via Travel and Expense Management.
- Allows sophisticated expense policy rules to be set up to meet national tax, fiscal, and legal requirements.
- Offers a ready-to-run version for 18 countries with pre-configured settings based on legal requirements, thereby accelerating implementation.
- Provides flexible configuration parameters for easy adoption of further company-specific or international statutory needs.
- Features credit card clearing interfaces to the leading card providers for personal cards, corporate cards, and lodged cards.

- Allows setting up control procedures in order to comply with Sarbanes Oxley and IRS requirements.

It also provides an offline solution, which enables travelers to record their working hours and travel expenses offline based on SAP's time management (CATS) and travel management applications via Mobile Time & Travel (MTT).

- Synchronizes data with the SAP systems using the SAP Mobile Infrastructure.
- Integrates customers' mobile employees with their main SAP systems - anytime, anywhere - to increase employee efficiency, improve data quality, and streamline business processes.
- Enables travelers on the road to access the itinerary data transferred from the travel planning solution, and create expense reports from these.

6. How FI-TV enables 'Global Travel Policy Compliance'?

With **travel planning**, you can control online booking by corporate travel policy parameters, helping travel managers to bundle travel volumes to preferred providers and negotiated fares. The system provides a better compliance with travel policy, which in turn facilitates a better negotiation position for central travel service procurement and has an immediate effect on direct purchasing costs.

With **travel expenses**, it allows the management to implement effective travel policy strategies and controls travel budgets for the global enterprise or institution. Helps to handle trips to locations all over the world, and can also be used in many countries throughout the world. Also permits the international standard version to be configured to meet country-specific requirements.

7. What is 'Travel & Expense Analytics' in SAP Travel Management?

The **travel & expense analytics** in SAP FI-TV keeps all booking and expense data in one place so users can benefit from easy-to-use reporting tools and full data ownership. It also provides exact reporting for total travel cost control and analytical exception monitoring, besides rendering volumes with travel service providers transparent making it easier for users to negotiate and procure travel services.

8. Explain the overall process in SAP Travel Management.

The process flow cuts across the three sub-components, and can be better explained using the Table 7-2:

Table 7.2: Process Flow in SAP Travel Management

FI-TV sub-component	Overall Step #	Travel process flow
Travel requests	1	You use the SAP system to submit a ***travel request*** to your manager. The travel request supplies your manager (superior) with details like the date, destination, and purpose of the trip, the transportation and accommodations required, the requested advance and the estimated costs for the trip
	2	Your manager can approve the request, send it back for corrections, or reject it.
	3	If you have requested an ***advance*** approved, you have the following options for ***payment*** when the advance has been approved: ● Bank transfer to your bank account (via DME) ● Cash payment by cash office ● Check ● Forwarding of the amounts for payment to financial accounting
Travel planning	4	After your travel request has been approved, you then determine the available travel services like flight, hotel and car rental (if you are in Germany, this also covers train) in a ***travel plan*** and book them online in the SAP system. ● The reservation made in an external reservation system is transferred to the SAP system. ● During booking, the system checks to make sure they comply with the company's travel policies as defined in Customizing for Travel Management. ● The system applies any existing company-specific rates and rebate agreements.
	5	When you have recorded the travel plan, the booking code (PNR) is entered in the ***processing queue*** of the ***travel agency***. ● The travel agency checks the correctness and consistency of the booking
	6	If changes are made to the booking outside the SAP system, they are transferred to the SAP system in a ***synchronization process***.
	7	Your travel plan is also transferred to the appropriate manager for approval.

		• As soon as the manager has approved your travel plan, the travel agency issues the ticket and the trip documents and sends them to you.
Travel expenses	8	After you complete the trip, you are required to submit your ***travel expense report***, with all the necessary data and supporting documents. • The system applies all statutory and company-specific specifications stored in Customizing and checks the consistency of the entries against these specifications
	9	The expenses department checks your travel expense report and the original documents and receipts. • Now the travel expense report is sent to the manager for **approval**, who can then release it for settlement
	10	As soon as the trip is approved, it is settled in the SAP system: • On the basis of the trip provisions set for the individual travellers, the system determines the travel expense results, especially the amount for reimbursement. • To determine the reimbursement amount, it is possible to choose between per diem/flat rate reimbursement and reimbursement according to individual receipts for meals, accommodations and travel costs; for all other categories, reimbursement on the basis of individual receipts must be used
	11	The travel expense results are prepared to suit the ***method of payment*** chosen and made available to the corresponding components (Financial Accounting, Payroll Accounting, Controlling Funds Management) with the appropriate additional information
	12	The ***payment of reimbursement amounts*** can be: • By check • Through payroll accounting • Through financial accounting • By bank transfer to your (the employee's) bank account (via DME) The travel expense results are always transferred for posting to Financial Accounting. The amounts are transferred from Financial Accounting to Controlling.
	13	You receive a ***travel expense statement*** with the relevant trip data and the accounting results.

9. Explain the roles in SAP FI-TV.

From Release 4.6, **roles** (single or composite roles) are available in SAP Travel Management covering the most important tasks involved in processing the trip data. Assigning roles to users enables them to work in the SAP system purely on the basis of tasks and functions.

The roles in FI-TV support both the decentralized and central organization of the trip process, as well as a mixture of the two with the focus on decentralization:

- For the decentralized organization the travelers are responsible for entering their own travel requests, travel plans and travel expenses in the system.
- For a mixed or central organization these tasks are carried out by a travel assistant on behalf of several travelers.
- The role of the travel administrator allows the settlement of travel expenses to be organized centrally, whereby the settlements are entered and checked centrally.

The standard SAP comes delivered with the following roles for SAP Travel Management:

Role Name

Single role	Role name
SAP_FI_TV_ADMINISTRATOR	Travel Management Administrator
SAP_FI_TV_ADVANCE_PAYER	Trip Advance Payer
SAP_FI_TV_MANAGER_GENERIC	Approving Manager
SAP_FI_TV_TRAVEL_ASSISTANT	Travel Assistant
SAP_FI_TV_TRAVEL_MANAGER	Travel Manager
SAP_FI_TV_TRAVELER	Traveler

Figure 7.2: Roles in SAP FI-TV

Transaction Code
PFCG

10. Explain the technical set-up of the FI-TV application.

The following are the possibilities of setting up of FI-TV, from the technical point of view:

1. In combination with SAP Payroll Accounting (HR) and SAP Accounting (AC)
2. In combination with HR and separate from AC
3. In combination with AC and separate from HR
4. Separate from HR and AC

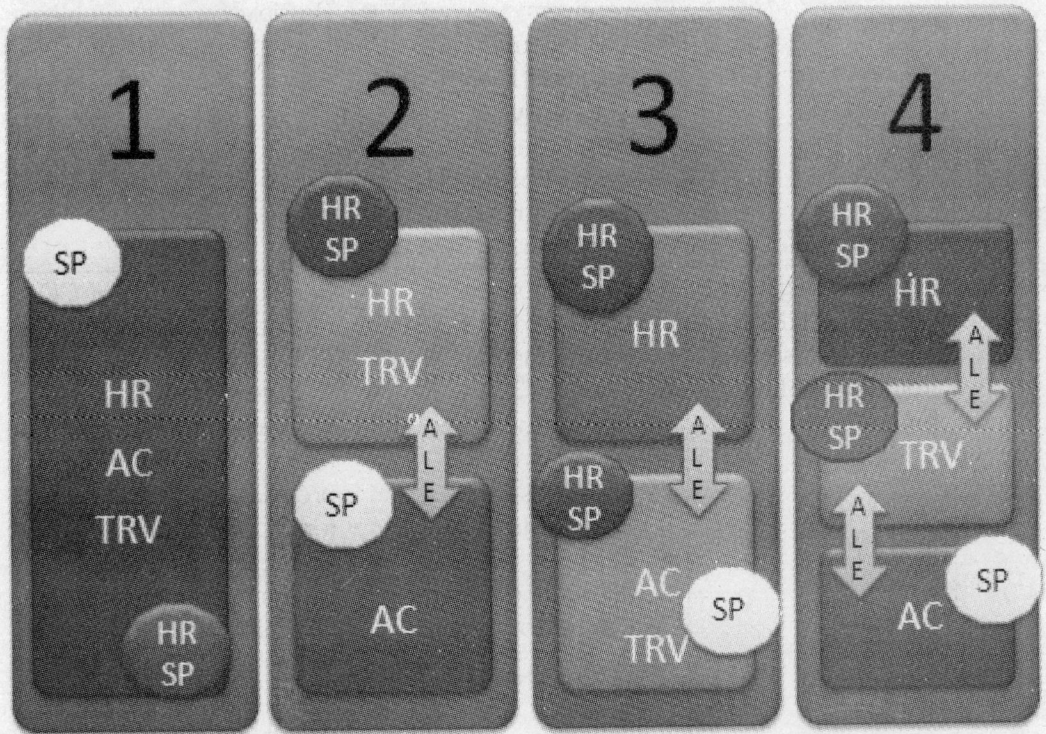

Figure 7.3: SAP FI-TV – Technical Set-up

Depending on the configuration, Support Packages (SP) and HR Support Packages (HR SP) have to be imported into the respective systems.

11. Outline the advantages / disadvantages of various technical setups of FI-TV.

The advantages / disadvantages associated with the each of combination of the technical set up of FI-TV are shown in Table 7-3:

Table 7.3: FI-TV Technical Setup Options – Advantages / Disadvantages

Option	Technical set up of FI-TV	Advantages	Disadvantages
1	Travel Management (TRV), HR, and Accounting (AC) in one system	• No need for distribution of HR master data, travel expense and results to Payroll CO receivers • Validation of CO receivers is carried out locally • Synchronous posting of travel expense results to Accounting	• Human Resources, Accounting, and Travel Management have to have the same release status • Lack of flexibility • Possible capacity problems
2	Travel Management (TRV) and HR in one system separate from Accounting (AC)	• No distribution of travel expense results for Payroll • Travel Management and Accounting can have a different release status • Existing accounting systems can be connected.	• Remote validation of CO receivers in Accounting via ALE • CO receivers have to be replicated in the Travel Management System to provide a correct input help for CO receivers • To create person-related vendors automatically, the HR master data (infotypes 0000, 0001, 0002, 0003, 0006, 0009, 0017, and 0105) has to be replicated in the Accounting system via ALE. • Asynchronous posting of travel expense results to Accounting via ALE. To ensure successful posting to the Accounting system in this case, the posting run must be validated before it is sent.
3	Travel Management (TRV) and Accounting (AC) in	• **No** distribution of CO receivers is required, CO	• HR master data (infotypes 0000, 0001, 0002, 0003, 0006, 0009, 0017, 0105)

	one system separate from HR	receivers are validated locally ● Payroll Accounting and Travel Management can have a different release status ● Synchronous posting of travel expense results to Accounting. In this case incorrect documents in a posting run can be rejected.	has to be replicated via ALE ● Travel expense results for Payroll have to be replicated via ALE ● Both the Support Packages and the HR Support Packages have to be imported into the Travel Management and or Accounting Systems.
4	Travel Management (TRV), Accounting (AC) and HR in separate systems	● Payroll Accounting, Travel Management, and Accounting can all have a different release status ● Maximum flexibility ● Existing Accounting and HR systems can be connected	● HR master data (infotypes 0000, 0001, 0002, 0003, 0006, 0009, 0017, 0105) has to be replicated in the Travel Management system via ALE ● To create person-related vendor master records in FI automatically, the HR master data (infotypes 0000, 0001, 0002, 0003, 0006, 0009, 0017, and 0105) has to be replicated in the Accounting system via ALE ● Travel expense results for Payroll have to be replicated via ALE ● Remote validation of CO receivers ● CO receivers have to be replicated in the Travel Management System to provide a correct input help for CO receivers ● Asynchronous posting of travel expense results to Accounting via ALE. To ensure successful posting to the Accounting system in

			this case, the posting run must be validated before it is sent.

12. Is there a guideline to select the system infrastructure for FI-TV?

You may use the guidelines outlined in Table 7-4 to decide on the system infrastructure appropriate for the technical set-up you need:

Table 7.4: FI-TV Technical Setup – Infrastructural Options

Criteria	FI-TV technical set up option			
	1	**2**	**3**	**4**
Replication of all HR Master Data via ALE	No	AC*	AC	TRV &AC*
Replication of CO Objects via ALE (for F4)	No	HR / TRV	No	TRV
Validation of CO Objects	Local	Remote via ALE	Local	Remote via ALE
Replication of TRV travel expense results in HR Via ALE	No	No	Yes	Yes
Transfer to AC	Synchronous	Asynchronous	Asynchronous	Synchronous
Different release status possible	No	HR/TRV & AC	HR/TRV & AC	HR & TRV & AC
Adaptability to existing system infrastructure	Poor	Good	Good	Very Good
HR Support Packages have also to be imported into AC	No	No	Yes	No

*Required only if the person-related vendor master records are to be created or maintained automatically.

13. What is 'Travel Manager'?

The **Travel Manager** is directed at occasional users who want to process their own trips or to employees who have a few travelers assigned to them. The Travel Manager covers all the process steps in Travel Management in a single transaction with a uniform interface design. Since the Travel Manager supports the entire Travel Management process, the data is fully integrated in Payroll (HR), Financial Accounting (FI), Cost Accounting (CO), and Funds Management (FM). You can obtain reporting data in the Business Information Warehouse (BW) and the reports in SAP Travel Management. The reporting data covers both pre and post-trip reports.

Depending on your Customizing settings, you can use the Travel Manager to:

- Create Travel Requests
- Create and Book Travel Services (with and without a template)
- Create Travel Expense Statements (with and without a template)
- Display an Overview of All Trips

In each section of the Travel Manager (travel request, travel planning and travel expenses) you can work through the screen from top to bottom as you are used to doing with printed forms. You carry out these actions in the processing area. You do not have to switch between tab pages or screens, all the data is available at all times in the overview.

Transaction Code
TRIP

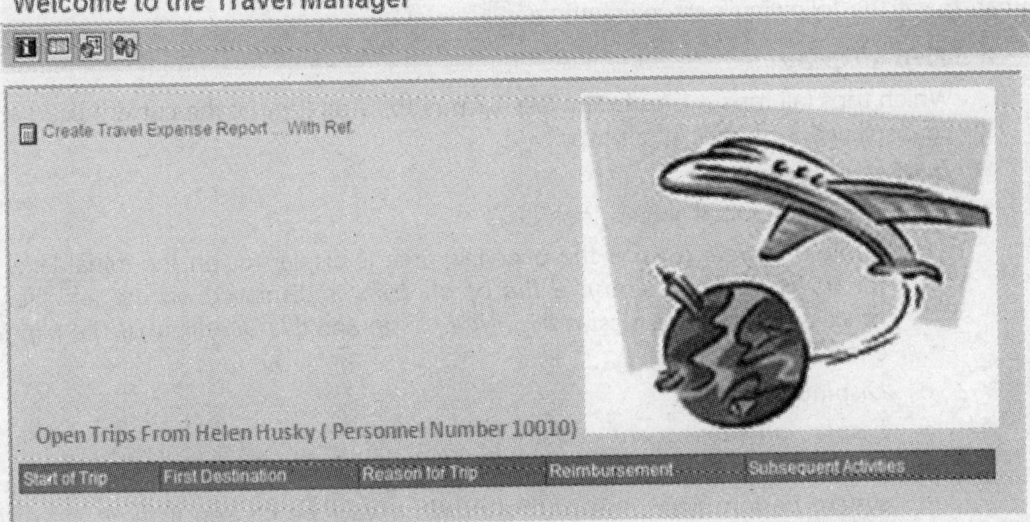

Figure 7.4: SAP Travel Manager – Initial Screen

Note that you will not be able go into the transaction unless you input a valid 'personnel number' when you start the transaction.

14. What is a 'Travel Request'?

Travel request, is a part of the travel manager supporting system-aided handling of the entire process of a business trip (from the initial request, planning, and booking until settlement) It is an information unit containing all the data that a traveller needs to submit to his or her manager for approval, advance payment, or booking, or that the manager needs to know before approving a trip. No paper form is required as the request is done electronically.

The travel request can include:

- Trip advance required
- Trip date / time
- Trip destination
- Trip itinerary (additional destination)
- Trip notes / comments
- Trip reason
- Trip's estimated cost

You can always keep track of the approval status of a travel request, besides looking at the trip details any time, by accessing the request from the overview area of the '*Travel Manager*'. The travel request is linked to the use of '*Travel Expenses*'.

15. What 'Personal Settings' you can make in 'Travel Manager'?

You can make the following personal settings

- ***Trip display***

  Which trips (all trips / trips in the last 12 months / all trips of the current year) are to be displayed in the list of all trips?

- ***Initial screen***

  How should the initial screen look like?

  - o *Show overview area*: If the overview area is displayed, on the initial level and for travel expenses entry, a *list of all trips* is displayed on the left. For the processing levels *Request a trip, Plan a trip* and the *Overview of the trip facts entered* is displayed.
  - o *Display screens*
  - o *Display all subsequent activity*
  - o *Basis HTML* (for display problems): Deactivated in the standard system for system performance, this setting should always be chosen if there are display problems.

- ***Storage of entries***

  How many entries are to be stored in the personal input help (F4 help): you can determine (for text fields, country and region fields and assignment objects) how many of the values you use are to be noted by the system and displayed, when you call the personal input help.

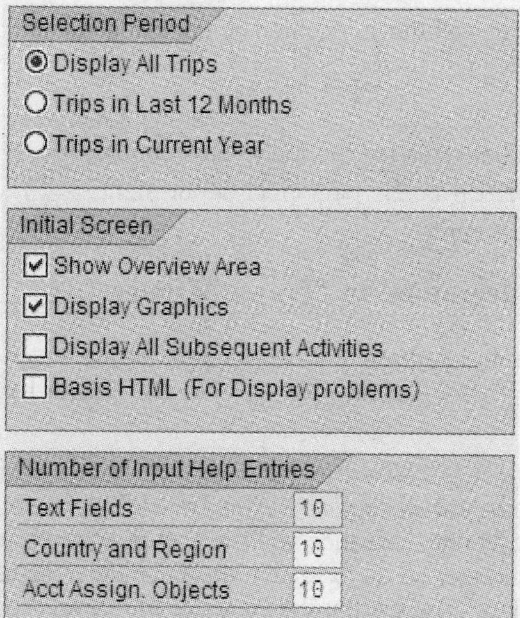

Figure 7.5: 'Personal Settings' in Travel Manager

16. What is an 'Infocenter'?

The **infocenter** is available in the 'Travel Manager', 'Planning Manager' and 'Travel Expense Manager'. The data is taken from Customizing or the specifications from '*Infotype 0001*' (Organizational Assignment).

Infocenter

Exch Rates | PDs/FRs | Traveler | Addnl Traveler Info

Currency Selection

From Currency GBP British Pound

To Currency INR Indian Rupee

Translation Date 10/10/2007

Results

100.00 GBP = 0.00 INR Rate

100.00 INR = 0.00 GBP Rate

Daily Spot Rate

Figure 7.6: Infocenter

Wherever you are, you can call the infocenter by choosing **H** (or Extras -> Infocenter), and the system will bring in:

- Exchange rates
- The per diems/flat rates for the individual countries
- Your contact person in the personnel department
- Your master cost center

17. Explain 'Data Integration' in 'Travel Manager'.

It is easy to explain the data integration, when we look at the status flow across the three sub-components namely the Travel Request, Travel Plan and Travel Expenses:

Travel Request

When a new *travel request* is created in the Travel Manager (Transaction Code: TRIP), the system also creates a similar *travel request* in the Travel Expense Manager (Transaction Code: PR05) transferring the basic data, advance and the cost assignment details to the travel request of the Travel Expense Manager so as to enable the payment / settlement of advances, if any. While doing this, the system ensures that the status of the travel request in the Travel Manager and in the Travel Expense Manager has the same value: if you approve the *travel request* of the Travel Manager, then the *travel request* in the Travel Expense Manager is also approved. This also applies the other way around: when the *travel request* status is approved in the Travel Expense Manager, then the status of the same *travel request* remains approved in the Travel Manager as well. This applies until a *trip* gets the status 'Trip Completed' or 'Trip Approved' from the travel request in the Travel Expense Manager.

Travel Plan

A *travel plan* needs to be created to book the required *travel item* (flight, hotel, rental car, train) for the travel request raised in the Travel Manager (Transaction Code: TRIP). Though a *travel plan* can have one of the three status viz., *open, approved* or *rejected*, these statuses do not normally affect the status of the *trip*: the status of a *travel plan* is independent of that of the *travel request*.

- Any change in the basic data, itinerary or the travel comments are not transferred back to the *travel request*.
- If the advance or the cost assignment in the *travel plan* is changed, then the *travel request* must be approved as this affects costs: now there will be two approval - approval of the *travel plan* and approval of the *travel request*. However, it is possible to simplify this if you approve a *travel request* when you approve the *travel plan* in the Travel Manager.

Travel Expenses

Once the *trip* has taken place, data is added to the *travel request* for the *trip* in the Travel Expense Manager (the status can be 'Trip Completed' or 'Trip Approved'). The itinerary data, trip comments and the ticket or booking data from the *travel plan* is added to the existing trip data. If there is no *travel plan*, the data (such as itinerary and trip comments) are transferred from any existing *travel request*.

18. What are the two statuses for a 'Travel Request' in the 'Travel Manager'?

Forming a part of the process control of Travel Management, the travel request status (in the Travel Manager) is used to determine whether different individual business procedures are permitted or not.

In the Travel Manager, a travel request can have either of the following two statuses:

- Request entered
- Request approved

Do not confuse the travel request status from the Travel Manager with the approval status value 'Request entered' from Travel Expenses.

19. What is a 'Travel Plan'?

The **travel plan** object constitutes the basis for all actions in Travel Planning: to start price and availability queries and book travel services. The general trip data (such as the personnel number, destination, reason for the trip, and the trip activity) are stored in the travel plan. Each travel plan is stored in the system with a trip number that identifies it uniquely, so that booked travel services have a unique assignment. The assignment of the travel services is also used for the object-specific transfer of the data to Travel Expenses. The travel plan thus has the same number as the trip to be settled.

You may create a travel plan from the Travel Manager or Planning Manager.

20. What is a 'Planning Manager'?

The **Planning Manager** is an entry transaction for creating and editing travel plans. With it you can:

- Check availability of flights, hotel rooms, car rentals, and trains
- Find out the best-price flight combinations for the whole trip
- Book flights, hotel rooms, and rental cars online
- Cancel and rebook reserved services

Planning Manager

Create | Change | Display | Copy | Cancel | Delete | Approve

PersonnelNo

Name

		Trip	Start Date	Time	End	Time	Destination	Reason	Approval	Booking Code

Figure 7.7: Planning Manager

- Update of data automatically in SAP Travel Management whenever changes are made by the travel provider

Transaction Code
TP01

When a travel plan is created, the system automatically creates the corresponding travel expense report. As soon as you book a travel service online in the reservation system and save the travel plan, a corresponding receipt for the travel service is created in Travel Expenses.

21. How 'Travel Expenses' is integrated with other application areas in SAP?

The travel expense transfer amounts can be reimbursed to the employee via Financial Accounting (FI), Payroll (HR), or via Data Medium Exchange. Within the Travel Expenses process, Travel Management accesses master data in SAP Personnel Administration (HR). To support the approval process, Travel Expenses is connected to the SAP Business Workflow component. Using ESS (Employee Self Service), the travellers can both request and plan their trip and enter the relevant data in an online travel expense report after the trip has been completed.

Using travel expenses, you can:

- Allocate travel expenses to SAP Controlling (CO)
- Allocate travel expenses to SAP Funds Management (FM)
- Calculate taxation in SAP Payroll (HR)
- Post travel expenses to SAP Financial Accounting (FI)

22. What are the elements of a 'Trip'?

An **employee trip** is a business trip taken by an employee, involving a change of location, including the outbound trip and return trip, for reasons of a temporary external activity. A **business trip** can be initiated by Personnel Development (HR) or Shift Planning (HR). You can forward the travel expense results produced by Travel Expenses for proper posting to Financial Accounting (FI) and to Payroll (HR) for tax calculation. You can reimburse the trip transfer amount to the employee via Financial Accounting (FI), Payroll (HR), or data medium exchange. You can forward the trip costs assignment specifications for internal cost accounting to Controlling (CO) or for cash budget management to Funds Management (FM).

A trip includes:

- *Trip data*-contains the facts about a trip (such as miles travelled and accommodation expenses) that are relevant for the settlement of travel expenses or that document the trip.
- *Travel expense assignments*
- *Travel expense results and trip transfer amount* created by SAP Travel Expenses

on the basis of the trip data

- *Trip status* indicating the state of the trip to control the permissibility of certain business transactions

23. Do you need an employee's HR master record for entering the 'Trips'?

As the Travel planning accesses a minimal HR master data record, the use of SAP Human Resources (HR) is not an absolute prerequisite for the use of SAP Travel Management. Remember that the person-related master data is stored in 'infotypes' that enable structured processing of this data. The special infotypes in SAP Travel Planning is based on the same logic as the infotypes in SAP Human Resources. They are however independent of HR infotypes and have no influence on existing infotypes in Human Resources.

Travellers abide automatically by the 'enterprise-specific trip rules' stored in the system. However, for planning and booking travel services, they can also enter personal preferences that are taken into consideration by the travel service provider, if possible. These personal preferences are only taken into consideration if they comply with company travel policy.

24. What is 'Personnel Mini-master'?

To store person-related master data, you create a **personnel 'mini-master'** record directly in SAP Travel Planning. You do not need to use the Human Resources component. You can simply create all the infotypes necessary for SAP Travel Planning via the personnel action 'Travel planning setting'. When you enter infotypes for the first time you are guided through these actions step by step. HR master data you have already created can be changed or supplemented at any time.

25. What are all the mandatory / optional 'Infotypes'?

The following infotypes are mandatory (Table 7-5) for any employee for whom a trip is to be booked using Travel Planning:

- Organizational assignment (0001)
- Personal data (0002)
- Travel Privileges (0017)
- Addresses (0006)

Table 7.5: Infotypes: Mandatory / Optional

Infotypes	
Mandatory	**Optional**
0001	0009
0002	0027
0006	0470 - 0473
0017	0475

- It is not advisable to make a booking without infotype 0006, as the Telephone number field in this infotype is used to create the booking record. This infotype is also used with the infotype Bank details (0009) in Travel Expenses, if the settled trips are to be paid as a credit via Financial Accounting (FI).
- The infotype Cost Distribution (0027) is only used in Travel Expenses for distributing the total costs to different cost centers.
- The Travel Planning-specific infotypes 0470 - 0475 represent the personal preferences of the individual employees (The infotype Rail Preference (0474) has no meaning). Even though these infotypes are optional, they enable employees' personal preferences to be taken into consideration for each business trip booking.
  - The infotype Travel profile (0470) allows a direct assignment of a travel profile to an employee.
  - The infotype Flight preference (0471) contains information specific to a flight, such as meals, seat position and preferred departure airport.
  - The infotype Hotel preference (0472) contains information about the preferred room and hotel category.
  - The infotype Car rental preference (0473) contains information such as the preferred make of car and air conditioning.
  - The infotype Customer program (0475) can be created many times, as it relates to all the provider categories. Here, you can store information about frequent fliers or special car rental or hotel customer programs.
- The additional infotype Communication (0105), subtype 0001, is used to assign system users to the active SAP system directly (SAP Business Workflow, SAP Office and ESS). Subtype 011 is used for credit card.

26. Explain the approval process in 'Travel Planning'.

The approval (requires a special authorization for the person who is to approve the travel plan) of a travel plan can be done in two ways:

- **Manual Approval** (through the entry transactions of Travel Planning).

  The traveller can see in the respective entry transactions by the approval status in the overview of his trips, which travel plans has been approved or rejected.

  The superior calls the appropriate travel plan in the entry transaction and carries out the 'Approve' function. The process flow is as shown in Table 7-6.
- By **SAP Business Workflow** (SAP Travel Management supports the approval process with a 'reference approval procedure' that can be adapted to suit any company's requirements at any time)
  - The travel planning data is entered in the system by traveller / travel assistant
  - The superior approves the travel plan: determined by the system automatically based on the maintained structural organization.
  - The superior can approve the travel plan, return it to the traveller for correction or reject it.

Table 7.6: Approvals in Travel Planning

Planning Manager	
Travel plans can be ● Approved ● Rejected	1. Call the *Planning manager.* 2. In the overview table, select a travel plan. 3. Choose *Travel plan -> Approve.* 4. On the popup that appears decide whether you want to *approve* or *reject* the travel plan.
Travel Manager	
Travel plans can be ● Approved	1. Call the *Travel manager.* 2. Position the cursor in the overview area (on the left-hand side or can be called up via *List of all trips*) on a travel plan. 3. Choose *Change.* 4. Choose *Travel plan -> Approve.*

- o When the superior has approved the travel plan, the traveller is informed of this via an automatically generated mail. The booking record is put in a processing queue of the connected travel agency.
- o If a correction is necessary the superior appends a message to this effect to the workflow. The employee receives a work item with this attachment. When the work item is executed the transaction to change the travel plan is started.
- o If the travel plan is rejected the superior enters a message that the traveller receives as a mail. The booking is then cancelled.

The approval status of a travel plan is displayed in the respective overview screens of the Planning Manager and Travel Manager. The various statuses for the approval process are shown in Table 7-7.

Table 7.7: Approval Process Statuses

Status	Meaning
Open	The superior responsible has not yet processed the trip.
Approved	The superior has approved the trip.
Rejected	The superior has rejected the trip.

27. What is known as 'Trip Transfer Document'?

A **trip transfer document** contains the summarized and formatted settlement results for one or more trips for transfer to Accounting. From the data in a trip transfer document, Accounting creates posting documents for G/L accounting, sub-ledger accounting and Controlling etc.

The system assigns a unique key to each trip transfer document. This key is transferred as a reference to the header data of the corresponding posting documents of Accounting. With this key, you can find the corresponding trip transfer document and the trips referred to in the posting document from the Accounting posting document at any time. Every trip transfer document belongs to exactly one posting run.

The physical structure of a trip transfer document depends on the conditions that you specify for the summarization of posting lines and documents when you create a posting run:

- You can decide separately for the expense posting and the off-setting entry whether the system should summarize the data within the posting line per trip, per employee, or per account assignment object.
- You can decide whether the system creates a trip transfer document per trip, per employee, per account assignment object, or per company code.

Every trip transfer document consists of at least two posting lines: in one posting line, all of the settlement results are collected that have the same G/L account, the same input tax code and the same account assignment objects.

28. What is a 'Posting Run'?

A **posting run** is a container for trip transfer documents. It has a unique number and a status (like 'posting with zeros', 'no documents selected', 'all documents checked' etc)

In a posting run, the results of travel expense settlement are collected as trip transfer documents for transfer to Accounting. The posting run status keeps you informed of the transfer process and influences whether a trip can be changed or not. You can not change the trips contained in a posting run until you have posted the complete posting run.

29. Can you cancel a 'Trip' that has been posted in Accounting?

Yes, it is possible to cancel a trip that has been posted in Accounting. To effect cancellation, you have to change the trip status to settlement status 'Cancelled'. This can be done using the entry scenarios or the approval program. In the approval program, the trips and requests are given the settlement status '*Po.can.*' (Posting cancelled) and the status '*Corr.*' (corrected).

The next settlement run also includes trips that have the settlement status 'Cancelled'. The settlement program replaces the old payroll period of these trips with the payroll period with which the settlement program was started.

The next time settlement results are transferred to Accounting after the settlement run, the system includes the trips that have settlement status 'Cancelled' in the posting run. Cancellation of postings in Accounting takes place when the posting run is posted. In the approval program, finally, the trips and requests are given the settlement status '*Can.po.*' (Cancellation posted).

30. How to post the 'Private Expenses' paid by the company?

You may use the 'Receipt Wizard' to post the private expenses that are not applicable for reimbursement. SAP has provided two new expense types for receipts that have already paid by the company:

- PRIV Private Shares (expenses), that need to be paid back
- PRBZ Private shares (expenses), that were paid by the company

By using these two expense types PRIV & PRBZ you can ensure that:

- Private expenses, that are not applicable for reimbursement, are shown as debits for travelers, and must, therefore, be paid back to the company.
- Private expenses for receipts that have already been paid are shown as credits in the expense account assigned to the paid receipt (this means that the expense is reduced by this amount), or that the expense account is not debited with the private expense in the first place.
- The travel expense form shows the correct figures for the reimbursement amount, the amount paid by the company and the total expenses for the trip.
- Data entry and usage is as easy and simple as possible for the user.

31. Explain 'Travel Information System'.

The **Travel Information System** in Travel Expenses supports the user for monitoring and analyzing the travel expenses incurred. Within the SAP system you can also use travel expense reports from the Manager's Desktop in HR Personnel Management. You can also use the data from Travel Expenses if you use the reports from Business Information Warehouse (BW). However, to use the data from Travel Expenses for reports, you need to have made the appropriate settings in Customizing for Travel Management under *Travel Expenses* > *Define Structure of Trip Statistics*.

Several reports and queries are available for you to use in the Travel Expenses Information System (Table 7-9).

Table 7.8: Reports / Queries in Travel Expenses Information System

Trip statistics	• General trip data/trip totals • Trip receipts • Trip receipts without general data • Cost assignment for trip • Cost assignment for trip without general data • General trip data/totals/receipts/cost assignments • Who is where? Search for trip destinations • Search for receipts using maximum rate
Diverse trip reports	• Reporting trip costs by periods • Statement for income-related expenses • Input tax recovery • Determination of employees with exceeded trip days

8

SAP FI Tables

Table 8.1: SAP FI Tables

#	Are you looking for:	Table
1	Account Assignment Templates for GL Account items	KOMU
2	Account Master (Chart of Accounts)	SKA1
3	Accounting Correspondence Requests	BKORM
4	Accounting Data – A/R and A/P Information System	RFRR
5	Accounting Document Header	BKPF
6	Accounting Document Header (docs from External Systems)	EBKP
7	Accounting Document Header	BKPF
8	Accounting Document Segment	BSEG
9	Accounting secondary index for customers	BSID
10	Accounting secondary index for customers - cleared items	BSAD
11	Accounting- Secondary Index for GL Accounts	BSIS
12	Accounting- Secondary Index for GL Accounts (Cleared Items)	BSAS
13	Accounting secondary index for vendors	BSIK
14	Accounting secondary index for vendors - cleared items	BSAK
15	Accounts Blocked by Dunning Selection	MAHN
16	Asset Accounting: Basic Functions	FI-A
17	Asset Class: Depreciation Area	ANKB
18	Asset classes- Description	ANKT
19	Asset Classes: Field Cont Dependent on Chart	ANKP
20	Asset Classes: General Data	ANKA
21	Asset Classes: Insurance Types	ANKV
22	Asset down payment settlement	ANEV
23	Asset Line Items	ANEP

24	Asset Master Record Segment	ANLA
25	Asset Master Record Segment	ANLX
26	Asset Master Record User Fields	ANLU
27	Asset Periodic Values	ANLP
28	Asset Texts	ANLT
29	Asset Type Text	ANAT
30	Asset Types	ANAR
31	Asset Value Fields	ANLC
32	Bank master record	BNKA
33	Business Partner Master (General Data)	BP000
34	Cash Management Line Items in Payment Requests	FDZA
35	Create GL account with reference	TSAK
36	Credit Management : FI Status data	KNKK
37	Customer / Vendor Linking	KLPA
38	Customer master - general data	KNA1
39	Customer master - partner functions	KNVP
40	Customer master - sales data	KNVV
41	Customer master - sales request form	KNVD
42	Customer Master (Company Code)	KNB1
43	Customer Master Bank Details	KNBK
44	Customer Master Credit Management : Central Data	KNKA
45	Customer Master Credit Management : Control Area Data	KNKK
46	Customer Master Dunning Data	KNB5
47	Customer Master Special GL Transactions Figures	KNC3
48	Customer Master Transaction Figures	KNC1
49	Customer Payment History	KNB4
50	Depreciation Terms	ANLB
51	Document Header Asset Posting	ANEK
52	Document Header for Document Parking	VBKF
53	Document Header Supplement for Recurring Entry	BKDF
54	Document Type Texts	T003T
55	Dunning Data (Account Entries)	MHNK
56	Electronic Bank Statement Line Items	FEBEP
57	Financial Accounting 'Basis'	FBAS
58	GL Account Master (Chart of Accounts –Description)	SKAT
59	GL Account Master (Chart of Accounts –Key Word list)	SKAS

60	GL Account Master (Chart of Accounts)	SKA1
61	GL Account Master (Company Code)	SKB1
62	General Ledger Accounting: Basic	FI-G
63	General Ledger Accounting: Basic	FI-G
64	Global Settings for Payment Program for Payment Requests	F111
65	Index for Vendor Validation of Double Documents	BSIP
66	Insurable Values (Year Dependent)	ANLW
67	Inter Company Posting Procedure	BVOR
68	Main Asset Number	ANLH
69	Management Records for the Dunning Program	MAHNV
70	Name of Transaction Type	AT10T
71	One-Time Account Data Document Segment	BSEC
72	Payment Medium File	PAYR
73	Payment Requests	PAYR
74	Pre-numbered Check	PCEC
75	Pricing Communication Header	KOMK
76	Run Date of a Program	FRUN
77	Secondary Index, Documents for Material	BSIM
78	Settings for GL Posting Reports	FIGL
79	Substitutions	GB92
80	Tax Code Names	T007S
81	TemSe - Administration Data	REGUT
82	Time Dependent Asset Allocations	ANLZ
83	Transaction Activity Category- Description	AT02T
84	Transaction Code for Menu TIMN	AT02A
85	Transaction type	AT10
86	Validation / Substitution User	GB03
87	Validation	GB93
88	Vendor Master (Company Code Section)	LFB1
89	Vendor Master (General Section)	LFA1
90	Vendor Master Bank Details	LFBK
91	Vendor master- dunning data	LFB5
92	Vendor Master Dunning Data	LFB5
93	Vendor master record: purchasing data	LFM2
94	Vendor master record: purchasing organization data	LFM1
95	Vendor Master Transaction Figures	LFC1

9

SAP FI Transaction Codes

This chapter lists some of the important Transaction Codes (T-Codes) in Financial Accounting, for your easy reference. The notable feature of these lists is the way these Transaction Codes have been arranged here: it is not an alphabetical list because such a list may not serve your purpose when you do not know the Transaction Code, but are looking for with some description in your mind. The Transaction Codes are arranged based on their functionality or usage or task so that it becomes easier for any one to search for it. Look for key words in the 2nd column of the Table ('are you looking for'), and then look at the corresponding Transaction Code under 'T-Code' column.

All the Transaction Codes are stored in the system in Tables TSTC & TSTCT.

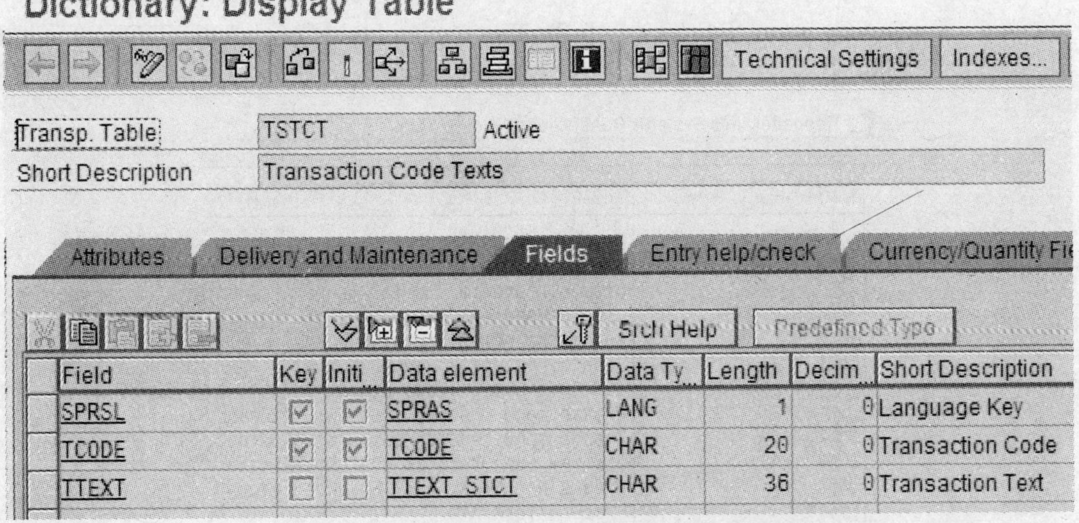

Figure 9.1: Fields in Table 'TSTCT'

It will not be practical to list all the Transaction Codes of SAP FI, and is not required as well. As you get to know, you will learn to look for Transaction Codes by going through the Transaction Code SE93. Should you want to know some Transaction Codes which are not listed in the following pages, use the Transaction Code SE93 for finding the same.

Transaction Code
SE93

There are two ways of finding the Transaction Codes using SE93:

1. When you know the application area: say, you want to list all the Transaction Codes starting with 'IQ'. Enter 'IQ*' in the initial screen (Figure 9-2).

Figure 9.2: Initial Screen in SE93

   a. Search using 'F4' (Figure 9-3). The system brings out all the T-Codes starting with 'IQ'.

Repository Info System: Transactions Find (31 Hits)

Transaction Code	Short text
IQ01	Create Material Serial Number
IQ02	Change Material Serial Number
IQ03	Display Material Serial Number
IQ04	Create Material Serial Number
IQ08	Change Material Serial Number
IQ09	Display Material Serial Number
IQM_CM_CONFIG	IQM Information Consistency
IQM1	Create cond. records qual.notificatn
IQM2	Change cond.records qual.notificatn
IQM3	Display cond.records qual.notificatn
IQS1	Create Notification - Extended View
IQS12	Process Task
IQS12_EWT	Process Task
IQS13	Display Task
IQS13_EWT	Display Task

Figure 9.3: Search using 'F4' in SE93

2. In case you do not know or do not have any clue about the Transaction Codes, but still want to find out, then you need to go via the 'Selection Screen' after you enter the Transaction Code SE93. Place the cursor in the 'Application Component' field on the pop-up (Figure 9-4):

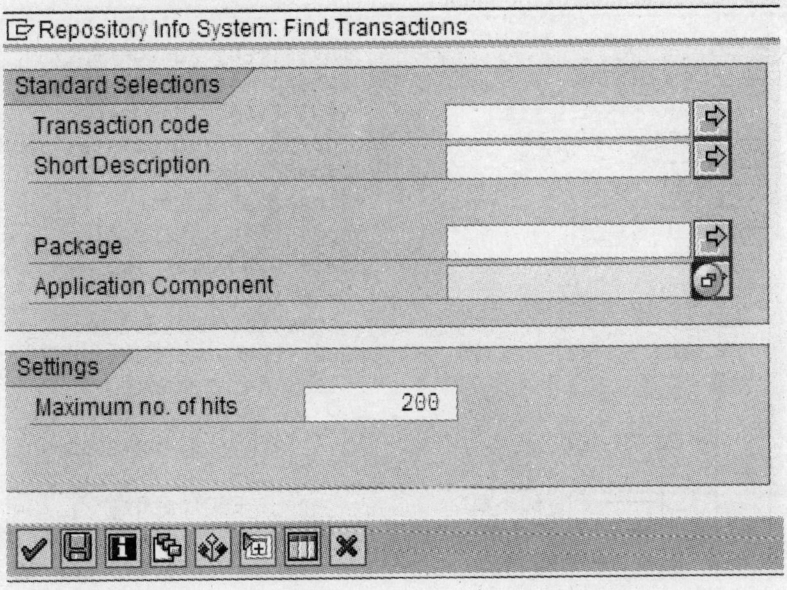

Figure 9.4: Search in an 'Application Component'

a. Press 'F4'. The system pops-up the 'Select Application Component' screen as shown in Figure 9-5.

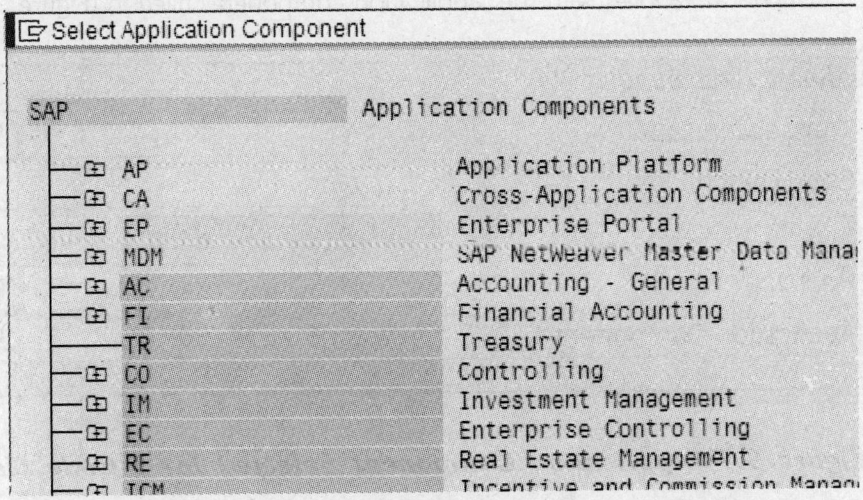

Figure 9.5: Select an 'Application Component'

b. Drill-down to the desired node (Figure 9-6). For example, consider you need to list down all the Transaction Codes under 'Equipment', then you will be drilling-down as shown below:

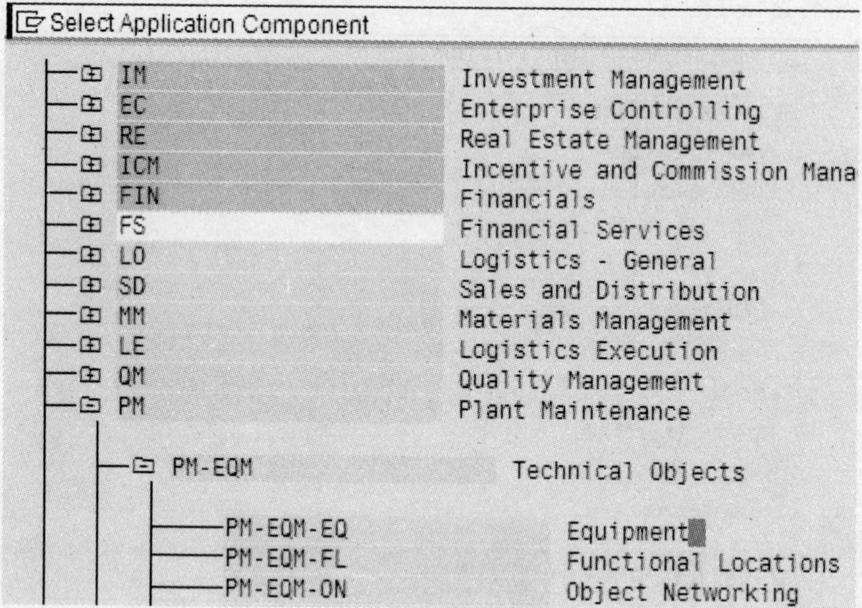

Figure 9.6: Drill-down to the desired Node of an Application Component

c. Select the node 'PM', then drill-down to 'PM-EQM and then to 'PM-EQM-EQ'. Now, double-click on the line. You are now taken back to the pop-up shown under (2) above, with the 'application component' filled in (Figure 9-7).

Standard Selections

Transaction code

Short Description

Package

Application Component PM-EQM-EQ

Figure 9.7: Application Component Selected for T-Code List

d. Press 'F8' and the system brings up all the Transaction Codes relating to this application sub-component (Figure 9-7).

Repository Info System: Transactions Find (31 Hits)

Transaction Code	Short text
IE01	Create Equipment
IE02	Change Equipment
IE03	Display Equipment
IE05	Change Equipment
IE07	Equipment List (Multi-level)
IE08	Create Equipment
IE10	Multiple Equipment Entry
IE25	Create Production Resource/Tool
IE31	Create Fleet Object
IE4N	Equipment Installation and Dismant.

Figure 9.8: T-Codes listed for the select Application Component

e. Continue to other application areas / sub-components to find all the Transaction Codes you need.

To save your time, and to provide a ready-reference, we have tabulated the most important Transaction Codes (432 in all) you may need in FI under two areas namely:

1. Customizing Transaction Codes (112)
2. Other Transaction Codes (320)

9.1. SAP FI Transaction Codes (Customizing)

Table 9.1 1: SAP FI Transaction Codes (Customizing)

#	Description	T-Code
1	Activate Functional Area Substitution	OBBZ
2	Activate Validations	OB28
3	Allocate a Company Code to Sample Account Rule Type	OB67
4	Assign Chart of Depreciation to Company Code	OAOB
5	Assign Country to Tax Calculation Procedure	OBBG
6	Assign Employee Groups to Credit Representative Groups	OB51
7	Assign GL Accounts to Reason Codes	OBXL
8	Assign Posting Keys to Document Types	OBU1
9	Assign Reference Interest Rates to Interest Indicators	OB81
10	Assign Tax Codes for Non-Taxable Transactions	OBCL
11	Assign Treasury Transaction Types to House Banks	OT55
12	Assign Users to Tolerance Groups	OB57
13	Automatic Account Assignment for Interest Calculation	OBV1
14	Automatic Account Assignment, Cross-Company Code	OBYA
15	Automatic Account Assignment, MM	OBYC
16	Automatic Postings Documentation	OBL1
17	Bank chain determination	FIBB
18	Cash Management Implementation Tool	FDFD
19	Configuration: Maintain Display Format	FAKP
20	Configuration: Show Display Format	FAKA
21	Configure Days in Arrears Calculation	OB39
22	Configure the Central TR-CM System	FF$X
23	Copy Chart of Accounts	OBY7
24	Copy Chart of Depreciation	EC08
25	Copy Company Code	EC01
26	Copy GL Accounts from Chart of Accounts to the Company Code	OBY2
27	Copy Vendor master Records Creation Program	FK15
28	Copy Vendor master Records Upload Program	FK16
29	Define Treasury Groupings	OT17
30	Define Additional Local Currencies	OB22
31	Define Asset Classes	OAOA
32	Define Base Method	OAYO

33	Define Cash Discount Accounts	OBXI
34	Define Cash Management Account Names	OT16
35	Define Check Lots	FCHI
36	Define Company Code (Create / Check / Delete)	OX02
37	Define Company Code Global Parameters	OBY6
38	Define Countries	OY01
39	Define Credit Control Areas	OB45
40	Define Credit Representative Groups	OB02
41	Define Credit Risk Categories	OB01
42	Define Currency Translation Ratios	GCRF
43	Define Customer Account Groups	OBD2
44	Define Customer Tolerance Groups	OBA3
45	Define Data Transfer Rules for Sample Accounts	FSK2
46	Define Depreciation Key	AFAMA
47	Define Document Types	OBA7
48	Define Financial Statement Versions	OB58
49	Define GL Account Groups	OBD4
50	Define GL Number Ranges	FBN1
51	Define House Banks	FI12
52	Define Line item Layouts	O7Z3
53	Define Lockbox Accounts	OB10
54	Define Number Range for Payment Request	F8BM
55	Define Number Ranges for Depreciation Postings	FBN1
56	Define Number Ranges for Master Classes	AS08
57	Define Number Ranges of Vendor Account Groups	OBAS
58	Define Number Ranges for Vendor Account Groups	XKN1
59	Define Posting Keys	OB41
60	Define Posting Period Variant	OBBO
61	Define Posting Rules for Electronic Bank Statement	OT57
62	Define Reason Codes	OBBE
63	Define Reference Interest Rates	OBAC
64	Define Screen Layouts for Asset Depreciation Areas	AO21
65	Define Sort Variants	O757
66	Define Source Symbols, for Treasury	OYOS
67	Define Special Fields	OBVU
68	Define Specify Intervals And Posting Rules	OAYR

69	Define Tax Accounts	OB40
70	Define Tax Codes for Non-Taxable Transactions	OBCL
71	Define Tax codes for Sales/Purchases	FTXP
72	Define Tax Jurisdiction Codes	OBCP
73	Define Tolerance Groups	OBA4
74	Define Vendor Account Groups	OBD3
75	Define Void Reason Codes for Checks	FCHV
76	Define Sample Account Rules	OB15
77	Depreciation Keys	OAYO
78	Determine Depreciation Areas in Asset Classes	OAYZ
79	Define Planning Groups for Treasury	OT13
80	Display Accounting Configuration	FBKA
81	Document Change Rules	OB32
82	Fast Entry Screens	O7E6
83	FI Configuration Menu (instead of IMG)	ORFB
84	Field Status Variants	OBC4
85	Integration with GL	AO90
86	Interest Indicator (Arrears Interest) for Int. Calculation Program	OB82
87	Internal Number Range for Payment Orders	FBN2
88	Loans Customizing	FDCU
89	Maintain Accounting Configuration	FBKF
90	Maintain Accounting Configuration	FBKP
91	Maintain Bank Chains for Account Carry-over	FIBTU
92	Maintain Bank Chains for House Banks	FIBHU
93	Maintain Bank Chains for Partner	FIBIPU
94	Maintain Bank Chains for Partner	FIBPU
95	Maintain Business Area	OX03
96	Maintain Client Dependent User Exits	GCX2
97	Maintain Currency Translation Type	FDIC
98	Maintain Currency Translation Type	FGIC
99	Maintain Currency Translation Type	FKIC
100	Maintain Dunning Procedure	FBMP
101	Maintain Fiscal Year Variant	OB29
102	Maintain Functional Areas	OKBD
103	Maintain Key Figures	FDIK
104	Maintain Payment Program Configuration	FBZP

105	Maintain Substitutions	GGB1
106	Maintain Text Determination Configuration	FBTP
107	Maintain Validations	GGB0
108	Real Estate Implementation Guide	FEUI
109	Retained Earnings Variant	OB53
110	Scenarios for Bank Chain Determination	FIBC
111	Structure for Tax Jurisdiction Codes	OBCO
112	Transport Chart of Accounts	OBY9

9.2. SAP FI Transaction Codes (Others)

Table 9.2 1: SAP FI Transaction Codes (Others)

#	Details	T-Code
1	Account Balances , A/P	F.42
2	Account Balances, A/R	F.23
3	Account List, A/P	F.40
4	Account List, A/R	F.20
5	Accounting Editing Options	FB00
6	Acquisition from Purchase with Vendor	F-90
7	Advance Tax Return	F.12
8	Archive Bank Master Data	F041
9	Archive Customer	F043
10	Archive Transaction Figures	F046
11	Archiving Bank Data Storage	F66A
12	Archiving Banks	F61A
13	Archiving Check Data	FCHA
14	Archiving GL Accounts	F53A
15	Archiving Payment Request	F8BO
16	Archiving Vendors	F044
17	Asset Acquisition to Clearing Account	F-91
18	Asset Depreciation Run	AFAB
19	Asset Explorer	AW01
20	Asset Master Creation	AS01
21	Asset Retirement from Sale With Customer	F-92
22	Asset Scrapping	ABAVN
23	Asset Transfer	ABUMN
24	Asset, Create Sub-Asset	AS11
25	Automatic Clearing: ABAP/4 Report	F.13
26	Balance Interest Calculation, A/P	F.44
27	Balance Interest Calculation, A/R	F.26
28	Balance Sheet- ABAP/4 Report	F.01
29	Balance Sheet Adjustment: ABAP/4 Reporting	F101
30	Balance Sheet/P&L with Inflation	FJA3
31	Bill of Exchange List	F.25
32	Bill of Exchange Payment	F-36

33	Bill of Exchange Payment Request Dunning	F.70
34	Bill of Exchange Payment -Header Data	F-40
35	Bill of Exchange Presentation - International	FBWE
36	Block Customer (Accounting)	FD05
37	Block Vendor (Accounting)	FK05
38	Cash Concentration	FF73
39	Cash Journal	FBCJ
40	Cash Management and Forecast - Initial Screen	FF72
41	Cash Management Position / Liquidity Forecast	FF70
42	Cash Management Summary Records	FF-3
43	Cash Position	FF71
44	Change Bank	FI02
45	Change Check / Payment Allocation	FCHT
46	Change Check Information/Cash Check	FCH6
47	Change Credit Limits	FD24
48	Change Current Number Range Number	FI07
49	Change Customer (Accounting Data)	FD02
50	Change Customer Credit Management	FD32
51	Change Customer Line Items	FBL6
52	Change Document	FB02
53	Change GL Account Line Items	FBL4
54	Change Intercompany Document	FBU2
55	Change Last Adjustment Dates	FJA2
56	Change Line Items -Customer / Vendor / Asset / GL	FB09
57	Change Parked Document (Header)	FBV4
58	Change Parked Document	FBV2
59	Change Payment Advice	FBE2
60	Change Pricing Report	F/LB
61	Change Recurring Entry	FBD2
62	Change Report Settings for Transaction Figures	FDI2
63	Change Report: Settings	FGI2
64	Change Report: Settings	FKI2
65	Change Sample Document	FBM2
66	Change Vendor (Accounting Data)	FK02
67	Change Vendor Line Items	FBL2
68	Check Extract - Creation	FCHX

69	Check if Documents can be Archived	FB99
70	Check Register	FCHN
71	Check Retrieval	FCHB
72	Check Tracing Initial Menu	FCHK
73	Clear Customer Down Payment	F-39
74	Clear Customer: Header Data	F-32
75	Clear GL Account: Header Data	F-03
76	Clear Vendor Down Payment	F-54
77	Clear Vendor: Header Data	F-44
78	Confirm Customer Individually (Accounting)	FD08
79	Confirm Customer List (Accounting)	FD09
80	Confirm Vendor Individually (Accounting)	FK08
81	Confirm Vendor List (Accounting)	FK09
82	Correspondence: Delete Requests	F.63
83	Correspondence: Maintain Requests	F.64
84	Correspondence: Print Interest Documents	F.62
85	Correspondence: Print Letters (Customer)	F.65
86	Correspondence: Print Letters (Vendor)	F.66
87	Correspondence: Print Requests	F.61
88	Create Bank	FI01
89	Create Check Information	FCH5
90	Create Customer (Accounting)	FD01
91	Create Payment Advice	FBE1
92	Create Payment Runs Automatically	F8BU
93	Create Planning Memo Record	FF63
94	Create Reference for Check	FCHU
95	Create Vendor (Accounting Area Data)	FK01
96	Credit Management - Mass Change	F.34
97	Credit Management - Mass Change	FD37
98	Credit Management - Master Data List	FDK43
99	Credit Management - Missing Data	F.32
100	Credit Management - Overview	F.31
101	Credit Master Sheet	F.35
102	Customer Account Analysis	FD11
103	Customer Account Balance	FD10
104	Customer Balance Confirmation: ABAP/4 Report	F.17

105	Customer Balance Display	FD10N
106	Customer Balance: Display with Worklist	FD10NA
107	Customer Changes (Accounting)	FD04
108	Customer Down Payment Request	F-37
109	Customer Interest on Arrears: Post (w/ Open Items)	F.2B
110	Customer Interest on Arrears: Post (w/o Open Items)	F.2A
111	Customer Interest on Arrears: Post (w/o postings)	F.2C
112	Customer Line Items	FBL5N
113	Customer Noted Item	F-49
114	Customer/Vendor Statistics	F.1A
115	Customers Drilldown Reports: Background Processing	FDIB
116	Customers: FI-SD Master Data Comparison	F.2D
117	Customers: Report Selection	F.99
118	Customers: Reset Credit Limit	F.28
119	Data Extract for FI Transfer	FC11
120	Delete A/R Summary	FCV2
121	Delete Cashing/Extract Data	FCHG
122	Delete Manual Checks	FCHF
123	Delete Payment Advice	FBE6
124	Delete Payment Run Check Information	FCHD
125	Delete Recurring Document	F.56
126	Delete Voided Checks	FCHE
127	Display Account Determination Configuration	FBBA
128	Display Bank Chains for House Banks	FIBHS
129	Display Bank Chains for Partners	FIBPS
130	Display Bank Changes	FI04
131	Display Bank	FI03
132	Display Check Information	FCH1
133	Display Customer (Accounting Data)	FD03
134	Display Customer Credit Management	FD33
135	Display Customer Line Items	FBL5
136	Display Document	FB03
137	Display Document/Payment Usage	FB03Z
138	Display Dunning Procedure	FBMA
139	Display Electronic Bank Statement	FF.6
140	Display FI Amount Groups	F8+2

141	Display FI Main Role Definition	F8+0
142	Display GL Account Line Items	FBL3
143	Display House Banks/Bank Accounts	FI13
144	Display Intercompany Document	FBU3
145	Display of Payment Requests	F8BS
146	Display Parked Document	FBV3
147	Display Payment Advice	FBE3
148	Display Payment Document Checks	FCH2
149	Display Payment Program Configuration	FBZA
150	Display Payment Requests	F8BT
151	Display Payment Run	FBZ8
152	Display Pricing Report	F/LC
153	Display Recurring Entry Changes	FBD4
154	Display Recurring Entry	FBD3
155	Display Sample Document Changes	FBM4
156	Display Sample Document	FBM3
157	Display Text Determination Configuration	FBTA
158	Display Vendor (Accounting Data)	FK03
159	Display Vendor Line Items	FBL1
160	Display/Edit Payment Proposal	FBZ0
161	Document Archiving	F045
162	Document Changes of Parked Documents	FBV5
163	Document Changes	FB04
164	Down Payment Request	F-47
165	Download Documents	FBF4
166	Dunning Run, A/R	F150
167	Enter Accrual/Deferral Document	FBS1
168	Enter Bill of Exchange Payment Request	FBW1
169	Enter Customer Credit Memo	F-27
170	Enter Customer Invoice	F-22
171	Enter GL Account Posting	F-02
172	Enter Incoming Credit Memos	FB65
173	Enter Incoming Invoices	FB60
174	Enter Noted Item	FB31
175	Enter Outgoing Credit Memos	FB75
176	Enter Outgoing Invoices	FB70

177	Enter Payment Request	FBP1
178	Enter Recurring Entry	FBD1
179	Enter Sample Document	F-01
180	Enter Statistical Posting: Header Data	F-38
181	Enter Transfer Posting: Header Data	F-21
182	Enter Vendor Credit Memo	F-41
183	Enter Vendor Invoice	F-43
184	Evaluate Info System, A/P	F.46
185	Evaluate Info System, A/R	F.30
186	Exchange Rates Table Maintenance	F-62
187	F111 Customizing	F8BZ
188	Failed Customer Payments	FBZG
189	FI Account Assignment Model Management	FKMT
190	FI Display Structure	FINA
191	FI Easy Access - Banks	FBME
192	FI Easy Access - Customers	FDMN
193	FI Easy Access - Vendors	FKMN
194	FI Information System	F000
195	FI Initial Consolidation Menu	FCMN
196	FI Valuation Run	F107
197	Financial Statements Comparison	FC10
198	Financial Transactions	FBF2
199	Foreign Currency Valuation: Open Items	F.05
200	Generate MultiCash Format	FEBC
201	Generate Payment Request from Advices	FF.D
202	GL Account Assignment Manual	F.53
203	GL Account Balance Interest Calculation	F.52
204	GL Account Balances	F.08
205	GL Account Cashed Checks	FF.3
206	GL Account Interest Scale	FF_1
207	GL Account Line Items	FBL3N
208	GL Account List	F.09
209	GL Account Posting: Single Screen Transaction	FB50
210	GL Accounts Archiving	F042
211	GL Advance Report on Tax on Sales/Purchase with Jurisdiction	F.5I
212	GL Balance Carried Forward	F.07

213	GL Balance Sheet Adjustment Log	F.5F
214	GL Chart of Accounts	F.10
215	GL Compact Journal	F.02
216	GL Create Foreign Trade Report	F.04
217	GL Delete Sample Documents	F.57
218	GL Drilldown Reports: Background Processing	FGIB
219	GL General Ledger from Document File	F.11
220	GL GR/IR Clearing	F.19
221	GL Open Items	F.51
222	GL Post Balance Sheet Adjustment	F.5E
223	GL Profitability Segment Adjustment	F.50
224	GL Report Selection	F.97
225	GL Structured Account Balances	F.54
226	GL Update Balance Sheet Adjustment	F.5D
227	Import Electronic Bank Statement	FF.5
228	Import Electronic Check Deposit List	FFB4
229	Import Forms from Client 000	FDIR
230	Import Lockbox File	FLB2
231	Import Reports from Client 000	FDIQ
232	Incoming Payments Fast Entry	F-26
233	Interest for Days Overdue, A/R	F.24
234	Invoice/Credit Fast Entry	FB10
235	Maintain Bill of Exchange Liability	F.93
236	Manual Bank Statement	FF67
237	Manual Check Deposit Transaction	FF68
238	Mark Bank for Deletion	FI06
239	Mark Customer for Deletion (Accounting)	FD06
240	Mark Vendor for Deletion (Accounting)	FK06
241	Mass Reversal of Documents	F.80
242	Online Cashed Checks	FCHR
243	Open Item Balance Audit Trail: from Document File	F.58
244	Open Item Sorted List, A/R	F.22
245	Open Items, A/P	F.41
246	Open Items, A/R	F.21
247	Outstanding Bills of Exchange	FF-2
248	Parameters for Automatic Payment	F110

249	Parameters for Payment of Request	F111
250	Park Customer Credit Memo	F-67
251	Park Customer Invoice	F-64
252	Park Document	FBV1
253	Park Vendor Credit Memo	F-66
254	Park Vendor Invoice	F-63
255	Payment Advice Comparison	FF.7
256	Payment Advice Journal	FF-8
257	Payment Card Evaluations	FCCR
258	Payment Cards: Settlement	FCC1
259	Payment Request	F-59
260	Payment with Printout	F-18
261	Periodic Account Statements, A/R	F.27
262	Post Bill of Exchange Usage	F-33
263	Post Collection	F-34
264	Post Customer Down Payment	F-29
265	Post Document	FB01
266	Post Electronic Bank Statement	FEBP
267	Post Electronic Check Deposit List	FFB5
268	Post Foreign Currency Valuation	F-05
269	Post Forfaiting	F-35
270	Post Held Document	FB11
271	Post Incoming Payments	F-06
272	Post Lockbox Data	FLBP
273	Post Outgoing Payments	F-07
274	Post Parked Document	FBV0
275	Post Payment Orders	FF.9
276	Post Tax Payable	FB41
277	Post Vendor Down Payment	F-48
278	Post with Clearing	F-04
279	Post with Reference Document	FBR1
280	Posting Period Table Maintenance	F-60
281	Preliminary Posting	F-65
282	Print Check For Payment Document	FBZ5
283	Print Payment Orders	FF.8
284	Realize Recurring Entry	FBD5

285	Recurring Entries: ABAP/4 Report	F.14
286	Reject Parked Document	FBV6
287	Release for Payments	FB13
288	Renumber Checks	FCH4
289	Report Painter	FGRP
290	Report Painter: Change Form -Customer	FDI5
291	Report Painter: Change Form -GL	FGI5
292	Report Painter: Change Form -Vendor	FKI5
293	Report Writer Menu	FGRW
294	Reprint Check	FCH7
295	Request from Correspondence	FB12
296	Reset Cleared Items	FBRA
297	Reset Cleared Items: Payment Requests	F8BW
298	Returned Bills of Exchange Payable	FBWD
299	Reversal of Bank-to-Bank Transfers	F8BV
300	Reverse Bill Liability	F-20
301	Reverse Check Payment	FCH8
302	Reverse Check/Bill of Exchange	F-25
303	Reverse Cross-Company Code Document	FBU8
304	Reverse Document	FB08
305	Reverse Posting for Accrued /Deferred Documents	F.81
306	Reverse Statistical Posting	F-19
307	SAP Office: Short Message -Create and Send	F00
308	Special Purpose Ledger Menu	FGM0
309	Summary, A/R	FCV1
310	Vendor Account Balance	FK10
311	Vendor Balance Confirmation: ABAP/4 Report	F.18
312	Vendor Balance Display	FK10N
313	Vendor Cashed Checks	FF.4
314	Vendor Check/Bill of Exchange	FBW6
315	Vendor Down Payment Request	FBA6
316	Vendor Interest on Arrears: Post (w/ Open Items)	F.4B
317	Vendor Interest on Arrears: Post (w/o Open Items)	F.4A
318	Vendor Interest on Arrears: Post (w/o postings)	F.4C
319	Vendor Line Items	FBL1N
320	Vendor Noted Item	F-57

Tables

Figures

Index

A

B

O

P

Q

U

V

Notes